KENTUCKY

On-the-Road Histories

KENTUCKY

Brad Asher

Interlink Books

First published in 2007 by

INTERLINK BOOKS
An imprint of Interlink Publishing Group, Inc.
46 Crosby Street, Northampton, Massachusetts 01060
www.interlinkbooks.com

Library of Congress Cataloging-in-Publication Data
Asher, Brad, 1963–
  Kentucky / by Brad Asher.
     p. cm.— (On-the-road histories)
  Includes bibliographical references and index.
  ISBN 1-56656-638-X (pbk.)
  1. Kentucky—History. 2. Kentucky—Description and travel. I. Title. II.
Series.
  F451.A84 2006
  976.9—dc22
                                      2005036392

*Color images © Photovault/Wernher Krutein Productions, Inc. unless otherwise
noted in the text*
Black and white historical images provided by the Kentucky Historical Society

Printed and bound in China

Contents

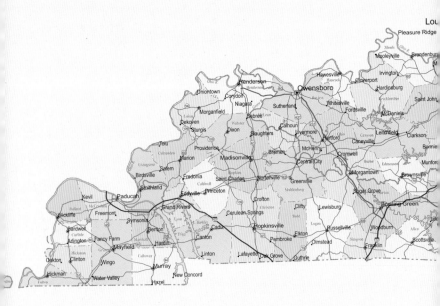

★ **State Capitals**
⊙ County Seat
● **Cities 100,000-499,999**
● Cities 50,000-99,999
• Cities 10,000-49,999
∙ Cities 0-9,999

1

Kentucky: Real and Imagined

In 1775, a Virginia preacher groped for a metaphor for heaven during a sermon to his congregation. He hit upon it finally when he described paradise as a "Kentucky of a place." The preacher knew his audience; Virginia in 1775 seethed with Kentucky fever as families sought what Daniel Boone and others had labeled a "good poor man's country." Despite the hardships and dangers of settling the trans-Appalachian country, hopeful emigrants flocked to Kentucky even during the years of the American Revolution.

Despite its heavenly reputation, Kentucky disappointed many emigrants looking for an American Eden. Transformed in short order from a "howling wilderness to a civilized society," as one 1818 guidebook writer put it, Kentucky went from a poor man's paradise to a commercial society that enriched speculators and lawyers far more often than the common settler.

Furthermore, from the viewpoint of those people displaced by the early settlers, the years after 1775 could hardly have seemed less heavenly. Brutal frontier warfare between the settlers and the various Native American tribes that claimed Kentucky as a hunting ground culminated in the forced ejection of the Native Americans from the land.

Stereotypes: The Colonel and the Hillbilly

If not heaven, what kind of place is Kentucky? To get an answer, take a close look at the Colonel and the Hillbilly, two common Kentucky stereotypes. The Colonel, most often imagined as a white-suited, goateed country gentleman, sits "on the veranda of his white-columned mansion, drinking a mint julep or bourbon and water, watching his thoroughbreds run in the fields of bluegrass," as the writer of *A New History of Kentucky* puts it. The Hillbilly, barefoot, raggedly clothed, and usually shown armed, sits "propped against a log cabin instead of on the porch of a mansion, [drinking] moonshine rather than bourbon, and [enjoying]... feuding over racing." Forget for a moment that no one in the state lives like either of these depictions, and few perhaps ever did. The key elements of these imagined Kentucky characters still reveal something about the state's culture, a culture rooted in history.

First, both these images are southern. Indeed, the stark difference between the two images shows the ambiguous place of the South in the popular mind. The leisured gentility of the Colonel evokes the South of *Gone With the Wind*. The poverty-bred violent dysfunction of the Hillbilly, on the other hand, evokes the South of *Deliverance*.

Kentucky's southernness is beyond question. It was initially part of Virginia, and most of Kentucky's early settlers hailed from the Old Dominion. These settlers brought with them the quintessential southern institution: slavery. Today, travel guidebooks categorize Kentucky as part of the Southeast and the University of Kentucky's sports teams play in the Southeastern Conference.

Straddling the great cultural divide between North and South, however, gives Kentucky's southernness a schizophrenic quality. Despite its southern roots, its early residents developed—through migration and trade—strong family and economic connections to Indiana, Ohio, and other midwestern states. Prior to the Mexican War, Americans thought of Kentucky more as the West than the South, and its political leaders talked up the clash between the newer states and the older coastal states, not the sectional differences between North and South. During a debate with a political opponent in 1818, for example, Kentucky's most famous pre-Civil War statesman, Henry Clay, asked, "[A]m I... who come from the great interior of the country, to be told that the Constitution was made for the Atlantic margin of the country only[?]... We, who are not washed by tide water, have as much right to the benefit of its provisions as any other part of the country." Most significantly, when the trial of fire came in 1861, Kentucky stayed in the Union, despite being a slave state.

It was after the Civil War that Kentucky really embraced its southern identity, celebrating the Confederate cause as worthy and honorable and erecting monuments to the state's Confederate war dead. In part, this was a practical matter; left relatively unscathed by the war, Louisville—the state's largest city—intended to make itself the hub of southern commerce, and making sales in the South was easier if it was seen as a southern city rather than a Yankee one. But it was also a genuine reflection of the state's cultural origins and strong southern sympathies. As the state's most prominent historian, Thomas D. Clark, has written, "to make Kentucky in the images of Ohio and Indiana was a spiritual impossibility."

A second common element in the images of the Colonel and the Hillbilly is that both are rural characters. As with its southernness, Kentucky's rural nature is beyond question; indeed, its pastoral countryside draws tourists by the thousands every year. The majority of Kentucky's population did not live in urban areas until 1970, some 50 years after that benchmark was reached in the nation as a whole. Kentucky has only one major city—Louisville—with the economic and demographic diversity typical of large urban centers. Population statistics show that the state has actually become more rural in the last three decades. "Many Kentuckians still prefer to see before them a rural landscape than an urban one," concludes the standard textbook on the state's history, *A New History of Kentucky*. "The city still has not won the hidden heart of the state."

"Rural" may evoke peaceful pastoralism, but it also connotes isolation and provincialism. The idea of "rural" slides easily into the idea of redneck, and neither the Colonel sitting on his veranda nor the Hillbilly in his mountain shack was too open to outside influences.

A third element shared by the Colonel and the Hillbilly is that both are nostalgic images, conjuring up an imagined and idealized past. For if the Hillbilly is violent, he is also self-reliant and independent—a repository of lore and skills long forgotten in this softer age. And the Colonel beckons us back to a less hurried time, when leisured conversation and good manners mattered more than efficiency. The state's bourbon distillers play up this theme consistently in their advertise-ments, stressing the small populations of the towns where their liquor is distilled and the absence of modern intrusions like computers, fax machines, and cell phones.

Like all nostalgia, there is willful denial and ambiguity here. Much of modern Kentucky life is as harried and

Must-See Sites:
Thomas D. Clark Center

"A Kentucky Journal," the permanent exhibit at the Thomas D. Clark Center for Kentucky History in Frankfort, uses 3,000 artifacts and 14 interactive displays to tell the state's history from prehistoric times to the present. It divides the state's history into eight periods, allowing visitors to walk from the time of the Paleoindians to the 21st century. Through room-sized displays meant to capture ordinary life, the exhibit attempts to give visitors a taste of how Kentuckians lived during each of these historical periods.

Another section of the exhibit, entitled "Pure Kentucky," highlights famous Kentuckians and houses memorabilia from several well-known entertainers and sports figures. Finally, a portion of the permanent exhibit—built to look like a historic black church—focuses on the civil rights movement in Kentucky and its relationship to the national movement for African American freedom. Another gallery, the Keeneland Changing Exhibits gallery, hosts temporary exhibits.

Run by the Kentucky Historical Society, the center is located at 100 W. Broadway in Frankfort. Call (502) 564-1792 or toll-free at (877) 444-7867 or visit www.kyhistory.org/museums/Kentucky_History_Center.htm.

hurried as modern American life anywhere. Distillers selling their wares worldwide rely as much on modern communication and computing technology as do brokers on Wall Street. But the nostalgia and the images remind people that the modern way might actually be a fairly unsatisfying way to live. Kentucky's notable authors, from Robert Penn Warren to Wendell Berry, have repeatedly returned to this theme. Fittingly, their works are all available through Amazon.com.

GEOGRAPHY AND POPULATION

Kentucky contains a great deal of geographic diversity within its 40,000 square miles of territory. Those who spend their time mapping different physiographic regions have determined that Kentucky has five big ones (with innumerable subregions). In the eastern portion of the state, bordering Virginia and West Virginia, is the Eastern Coalfield, which makes up about a quarter of the state's land area and contains about 18 percent of the population. A mountainous region rich in coal and timber, the Coalfield's southeastern corner contains the Cumberland Gap, a 1,000-feet deep notch in the mountains that provided passage for the early settlers into Kentucky.

Most of those early settlers hightailed it for the Bluegrass, which is set off from the Eastern Coalfield by a row of conical hills called the Knobs. The 8,000 square miles in the Bluegrass account for only about one fifth of the state's land area, but the region dominated early settlement and continues to be the economic and political center of the state. It contains half the state's population and its finest agricultural land—as well as its two largest cities, Louisville and Lexington, and the state capitol, Frankfort. For many visitors the Bluegrass—with its thoroughbred farms and gently rolling landscape—*is* Kentucky, which irritates to no end those who do not live in the region.

The Pennyroyal sits like a crab at the bottom of the state, with the southern end of the Eastern Coalfield at its back and its claws encircling the Western Coalfield. The region contains 12,000 square miles and about 17 percent of the state's population. High stone escarpments mark its boundaries, producing some impressive waterfalls. Cumberland Falls, now the site of a state resort, plummets 67 feet to create a "moonbow" on clear nights with a full moon. The central Pennyroyal is Kentucky's cave country, marked by numerous caverns and sinkholes, underground rivers, and the like. Mammoth Cave, the world's longest, is in this region. John Filson, a 1784 guidebook author, listed the numerous "amazingly large" caves as one of Kentucky's notable "curiosities."

The Western Coalfield sits inside the Pennyroyal's embrace. Rich in coal, it is also one of the state's prime agricultural regions. It covers 4,600 square miles—about one tenth of the state's total area—and contains a little over 8 percent of the state's people.

The final region, known as the Jackson Purchase after the president who bought the land from the Native

Americans, sits at the western tip of the state. It is virtually a peninsula, surrounded to the north, east, and west by major rivers. It contains just 2,400 square miles of land, but much of it is fertile bottomland, very flat and low and good for farming. Roughly 5 percent of the state's people reside in the Purchase.

The 2000 Federal Census pegged Kentucky's population at just over 4 million people. As it had since the Civil War (with the exception of the 1970s), the growth rate of Kentucky's population during the 1990s lagged behind the nation's growth rate. Almost all the population growth in the state comes from natural increase rather than im-migration; after the initial population boom of the "settling-up" period ended in the 1820s, the number of people leaving the state has typically been larger than the number coming in.

Demographically, Kentucky largely fits the stereotype of the rural American Midwest—white, Anglo-Saxon, and Christian. In racial terms, Kentucky remains over-whelmingly white, even as the country as a whole has become more diverse. The 2000 census reported that the United States' white population made up just over 75 percent of the total, but Kentucky remained over 90 percent white. While African Americans totaled 12.3 percent of the national population, they made up just 7.3 percent of Kentucky's. And the other races that made up the remaining 13 percent or so of the national population comprised only about 2.5 percent of the state's population.

The relative lack of diversity among the population forms part of a long trend. The African-American population peaked during slavery times at about one quarter of the state's population and has fallen steadily ever since—from 17 percent right after the Civil War to 13 percent in 1900 to around 7 percent today. The decline stemmed largely from blacks leaving the state in search of more hospitable surroundings.

Likewise, the repeated waves of immigration—during the 1840s, the 1890s and early 1900s, and from the 1960s onward—that altered the nation's population had little effect on Kentucky. Substantial numbers of Irish and Germans settled in the Ohio River towns during the antebellum period—accounting for up to one fifth of the population in Louisville, Covington, and Newport—but

Literary Extracts
Jesse Stuart

Jesse Stuart was born in 1906 in Greenup county. He started publishing poems and stories about his people—the people of Kentucky's eastern mountains—in the 1930s. In the following excerpt from his 1975 memoir, *My World*, Stuart sums up the geographical, social, and cultural differences between the mountains he knew so well and the Bluegrass region that dominates the state:

I can change worlds in two hours in Kentucky. All I have to do is drive up scenic Route 1, along the Little Sandy… and arrive at Interstate 64 at Grayson. From Grayson I follow I-64 westward across East Kentucky's high hills and knobs. Without speed limits this could be a fast road. But who wants to drive fast along this scenic route? Better to go slower and see the cliffs, the hardwood trees, the tough-butted white oaks that hold their leaves in winter, the sawbriars and blackberry briars, old fences, old houses, country cemeteries, valleys, and streams. This is a country where stubborn people cling tenaciously to their stubborn soil.

Now in an hour and a half, just beyond Morehead, we drive into the Outer Bluegrass world. Here everything is different. Here we find excellent cattle farms, and tobacco barns painted black with red roofs. Here we see evidence of wealth spread over the land and the buildings….

The early settlers of the Bluegrass and the English were just a step apart; perhaps, not so much as a step, in their social divisions. This was and is (to a lesser extent today) typical of the Bluegrass people. No wonder it is a little difficult for the East Kentucky mountaineer, who is far removed from any desire for an aristocracy, to understand the people here.

they made up only 5 percent of the state's total population in 1870. The later waves of immigration mostly bypassed Kentucky, although Louisville absorbed a small share of the newcomers. In 1910, nearly 90 percent of those living in Kentucky had been born in Kentucky—the fifth highest rate in the nation. In 1990, things had not changed much;

Kentucky ranked fourth among the states in the percentage of natives living in their home states.

In religious terms, Kentucky in 1990 ranked thirteenth among the states in the percentage of its population that identified itself as Christian, with 60 percent of the population specifying membership in a particular religious group (the nearly one million Baptists in the state being the largest single group). The religious culture of the state has a long historical tradition; fervent religiosity has marked Kentucky since the first revivals began soon after Daniel Boone and friends opened the floodgates of settlement.

For the traveler, Kentucky might not provide a preview of heaven, but its place in the earthly domain offers some this-worldly rewards. As the borderland between Midwest and South, Kentucky fits neatly into neither box. The state's history offers paradox, contradiction, and contrast—in short, an enriched cultural grist for the historical mill. And if that is not exactly a proxy for paradise, at least a sojourner in Kentucky can also have a good glass of whiskey and watch a fast horse.

Louisville skyline at night

THE FIRST KENTUCKIANS

Nobody knows who the first European was to set foot in Kentucky. But whoever he was, he stepped into over 10,000 years of previous history and human habitation. Before the coming of the Europeans, these early inhabitants left their story behind in stones, bones, and piles of garbage. After 1700, they figure prominently in the stories told by the European adventurers, explorers, and traders who made their way into Kentucky.

FROM PALEOINDIANS TO THE ARCHAIC PERIOD (9500 BCE TO 1000 BCE)

Archaeologists call the earliest humans to live in Kentucky Paleoindians. The reigning theory suggests that their ancestors came from Asia, probably migrating by way of a land bridge that connected Siberia and North America during the last Ice Age (although archaeologists are challenging this theory on numerous fronts). Over several thousand years moving south and east, the descendants of those first migrants arrived in Kentucky in about 9500 BCE.

At that time, Kentucky was cooler and moister than it is now, and huge game animals walked through its mix of open grasslands and dense forests. Mammoths, mastodons, Pleistocene bison, enormous ground sloths, and other megafauna lured early Paleoindians to the hunt. Most of the early archaeological sites are hunting camps, situated near watering places or salt springs. One of the best known of these is Big Bone Lick salt springs, located in present-day Boone County and now a state park. Other sites are located near outcrops of chert, the stone from which early Paleoindians made most of their tools.

Kentucky's mammoth-hunters did not differ markedly from the Paleoindians hunting mammoths in other parts of the continent. In fact, they did not really differ very much from their Eurasian ancestors. They used largely the same tools in the same way, and for one simple reason: They worked. Why mess with success when you've found an effective way to kill a mammoth?

To bring down an 11,000-pound mammoth or any other big game, Paleoindian hunters used a spear with a detachable foreshaft. At the tip of the foreshaft, they tied on a stone point with fluted edges. They then drove the spear into the animal's hide (modern tests of such weapons have proved that they could penetrate even the thickest of animal hides), and pulled out the main shaft of the lance, leaving the detachable foreshaft with its barbed point stuck deep inside the animal's skin. The weapon could quickly be reloaded, allowing the hunters to stick the animal repeatedly. These fluted stone points—along with stone knives and scrapers for processing the hides and flesh of the dead animal, as well as the stone hammers used to make these tools—make up a large portion of the artifacts that these early hunters left behind in Kentucky.

Paleoindians moved around a lot, so they kept their gear small and light. Almost everything a hunter needed could be kept in a small pouch. They moved in bands of 20–50 people and did not stay long in any one place. Their archaeological remains do not show houses or accumulated garbage or fire pits that indicate an extended stay. Another sign of their mobility is that some of the stone points they left behind in Kentucky were made from stone located hundreds of miles away.

Around 9000 BCE things started to change for the Paleoindians. The general warming that accompanied the retreat of the Ice Age glaciers spawned changes in the mix of grassland and forest. Some of the big game animals died out, and others migrated north after the glaciers, leaving a different mix of animals for hunting. Kentucky's Paleoindians came to rely on a broader mix of large and small game animals and they foraged more widely for plant foods, and so their archaeological remains are more widely distributed than those of their earlier ancestors.

These "middle Paleoindians," as archaeologists call

them, also altered the way they made their tools. By changing the way they fashioned their knives, they found they were able to use poorer-quality stone and still get an effective tool. They also earned their archaeological moniker by changing the design of the projectile points that fit on the end of their spears. Of such changes are archaeological periods made.

But what the middle Paleoindians went through was nothing compared to what came later. "Late Paleoindians" had to adapt to an even more dramatic set of environmental changes that occurred around 8500 BCE The Ice Age ended, and most of the Ice Age megafauna melted away with the glaciers. That left smaller, more mobile, and more dispersed game animals as a principal food source. Since these animals were more evenly spread out over the landscape than the older herds of mammoths and other Pleistocene big game, the late Paleoindians moved less often and less far than their ancestors. They also moved into areas that the early Paleoindians had only passed through, like the mountains, using rock shelters on a regular basis, and changing their hunting tools.

With mammoths and mastodons gone, ivory could no longer be used for the foreshafts of spears. Late Paleoindians substituted wood and bone. The classic fluted projectile point disappeared as well, replaced by a variety of styles reflecting the new mix of animals to be hunted. Their knives and scrapers also became smaller, like the animals being processed. These adaptations ensured the Paleoindians' survival, and their technological innovations shaped the way their descendants hunted for the next two millennia.

With the Ice Age over, Kentucky's flora and fauna essentially took on their modern forms; and thus began the Archaic period of archaeological history. The Archaic period is a catch-all time frame used to describe post-Ice-Age peoples who had not yet discovered the manufacture of pottery. It lasted from about 8000 BCE to about 1000 BCE. In Kentucky, late Paleoindian peoples unknowingly stepped over a historical threshold and became Early Archaic peoples. As such, they made few modifications to their basic lifestyle but did witness growing success, as evidenced by an increase in the size and number of Early Archaic bands.

Must-See Sites:
Archaeological Explorations

The William S. Webb Museum of Anthropology

The museum houses representative artifacts from the major archaeological periods in Kentucky, including projectile points, stone tools, pottery, ornaments, and other material remains. Through informational placards, the museum reconstructs the culture and life of Native Kentuckians during each of the five principal archaeological periods: Paleoindian, Archaic; Woodland; Late Prehistory; and the historic post-contact period. A series of maps shows the locations of various archaeological sites across the state.

The museum was founded in 1931 by Webb, a professor of physics, and William Funkhouser, a professor of zoology. The two shared a passion for Kentucky's prehistory and had done a county-by-county archaeological survey of Kentucky during the 1920s. They collaborated to establish the University of Kentucky's Department of Anthropology in 1927, which runs the museum.

The Webb Museum is a traditional display-case and reading type of museum. It brings together in one place the essential materials for an excellent introduction to Kentucky archaeology and is the major facility in the state for curating archaeological findings—a designation granted it by the Kentucky Heritage Council. In addition to the items on display, the museum serves as the repository for over 5,800 separate collections of artifacts and plays an active role in current collecting and research around the state and elsewhere.

The museum is located in Lafferty Hall near the center of the university's campus in Lexington. Call for information at (859) 257-8208 or visit www.uky.edu/AS/Anthropology/museum/museum.htm.

Living Archaeology Weekend

This event brings together archaeologists, Native Americans, and local craftsmen to demonstrate the life and culture of ancient native peoples. In an area close to where some of the first Kentuckians lived, artisans demonstrate the making of arrowheads and other projectile points, the use of a bow and arrow, and how to throw an *atlatl*. On the more domestic side, there are displays of prehistoric dwellings, as well as demonstrations of hide tanning, mat and basket weaving, pottery making, and the medicinal use of native plants and herbs.

Living Archaeology Weekend takes place in September (usually the second-to-last weekend) at the Gladie Historic Site in Red River Gorge. In the late 1800s a logging community existed in this area, but the Gladie Cabin, a reconstructed log house from the 1880s, is the only remaining structure. It now serves as a visitor's center.

Red River Gorge is located in the Daniel Boone National Forest near Natural Bridge State Park. The gorge—nicknamed "The Grand Canyon of the East"—contains over one hundred natural stone arches and numerous waterfalls. The gorge is extremely popular with outdoor-adventure enthusiasts, with kayaking and canoeing available in Red River and rock climbing on the sheer cliffs of the gorge. Information on the Living Archaeology Weekend can be obtained at (895) 745-3100 or at www.fs.fed.us/r8/boone/events.

Wickliffe Mounds State Historic Site

Wickliffe Mounds sits on the location of a Mississippian village built around 1100 CE. One display houses the artifacts found at Wickliffe; another allows visitors to see the interior of a mound; a third, the Cemetery Building, gives a glimpse of the village burial ground and an explanation of Mississippian burial practices. There is also a visitor center that contains a mural depicting typical Mississippian village life.

Prehistoric native people lived in the village for two hundred years. It was built in typical Mississippian style, with a central plaza highlighted by several earthen mounds. The peak population at Wickliffe was probably several hundred. The village was abandoned for reasons unknown during the mid 1300s.

The mounds were undisturbed for centuries until, in the 1930s, they were excavated by Paducah businessman Colonel Fain White King. The artifacts and the site itself were displayed to the public, and King sought to build the site into a tourist attraction. In 1946 a local hospital gained the deed to the property and in 1983 Murray State University gained control of it. The university ran the site as a research and education center before handing it over to the state park system in 2004.

Wickliffe Mounds is located in the town of Wickliffe on US Highway 51/60/62. Call (270) 335-3681 or visit parks.ky.gov/statehistoricsites/wm.

These bands, like their Paleoindian predecessors, moved around a lot. Most of the remains they left behind are from temporary hunting camps or seasonal foraging camps. In many places, such as the Longworth-Gick site on the Ohio River near Louisville, the remains are layered on top of one another, suggesting repeated and regular use by Archaic peoples.

Some two thousand years later, Archaic peoples had prospered to such an extent that regionally distinct archaeological cultures began to develop. These new cultures came about as people all over the eastern United States made specific adaptations to their own particular local climates and geographies. One of the most telling of these adaptations, at least to archaeologists' eyes, was the regional variation in projectile points. The predominant styles of projectile points used in eastern and central Kentucky, for example, differed from those used in western Kentucky. Other specialized tools used to process plant foods—such as axes, grindstones, mortars, and pestles—also show regional variation. Sameness within a region and diversity between regions probably signal a good deal of communication between Middle Archaic bands, as those people living in a similar environment learned from each other which tools worked best.

Middle Archaic people used more of their environment than their predecessors. While game remained important, they ate more plant foods, as well as fish and shellfish from the rivers. They developed the *atlatl*, or spear-thrower, which enabled a hunter to throw his weapon a much farther distance. They also stayed in one place for longer periods of time than their ancestors. Large Middle Archaic sites in the Ohio River valley near Louisville may have been occupied almost year-round. Hunters and food-gatherers dispersed from these "base camps" to temporary hunting camps at particular times of year. The concentration of population in large, semi-permanent camps may have been triggered by a four-thousand-year warming trend between 7000 and 3000 BCE that dried out much of the state, causing grasslands to replace forests and inducing Middle Archaic peoples to gather in river valleys where food sources were more reliable and varied.

At Falls of the Ohio State Park, just across the river from Louisville in Clarksville, Indiana, the permanent exhibit details the lives of Archaic hunter-gatherers along the river with artifacts and textual interpretation. While the exhibit covers the other periods of Native American prehistory, the Archaic saw the most sustained and intense use of the area around the Falls.

When the Middle Archaic warming trend ended, Archaic peoples spread out again, increasing in number and developing a more complex and sophisticated society over the course of the so-called Late Archaic period. In some areas, they built permanent houses in their winter settlements, to which they returned year after year. They developed a wider variety of regionally specialized tools as they settled into their local environments. Since squash rinds were found in some garbage piles, archaeologists think Late Archaic people may have begun to experiment with gardening. On occasion, they buried their dead with more objects alongside them—and presumably with more ceremony—and so they may have recognized some status distinctions among people, a social innovation in a generally egalitarian society. Some of the objects in the graves included copper items and marine shells, which would only be available through long-distance trade networks.

Continuing the trend started by their Paleoindian ancestors, Late Archaic people expanded the range of foods they ate. Whitetail deer and hickory nuts were staples, but they also ate smaller game animals, river mussels, and a variety of plant foods. Garbage mounds along the Green River in Kentucky contained the remains of 73 different kinds of plants, although most of those remains came from the 10 or so most important plants. All in all, Late Archaic peoples were fairly healthy, and it shows in the bones of their dead.

The earliest native artifacts from inside Mammoth Cave date from the Late Archaic period. Late Archaic natives traveled miles within the cave to collect various minerals for some unknowable purpose. Anthropologists speculate that the minerals might have been used in ceremonies, in curing rituals, or in long-distance trade. Native explorations of the cave continued through the end of the Archaic period, but then—again for unknown reasons—evidently ceased.

Mammoth Cave, Kentucky © Mark Gibson/Photos to Go

WOODLAND PEOPLE (1000 BCE TO 1000 CE)

Around 1000 BCE, people in eastern Kentucky learned a vital new skill: How to make pottery. The forms of this earliest Kentucky pottery bear similarities to ceramics found in other places in the Midwest and Northeast, so Kentucky people may have learned the skill from travelers or during their own travels. By 500 BCE, ceramics had spread throughout the state. For the Native Americans, the introduction of pottery made it easier to carry, store, or cook food, water, and other items. For archaeologists, the introduction of pottery marks the beginning of the Woodland period.

Early Woodland people made some other pioneering technological discoveries. The first fabrics, made of twisted and twined plant fibers, date from this period. They made further refinements to the design of projectile points, improving on the stemmed and notched bases of their Late Archaic predecessors. And they expanded on the initial steps toward gardening taken by those predecessors to develop full-fledged cultivation of plant foods.

Despite the technological changes, Early Woodland people lived much like their ancestors. Like Late Archaic people, they built semi-permanent base camps and winter villages, usually in the major river valleys. In other areas, like the Bluegrass region, they congregated on the ridge tops because the river valleys were too narrow. There they shifted about among smaller camps and settlements, not consolidating into more permanent settlements until later. Like their ancestors, they still hunted and still gathered wild plant foods, especially nuts. Gardening was an adjunct to this staple diet, contributing squash, gourds, and edible seeds to mealtimes.

What Woodland people did do very differently from their ancestors was to bury their dead in sacred mortuary grounds separated from the settlements. These sacred grounds developed from simple gravesites to more elaborate burial mounds, sometimes enclosed by palisades, in the five centuries between 1000 BCE and 500 BCE. In addition to providing a ceremonial center for a local community, a burial ground may have also served as a territorial marker. Populations increased during the Early Woodland period, and these sacred areas may have staked the claim of a local group to the use of a particular region.

Over the next five centuries or so, burial mounds became all the rage in the central and eastern parts of Kentucky. During the Middle Woodland period (200 BCE to 500 CE), people built hundreds of these mounds, along with other earthworks, all over the Bluegrass and northeastern Kentucky. Their less fashionable neighbors in southern and western Kentucky resisted the fad, and continued to live in their central base camps and constructed very few burial mounds. Some western people eventually did decide to see what all the fuss was about; burial mounds from the western part of the state are later constructions, after the mound-building boom had tapered off in the Bluegrass.

In the Bluegrass, the mounds served as ceremonial centers for people living in dispersed villages, and the majesty of the earthworks contrasted with the absence of large villages. The mounds probably served to reinforce a sense of group identity among several widely scattered communities as well as to warn other people from encroaching on the locals' lands.

Archaeologists call the culture of the mound-builders the Adena culture, and they continue to argue about its relationship to the more extensive mound-building Hopewell culture, which spread throughout much of the eastern United States. Without entering into the archaeological arcana of projectile points and potsherds, the general conclusion seems to be that Adena was either a predecessor of Hopewell or that it was simply an early regional variation of the larger Hopewell culture. The important historical point is that the mound-building craze grew out of the interactions between Kentucky's Middle Woodland peoples and other peoples from all over the eastern United States. Together they built a common culture, in which they exchanged ritual practices, sacred items, and probably ideas about life and afterlife.

Although many have been bulldozed, these mounds still exist in lots of locations around the Bluegrass region. To the untrained eye, they appear merely as wooded hillocks, but the state highway department has posted informational signs at some of them—like Gaitskill Mound near Mount Sterling in Montgomery County—to alert travelers to the fact that they are staring at 2,000-year old monuments, not just the rolling Kentucky landscape. The city park in Ashland, at the eastern edge of the state, likewise contains several ancient mounds.

Middle Woodland people outside the Bluegrass region participated less intensely in this common Hopewellian culture, but proximity had some impact. In the mountains of eastern Kentucky, people living on the Big Sandy River and along the Ohio built burial mounds and earthworks, while people in other parts of the mountains did not bother. Similarly, there are just a few mounds in western Kentucky, along the Green River in the southern part of the state and in the central cave country. In general, mound-building corresponded with dispersed settlements, as in the Bluegrass. People who lived in more concentrated or semi-permanent villages saw less need for the mortuary monuments of their neighbors.

Like most architectural fashions, burial mounds eventually fell out of favor. In the Bluegrass—the heart of the Adena culture in Kentucky—mound-building slacked off around 300 CE. This decline corresponded with the rise of clustered villages, particularly at the northern end of the Bluegrass, along the Ohio River. These villages became the focus of ritual life, taking that role away from the burial mound complexes. By 500 CE, mound-building construction had fallen so sharply—as had the long-distance trade of ritual items between Kentuckians and their Woodland neighbors to the north and east—that archaeologists decreed the beginning of the Late Woodland period.

Why the sudden end of mound building? No one knows for sure, but two rival hypotheses exist. One says that new construction and trade simply became less necessary because the Hopewell culture had stabilized; people had the burial mounds and ritual items they needed, so they didn't need to get any more. The other says the opposite. Demand increased, and when trade networks could not meet that demand, some groups decided to take what they wanted. The resulting hostility and conflict triggered the collapse of the exchange network, with the result that local groups tended to turn inward and focus more exclusively on their own local environments.

The transition from Middle to Late did not mean much for daily life. Late Woodland people still ate the same foods and used the same tools as before. Their hunting

Must-See Sites:
Natural Attractions

Big Bone Lick State Park

The park contains one of the many natural salt springs and salt bogs in Kentucky. These natural salt licks were favored hunting sites by everyone from Paleoindians to American frontiersmen. During the Ice Age, the salt in these areas lured many of the large Pleistocene megafauna hunted by Paleoindians. Over time, many animals became mired in the swampy land and died. Their bones, preserved in the bogs, eventually mineralized, preserving a fossil record of prehistoric Kentucky. The "big bones" of these animals gave the area its name.

Big Bone Lick became one of the first fossil-collecting sites in the young Republic. Even before the Revolution, French explorers had visited the place and written of bones literally lying on the ground. Later explorers, including Lewis and Clark, visited the site, collected fossilized remains, and shipped them to other locations. By 1840, the bones of hundreds of mammals had been removed from the area.

The state park contains hiking trails around the now dried-up salt bogs. A life-sized, diorama of some of those Pleistocene mammals stuck in the mud illustrates what drew Paleoindian hunters to the area. A small museum houses some native artifacts, though not all are from local sites, and some animal bones from digs at the site, including a mastodon skull uncovered in 1955.

The park is located near Union, Kentucky, off State Route 338 at 3380 Beaver Road. For information, call (859) 384-3522 (park) and (859) 384-3906 (museum), or visit parks.ky.gov/stateparks/bb.

Falls of the Ohio State Park

Actually in Clarksville, Indiana, the park is just across the Ohio River from Louisville. It is widely known for its Devonian-era fossil beds, and most visitors revel in their access to these ancient rocks, uncovered when the water levels of the river are lowest, from August to October.

The 16,000-square-foot interpretive center, which sits overlooking the fossil beds, has several exhibits that cover various facets of life and history at the Falls. The exhibits dealing directly with the prehistoric peoples of the area explain native uses of the various plants and animals, as well as their means of transportation and housing during different archaeological time periods. The park also holds an Archaeology Day in September, with plenty of hands-on demonstrations of native technologies and archaeologists available to explain the use and the historical context of ancient artifacts. In addition to Native American history, the interpretive center also offers information on the American conquest and settlement of the area around the Falls, as well as a wealth of natural history.

Falls of the Ohio State Park is located on Riverside Drive in Clarksville (Exit 0 off Interstate 65 after you cross the river from Louisville). Call (812) 280-9970 or visit www.fallsoftheohio.org.

Mammoth Cave National Park

This national park is home to the longest cave system in the world. Archaic-period natives ventured into the cave some 4,000 years ago and left behind archaeological evidence of their presence. They lit their way using cane torches; when one burned low, they lit another, proceeding ever deeper into the darkness. Their burned-out torches have been found in several locations in the cave. Some of these Archaic-period spelunkers did not come out, and their remains have been found at various points along the cave.

The cave contains over 350 miles of underground passageways mapped out on five levels, yet it still has not been fully explored. The Park Service offers a wide variety of cave tours that vary in length, theme, and difficulty. The Native American presence in the cave is covered most fully on the Historic Tour, which lasts about two hours.

The National Park encompasses 52,830 acres and, besides the cave itself, contains 70 miles of hiking and horse trails, a campground, and parts of the Green River and the Nolin River. The visitor center offers an introduction to the cave, the park's plants and animals, and the history of the area. It also sells the tickets for the cave tours.

The park is located ten miles west of Cave City on State Route 70. For information, call (270) 758-2328 or visit www.nps.gov/maca.

improved with the introduction of the bow and arrow sometime in the eighth century. Like their Middle Woodland predecessors, some Late Woodland people lived in villages and some lived in more dispersed and isolated camps. The most noticeable change from an archaeologist's point of view was the decline of nonlocal goods placed with the dead and the disappearance of distinctively Hopewellian decorations on pottery.

But the general picture of continuity masked the deeper changes that were occurring in Late Woodland societies. By the end of the period, many people had abandoned village life for dispersed settlements, the Late Woodland equivalent of suburbanization. Sometime in the ninth and tenth centuries, many of these settlements cultivated a new crop: maize. This new crop would become not only a staple food, but would revolutionize the societies that planted it, leading to full-blown field agriculture as the basis of subsistence and to the development of a complex social hierarchy and sophisticated village life.

LATE PREHISTORIC NATIVE AMERICANS (1000 CE TO 1600)

By about 900 CE, maize-based agriculture surpassed hunting and gathering as the primary base of subsistence for the native societies of Kentucky. As it did so, people gave up living in the dispersed settlements of the Late Woodland period and began to congregate in large planned villages. These villages became the centers of political power, religious ceremony, and social life during the Late Prehistoric period.

Two separate cultural traditions took hold in Kentucky during this time. In the western and southern portions of the state, the villages were part of the Mississippian culture, which existed throughout the southeastern United States along the Mississippi River drainage. In the Bluegrass and the eastern mountains, the villages were part of the Fort Ancient culture, a less extensive cultural tradition spread throughout the central part of the Ohio River valley. This was the heart of the Adena/Hopewell culture during the Woodland period, and Fort Ancient probably grew independently out of these older traditions.

Fort Ancient villagers moved around a little bit more,

practiced a little less intense ritual life, and had a less burdensome elite class than their Mississippian contemporaries. But Mississippians left behind more impressive monumental architecture and had a more stable village life.

The Mississippians may be the most famous prehistoric people of the eastern United States, thanks to the large size of some of their cities and the gigantic platform mounds they constructed. Cahokia, their "capital," near present-day St. Louis, Missouri, had a peak population of perhaps 10,000. It took until 1800 for a city in the United States to achieve that level of population.

But the cities tell only part of the story. Just like only a small percentage of modern Americans live in New York City, so only a small percentage of Mississippians lived in Cahokia. For every large town, there were dozens of smaller villages and isolated farmsteads. Archaeologists still ponder the relationships between these different settlements, but it appears to have been hierarchical. The farmsteads served the local village, and the smaller villages served the larger towns. In other words, just as New York City's reach extends into New Jersey and Connecticut, the larger Mississippian towns had extensive metropolitan areas.

The Mississippian sites in Kentucky vary from large towns to small villages to mortuary sites. The largest towns in Kentucky, such as the Adams site in Fulton County, Wickliffe in northern Ballard County, and Corbin in Adair County, shared a similar Mississippian town plan. A large plaza lay at the center of the town. On the edges of the plaza stood various platform and burial mounds. Houses, granaries, and work areas surrounded this ceremonial public space, with the agricultural fields lying just beyond. Mississippians liked to build their towns on bluffs and prominent river levees, highly visible sites that indicated the towns' central place in the region.

For a long time, archaeologists viewed smaller Mississippian outposts, such as Annis Village in Butler County, as just that: frontier "outposts" intended to colonize the local area on behalf of the regional metropolitan area. Now they are not so sure. For one thing, people lived in the "outposts" for a long time and, while the villagers sometimes built defensive fortifications, these appear to be reactions to sporadic local threats rather than the actions of a group of soldiers building an advance fort in hostile territory. While a determined band of frontier settlers dispatched to conquer new territory for the greater glory of Cahokia makes an exciting script, the real story might be a tad more mundane. Mississippian culture spread simply through everyday exchanges of goods and ideas that occurred when people came together.

One aspect of Mississippian culture gained only a limited hold in Kentucky. In the classic Mississippian tradition, the roles of chief, war leader, or shaman fell to a chosen few, usually members of a specific family or clan. Hereditary elite status marked a true Mississippian departure from the traditions of their Woodland ancestors. Mississippians in Kentucky did recognize status distinctions and the idea of hereditary chieftainship, but none of the Kentucky sites showed the extreme attention to status displayed in the burials at Cahokia, where dead elites were showered with treasures and joined in death by human sacrifices.

What did the elites do? Archaeologists guess that they bore the primary responsibility for designing, building, and keeping up the ceremonial mounds and central plazas at the heart of the Mississippian towns. Different clans probably oversaw different aspects of the work, and elites could call on the labor of their non-elite neighbors to make sure the work got done. But this was not a centrally directed society with an all-powerful ruling class. Most day-to-day decisions concerning individual communities stayed at the local level.

Over the course of the Mississippian period, some towns and villages survived and prospered, while others did not. With no written accounts explaining why people abandoned some settlements and persisted in others, archaeologists cannot explain the different fates of the various Mississippian communities in Kentucky. In general, the towns and villages in the Western Coalfield and Pennyroyal regions had shorter lives than those along the major river valleys. They survived only a century or two before they were abandoned, whereas people lived in some of the towns on the Ohio and Mississippi Rivers in the western part of the state for 500 years or more.

In either case, the Mississippian heyday ended when Europeans arrived in North America. Long before seeing their first European, Kentucky's Mississippians had fled their towns and villages or died trying. Fatal diseases preceded the arrival of actual European explorers and spelled doom for the natives. However, archaeological evidence suggests that some towns survived into the sixteenth and seventeenth centuries before the unique catastrophe of epidemic disease finally killed them off.

While their Mississippian contemporaries built large towns and elaborate mound complexes, the Fort Ancient people of central and northeastern Kentucky opted for a simpler life. As people in the Bluegrass and along the northern Ohio River began to come together in larger villages and rely more heavily on the classic Native American crop combinations of maize, beans, and squash, they did not construct majestic ceremonial spaces like the Mississippians. Nor did they organize their settlements into strict hierarchies or sort themselves out based on hereditary status differences. They built their houses either in a ring around a central plaza or in a line that followed the natural contours of a ridge or river valley. Between 1200 and 1400, the typical village, like the one at Fox Farm in Mason County, had 20 to 30 houses and maybe 300 inhabitants. A mural and artifact exhibit at the James Salato Wildlife Education Center in Frankfort depicts typical Fort Ancient village life around this time.

Not that the Fort Ancient people ignored status; after all, different people have different capabilities. When an important person died, Fort Ancient villagers might inter him in a burial mound, whereas the ordinary Joe got buried in front of the house. But village chiefs and other elders earned their places of prominence; they were not born to it. Moreover, these local chiefs and elders held predominantly local power. As opposed to the nested Mississippian hierarchy of farmstead-to-village-to-town, most Fort Ancient villages seemed to be roughly equal, suggesting that villages were mostly autonomous and could go about their business without interference from town-based elites.

Fort Ancient people also moved around more than the Mississippians. They periodically relocated their villages, perhaps as often as every 10 to 30 years as timber became scarce and soils became exhausted. They also migrated seasonally. Village populations dispersed in the fall into family groups, who would winter at smaller, more isolated hunting camps. Come planting time, they would return to the main village to prepare the fields.

Around 1400, the Fort Ancient world got smaller. Pottery throughout the central Ohio valley lost much of its regional distinctiveness, suggesting that Fort Ancient villages were becoming more closely integrated. The villages themselves during this time became larger but decreased in number. For whatever reason, these developments coincided with an increase in trade between Fort Ancient people and communities to the south and north.

Life in the villages also changed during this period. Dwellings became larger rectangular longhouses, in which two or more related families lived together. While earlier Fort Ancient people had built the occasional burial mound, their later relatives did not. They buried their dead near their houses in clan- or family-affiliated cemetery areas. Some of these villages, such as Hardin Village in Greenup County and Lower Shawneetown in Ohio, were occupied into the era of European exploration. European trade goods have been found at both places, and French and English traders left accounts of their visits to Lower Shawneetown in the 1750s.

Eventually, it was the impact of European trade and European-introduced disease that doomed the Fort Ancient culture. These impacts mostly preceded the physical arrival of Europeans in Kentucky. Germs followed trading routes and coastal natives infected inland ones. The diseases devastated large populations throughout the Ohio Valley before European traders ever got there. In addition, as Native Americans along the eastern seaboard and Great Lakes began to reorganize their lives around European trade, fierce intertribal conflicts erupted that contributed to the disruption and disappearance of the Fort Ancient tradition.

HISTORIC TRIBES

Although Native Americans occupied both Mississippian towns and Fort Ancient villages until after the arrival of Europeans into North America, it is extremely difficult to make direct links between these people and the tribes encountered by European explorers when they reached Kentucky. Epidemics wiped out whole villages, and the intertribal wars of the seventeenth century uprooted dozens

Road in Lexington, Kentucky

of native communities. Devastated by disease and warfare even before Europeans came among them, the tribes who the explorers did eventually encounter represented relatively recent social groupings, adaptations foisted upon them by forced migration and drastic population loss.

By around 1700, few Native Americans lived in Kentucky, although many tribes hunted there. Early settlers in Kentucky reported meeting members of at least a dozen tribes. However, four groups in particular had especially strong claims on the land: the Shawnee, Cherokee, and Chickasaw through occupation and use, and the Iroquois through conquest. Through years of warfare and diplomacy, Euro-American settlers eventually displaced most of these people. Present-day Native Americans celebrate their heritage, however, at festivals around the state, such as the Annie Tramper Festival in London and the Trail of Tears Indian Pow Wow in Hopkinsville.

Early pioneers made much of the fact that no permanent native settlements existed in Kentucky, thus justifying their own claims to the now "empty" land. This view conveniently ignored the fact that the Shawnee did have at least one town in Kentucky in the 1750s, and that the burial mounds, town sites, and abandoned villages of the Mississippians and Fort Ancient peoples showed that large numbers of Native Americans had previously lived in Kentucky. It also ignored the value of Kentucky as a hunting ground for the tribes.

In his 1784 guidebook, John Filson did note that "there are several ancient remains in Kentucke," but he argued that their existence proved "that this country was formerly inhabited by a nation farther advanced in the arts of life than the Indians." Filson, like some of his contemporaries, attributed these remains to the descendants of forgotten 12th-century Welsh colonists: "Having been expelled by the natives, [the Welsh] were forced to take refuge near the sources of the Missouri."

Of the historic tribes, the Shawnee probably had the strongest claim on Kentucky as a homeland. Many writers, although not all, trace the Shawnee back to the Fort Ancient people, and early French explorers said the Shawnee lived in the valleys of the Ohio River and of the Cumberland River. In fact, maps of the seventeenth and eighteenth centuries routinely identify the Cumberland as the "Shawnee River." That puts the Shawnee smack dab in the middle of Kentucky right about the time the intertribal wars of the seventeenth century began.

Those wars resulted from the impact of European trade on the more eastern tribes. The Europeans wanted furs, and tribes in the east had to secure an increasing number of skins to satisfy their desires for European manufactured goods. In short order, that meant expanding their hunting grounds. By the third quarter of the seventeenth century, the Iroquois Confederacy of upstate New York—a confederation of five separate tribes—had entered into a widening circle of hostilities with the tribes to their west and south in an aggressive effort to expand its hunting territory.

The Shawnee, pressed to the wall by the Iroquois, fragmented into different groups and moved in different directions, essentially abandoning Kentucky. Some moved west into the Illinois country; others moved into the southeast, establishing themselves in Georgia, where they frequently warred against the Cherokees and other neighboring tribes. By 1700 or so, a goodly portion of the Shawnee from the west and from the south had moved into Pennsylvania, where they shared space more or less peacefully with the Delaware, another tribe being pushed around by the Iroquois and by the colonists. By this time, the Iroquois claimed dominion over both the Shawnee and the Delaware, and by extension over the lands of Kentucky.

The colonial governments looked to the Iroquois to keep the subordinate tribes in line, but the Shawnee did not wear the Iroquois yoke easily. They frequently disregarded the agreements made by the Iroquois with colonial authorities, and around the 1720s or so they began a movement back down the Ohio River. They mostly settled north of the Ohio, but it was around this time, give or take a couple of decades, that some Shawnee settled Eskippakithiki, about 11 miles southeast of Winchester in present-day Clark County, the last permanent native settlement in Kentucky. Today, a state historical highway marker signals the site of Eskippakithiki. Whether north or south of the river, though, Shawnee men hunted throughout Kentucky.

The other tribe with strong claims to Kentucky was the Cherokee. While the traditional Cherokee homeland lay

Must-See Sites: The James C. Salato Wildlife Education Center

The center is one of the few places in the state where the Fort Ancient culture of Kentucky is interpreted for a general audience, although Native American history is not its primary mission. In 1992, Archaeologist A. Gwynn Henderson published a short book entitled *Kentuckians Before Boone*, which summarized in an easily readable form the available information about Fort Ancient life. At the Salato Center, the "Kentuckians Before Boone" mural depicts a Fort Ancient winter camp sometime in the late 1500s.

In addition to the mural, the center has a small display of artifacts. These include specimens of crops that the Fort Ancient people raised (primarily corn and squash), as well as shell gorgets, pottery, and tanned hides. In addition, the center offers regular weekday educational programs on Native American life in Kentucky.

The primary mission of the center is to educate visitors about natural life in Kentucky. It has inside and outside exhibits that introduce visitors to the diverse ecosystems within the state. Native plant and animal species are on display, both live and in dioramas. Hands-on exhibits and computer programs enhance the indoor displays. Live animals, restored native plant species, and short walking trails highlight the outdoor exhibits.

The center is administered by the Kentucky Department of Fish and Wildlife Resources. Dr. James C. Salato served for 28 years as a district Fish and Wildlife Resources commissioner, and devoted much of his free time to advancing the interests of hunting and fishing enthusiasts in the state. The Salato Center is located at 1 Game Farm Road off US Highway 60, just outside of Frankfort. Call the center at (502) 564-7863, or visit www.kdfwr.state.ky.us.

south of Kentucky, the Cherokee also hunted in the state and claimed at least the southeastern portion as part of their dominion. The Cherokee and the Shawnee were not friendly, and Kentucky served as a geographic buffer between the two traditional enemies. The Warrior's Path, a well-known Indian trail, ran directly through Kentucky from the Tennessee homelands of the Cherokee to the Ohio heart of Shawnee country. Its presence is acknowledged by a state highway marker in Jackson County, near the hamlet of Gray Hawk.

The Chickasaw also claimed lands in Kentucky. The heart of the Chickasaw homeland lay in northern Mississippi and Alabama, but their reach extended north up the Mississippi River to include that part of Kentucky west of the Tennessee River.

Quieting the various Native American claims to the land through treaty negotiations was part of the legal process that opened Kentucky to settlement by American pioneers. Yet signed treaties rarely avoided controversy. Colonial negotiators often excluded tribes with legitimate claims to the land from negotiations, or they talked only with cooperative tribal leaders, who did not speak for the entire tribe. Given the nature of authority within tribes, it was difficult for leaders to coerce acceptance of a treaty among all tribal members. Some of the treaties also had a *Godfather*-like quality to them; often negotiated at the point of a gun or on the verge of starvation, they were offers the Native Americans could not refuse.

The land hunger of the colonists drove negotiators to such tactics. To the colonists, the natives wasted Kentucky, using it only for hunting and not fully exploiting the land for all the bounty it might offer. The colonists were sure they could do better. It is a little ironic, therefore, that it was hunting that drew the first pioneers to the region.

3

EUROPEAN SETTLEMENT AND AMERICAN REVOLUTION

Kentucky's location isolated it from the earliest European explorations. The Spanish stuck to the southern coastlines and the Southwest, never pushing far enough east or north to make it to Kentucky. The English lay beyond the Appalachians, a forbidding barrier that relegated them to the eastern seaboard for much of the seventeenth century. And the French stuck largely to the Mississippi River drainage and the Great Lakes/St. Lawrence axis, allowing them to encircle Kentucky from the west and the north but not penetrate very deeply into the state.

The French had the best shot. In 1673, the Jesuit missionary Jacques Marquette descended the Mississippi and stopped at the mouth of the Ohio, noting that the river flowed from the east and was home to many Shawnee villages. During the eighteenth century, the French built settlements all around Kentucky—at Kaskaskia on the Mississippi River in Illinois, at Vincennes on the Wabash River in Indiana, and at the forks of the Ohio near modern-day Pittsburgh, Pennsylvania—but nothing on the Ohio River itself. In 1749, they sent a fairly large force under Pierre-Joseph Celoron de Bienville up the Ohio to remedy that situation. The best Bienville did was to bury some lead plates somewhere around the mouth of the Big Sandy River as evidence of the French claim to the region.

From the English side, the Virginian colonial authorities showed interest early in Kentucky. The royal charter granting land to Virginia's proprietors stated that Virginia's boundaries extended from sea to sea. With one sea at their back, Virginians naturally wondered where that other sea might be. In 1671, a Virginian exploring party crossed the

Blue Ridge Mountains and discovered the New River, which flowed to the west and presumably toward that elusive other sea. And in 1673, a young Virginian journeyed with a war party of Tomahittan natives up through Kentucky to attack a Shawnee camp in Ohio. Wounded and captured, he did not make it back to Virginia until five years later, bringing with him detailed information about Kentucky and the Native Americans who lived there.

But it was not formal exploration or missionary zeal that finally brought Kentucky into the wider world of European settlement and colonial competition. It was instead that great mover of men's hearts, money. Lacking the kind of instant wealth the Spanish had found in Mexico and Peru, the colonists in North America needed to find New World revenue producers. In the colonial backwoods, the best revenue producers were animal skins, and by the 1760s backwoodsmen from Pennsylvania, Virginia, and North Carolina routinely crossed the mountains to hunt in Kentucky.

THE LONG HUNTERS

By the latter half of the eighteenth century, several thousand of Kentucky's whitetail deer were killed, dressed, and shipped to Europe each year, where they became book bindings, gloves, and other leather items. Although it mattered little to the deer, it mattered greatly to the history of Kentucky whether Native American hunters or colonial backwoodsmen did the killing. For Native American hunters, the fur trade allowed them to participate in an altered but still recognizable traditional economy, in which men predominantly hunted and women tended the fields. In exchange for deerskins, European traders provided metal pots, knives, guns, cloth, beads, and other useful and not-so-useful items upon which the natives came to depend. Traders like John Findley and George Croghan succeeded because they established strong relationships with the natives who were their suppliers and customers. When they came back east to sell the skins, they also transmitted detailed reports about the abundance of fur-bearing animals in Kentucky.

From a trader's perspective, the Native American trade had certain disadvantages. You had to work within the cultural framework of the tribes to succeed, a framework that often viewed trade not as an economic relationship but as reciprocal gift-giving among friends. Once you mastered that, you had another problem. The native demand for durable metal goods and other essentials had a fairly low ceiling; bump into it and it was tough to get your hunters to hunt. As a solution, some traders introduced the ultimate nondurable commodity into the Native American trade—booze. Alcohol had its own drawbacks by creating disorder and unpredictability among your customers, but the natives might drink the proceeds of a season's hunt in just a few days, which would force them back out to procure more skins.

There was another way around these disadvantages, and that was to sidestep the Native Americans entirely. As traders' reports of Kentucky drifted back east, parties of "Long Hunters" from Pennsylvania, Virginia, and North Carolina crossed the mountains to see and hunt Kentucky for themselves. Long Hunters earned their name by disappearing into the wilderness for extended hunting trips. Long hunts initially developed in the backcountry settlements as a way to put meat on the table for the winter months, but the hunts took on a commercial flavor as the fur trade developed. It was risky business. Hunters needed at least one good hunting season to turn a profit, but the haul from a season's work might be lost in an instant to Native Americans, wild animals, or inclement weather. In 1769, one member of a group of twenty hunters from Virginia and North Carolina left this unhappy message carved on a Kentucky poplar tree: "2,300 deer skins lost. Ruination by God."

Long Hunters and Native Americans coexisted uneasily in the shared hunting grounds of Kentucky. The Native Americans resented the intrusion, the competition, and the tremendous waste that followed in the wake of the Long Hunters. They punished these infractions when they could, generally by confiscating the skins but usually letting the hunters themselves go. When a Shawnee party captured Daniel Boone and John Findley in December 1769, for example, they took their deerskins but released the men after giving them small gifts of moccasins, powder, and shot and a warning not to poach in Shawnee country again.

Must-See Sites: The Dr. Thomas Walker State Historic Site

This area was chartered by the Virginia-based Loyal Land Company to explore the more than 800,000 acres of western country that the company owned. Walker and his party only stayed in the area for about a week in 1750, but the replica cabin now located here is a faithful reproduction of a pioneer log structure. Its size is about twelve feet by eight feet; the door is hung without using iron hinges, and the wood is pegged together. The cabin was largely built to solidify the company's claims to the land. While at the site, Walker's party planted some corn—further evidence to support the Loyal Company's claim to the land—and successfully hunted some bear. They cured the meat for use during their further travels.

Walker's party left Virginia on March 6, and heavy spring rains forced them further south and west than many later pioneers would travel. High water thwarted their initial attempt to cross the Cumberland River (which Walker's party named for the Duke of Cumberland) at a well-known fording spot, and they moved down the south side of the river. When they came to a second fording spot also rendered unusable by high water, the party built a bark canoe and paddled across the river and into Kentucky. It was after getting out of the marshy land near the river and up onto the knolls that Walker's party stopped to build their cabin.

The Walker State Historic Site is located about six miles southwest of the town of Barbourville on State Route 459. The entire site contains just twelve acres of land. For information, call (606) 546-4400 or visit the website parks.ky.gov/statehistoricsites/dt.

Despite these conflicts, Long Hunters and Native Americans shared many values. Both prized toughness, marksmanship, and independence. Boone, the most famous of the Long Hunters, favored the "Indian life" to the life of a civilized farmer back in the colonies. Come hunting season, he was eager to be off, more at home in the woods than under a roof. As Boone put it, "I was happy in the midst of dangers and inconveniences." Being in the woods was like a tonic for him: "A tour through the country, and the diversity and beauties of nature I met with... expelled every gloomy and vexatious thought."

Boone, born in 1734 in Pennsylvania, first traveled to Kentucky in the company of Findley, an old friend and Indian trader. They departed the Upper Yadkin country of North Carolina in May 1769 and passed through the Cumberland Gap into Kentucky. Boone and his party hunted through the summer and fall before the run-in with the Shawnees in December 1769. Disregarding the Shawnee warning, Boone and his brother-in-law John Stuart stayed on and hunted in Kentucky. (Stuart disappeared in the winter of 1770; they found his skeleton five years later.) Boone's brother, Squire, twice traveled back east to sell the skins and renew their store of supplies. Daniel himself remained until March 1771, when he finally began the return trip laden with a last load of skins and accompanied by Squire. Unfortunately for the Boones, they met an unfriendly group of Cherokees who confiscated their skins and their horses.

Although he probably lost money on his two-year venture, Boone had gained an intimate knowledge and a deep love for Kentucky. "Soon after," he wrote, "I returned home to my family, with a determination to bring them as soon as possible to live in Kentucky, which I esteemed a second paradise, at the risk of my life and fortune."

Boone's case clarifies an important difference between Long Hunters and Native American hunters. Although Long Hunters liked the woods, they carried visions of settlement in their heads—of private property and individual farms—and that eventually eroded any commonality with the Native Americans. Boone is typical: celebrated as a natural man of the wilderness, he was also an avid land speculator and willing employee of large land companies looking to transform Kentucky from a hunters' paradise to a settled society.

TROUBLE WITH THE CROWN

Certain practical concerns stood in the way of such visions. First and foremost, there were the various Native

American claims on the land. The tribes might uneasily tolerate Long Hunters but they did not welcome the idea of giving up their hunting grounds to colonial settlers. Second, there was the ongoing conflict between the French and the English for control of the western country and, indeed, all of eastern North America.

The struggle between France and England culminated in the global struggle known as the Seven Years' War. In the North American theater, the English colonists called it the French and Indian War, since the French relied heavily on Native American auxiliaries to do their fighting. The English had Native American allies too—most of the Iroquois sided with them—but colonial militias also did a good deal of the fighting for the Crown. Although France held the upper hand early, England eventually won the war. In 1763, France and England signed the Treaty of Paris, in which France gave up all its claims in North America. Needless to say, France did not consult its Native American allies on the terms of the treaty.

The British planned on dealing with the tribes as conquered enemies. They figured that with the French gone, the Native Americans had no European ally to arm them and exhort them against the colonists, so there was no need to try and placate their demands. Such high-handed treatment triggered a multi-tribal uprising in 1763 that the British put down only with difficulty. The rebellion made it clear that the Native Americans in the Ohio Valley could not simply be ignored.

So the king drew the infamous Proclamation Line of 1763. The line ran down the crest of the Appalachians, and the Crown forbade any settlements west of the line. It ordered any existing settlements to be abandoned, and it disallowed any private purchases of land from the Native Americans. The Crown intended the line as a way to gain a little time while conflicting colonial claims to the western country were sorted out and to calm the Native Americans so they would negotiate the peaceable sale of their lands. Many Native Americans in the Ohio country saw the line as a vindication of their right to retain their lands and their traditional economy of mixed hunting and farming.

However, the colonists saw the line as a complete betrayal. Many had figured the prize for victory over the

French would be the opening of the land beyond the Appalachians to English settlement. Virginians especially detested the line, for they felt it violated their rights to the western country contained in the original colonial charter. Lacking money to pay its soldiers, Virginia had also induced men to fight in the war by promising them land. With much of the good land in the east already taken up, holders of these military land warrants looked with hungry eyes to Kentucky.

Hating it so, the colonists simply ignored the line. Backwoods settlements spread west of the Appalachians during the mid-1760s, and the Long Hunters trespassed even deeper into Native American country. "The white people pay no attention to the talks we have had," complained the Cherokee leader Oconostota to the king's Indian agent. "They are in bodies hunting in the middle of our hunting grounds…. The whole nation is filling with hunters, and the guns rattling every way on the path, both up and down the river. They have settled the land a great way this side of the line." The Crown, with only a handful of troops and with other problems on its hands, hardly bothered to attempt enforcement.

It did attempt to negotiate treaties with the Native Americans to cede the land. They turned first to their erstwhile allies in the war, the Iroquois. The Iroquois claimed great swaths of the Ohio Valley by dint of conquest and, being smart imperial overlords, they sold their underlings' land first. In the Treaty of Fort Stanwix of 1768, the Iroquois signed away all the lands between the Ohio and the Tennessee Rivers, essentially all of Kentucky, with bits of Tennessee, the Carolinas, Georgia, and Alabama thrown in. The Shawnee, who had never warmed to their status as Iroquois lackeys, understandably resented the sale of their lands, and they resisted the European settlement of Kentucky for the next three decades.

Like the Iroquois, the Cherokee also came under great pressure to cede their lands to the colonists after the French and Indian War. Although the Cherokee lands in Kentucky overlapped the land already ceded by the Iroquois, the Cherokee were too powerful simply to ignore, as the colonists tried to do with the Shawnee. In 1768 and 1770, the Cherokee signed treaties giving up their lands in

Scenic red barn in Kentucky

Kentucky east of the Kentucky River. "The land is now divided for the use of the red and the white people," Oconostota said after signing the 1768 treaty. He voiced his hope that "the white people on the frontier will pay attention to the line marked and agreed upon.... We have now given the white men enough land to live upon, and hope in return to be well used by them."

These treaties hardly quieted all the Native American claims to Kentucky, but land-hungry colonists paid little heed to such legal niceties. They wanted the land, and not just for their own modest homesteads. Many dreamed of cashing in on the anticipated land rush, and so they tried every means possible—both legal and illegal—to amass as much Kentucky land as they could.

THE LAND SPECULATORS

Already by the 1770s, land speculation had a distinguished pedigree in Kentucky. Well-connected Virginia gentlemen had dreamed since the 1740s of profiting from the empire to the west. These gentlemen joined together to form great land companies and then, using their political connections, gained rights to almost unfathomably large amounts of land. Between them, two rival land companies—the Ohio Land Company, founded in 1747, and the Loyal Company, chartered in 1749—claimed 1.3 million acres in the backcountry of Virginia and Kentucky. In 1750, the Loyal Company sponsored the first exploring party to cross through the Cumberland Gap into Kentucky. Led by a Virginia physician, Dr. Thomas Walker, the group built a cabin in present-day Knox County and explored the surrounding area. A replica of the cabin now stands at the Thomas Walker State Historic Site near Barbourville.

The companies' goals were to plant settlers on the land, subdivide it, and sell the lots off to the expected flood of immigrants. Although each company tried to locate colonists on its lands, neither enjoyed great success. When the American Revolution broke out, companies that held privileges granted by royal fiat did not fare well, and they had to abandon their plans.

Around 1775, when the great plans of the Ohio and Loyal Companies were foundering, Daniel Boone went to work for Richard Henderson, a prominent backcountry judge in North Carolina. Henderson dreamed of building an empire in Kentucky, and had recently organized the

Transylvania Company to colonize and speculate in western lands. Lacking the political resources of rival groups of land speculators, the Transylvania Company went directly to the Native Americans. At the Treaty of Sycamore Shoals, it purchased from the Cherokees all land between the Kentucky and the Cumberland Rivers for £10,000 in trade goods, despite the fact that the Cherokees held only a tenuous claim to the territory.

The constant grasping was enough for many of the younger Cherokees. Dragging Canoe, the son of one of the chiefs who signed the treaty, vented his anger in a long speech to the treaty council:

> We had hoped that the white men would not be willing to travel beyond the mountains. Now that hope is gone. They have passed the mountains, and have settled upon Cherokee land. They wish to have that usurpation sanctioned by treaty. When that is gained, the same encroaching spirit will lead them upon other land of the Cherokees. New cessions will be asked…. Such treaties may be all right for men who are too old to hunt or fight. As for me, I have my young warriors about me. We will have our lands.

Even before the negotiations were complete, the company dispatched Boone to cut a road into Kentucky and establish a settlement to solidify the company's claim. The company promised Boone 2,000 acres of prime land as reward. By April 1775, Boone had weathered rugged terrain, repeated Native American attacks, and a failure of nerve on the part of many in his party. Nonetheless, he wrote, "we proceeded on to Kentucky River without opposition; and on the first day of April began to erect the fort of Boonesborough at a salt lick, about sixty yards from the river." That outpost has long since deteriorated, but the state has recreated it near the original site at Fort Boonesborough State Park.

Henderson's dreams of empire faded, however, as other speculators heard of his bold bid to claim this most desirable section of Kentucky. They fought his claims in the legislative halls while Henderson's own empire-building alienated other pioneers in Kentucky. Outmaneuvered in Virginia, Henderson took his case to the Continental

Congress but lost there as well. In 1776, the Virginia legislators outlawed any purchases from Native Americans made without legislative approval, and they officially incorporated Kentucky into the Old Dominion as a separate county. The legislature specifically voided Henderson's treaty with the Cherokees two years later.

Smaller-scale land speculators actually played a more important role in the settlement of Kentucky than the great land companies. Although early pioneers made a great fuss over the machinations of large land companies, contrasting the companies' corruption with the simple virtue of the "actual settler," most pioneers also wore speculators' hats. Pioneers engrossed more land than they needed for actual subsistence in the hope of selling it off to latecomers at inflated prices. They served as the local agents of far-off eastern investors, buying up their neighbors' claims. In fact, few early settlers saw their claims through and actually obtained a land title; many took the easy money offered by speculators and went off to settle another piece of land. Indeed, Daniel Boone changed from a Long Hunter to a land hunter in the years after the Transylvania Company's demise, locating lands for absentee eastern owners.

THE FIRST SETTLEMENTS

The flagrant disregard of the Proclamation Line and the clear intention of colonists to settle in the lands west of the mountains led to almost constant friction between the Native Americans—primarily Shawnee and Cherokee—and would-be settlers. Pioneers rarely took the trouble to distinguish between peaceful and hostile tribes, and the frontier produced frequent reports of shocking murders of peaceful natives. These murders resulted in equally shocking and bloody counterattacks by Native Americans already angered by the trespasses and the occupation of their lands. Small war parties struck isolated farmsteads and backcountry settlements with regularity, which in turn produced retaliation by frontiersmen. "Two darling sons, and a brother, have I lost by savage hands," Daniel Boone once lamented, "which have also taken from me forty valuable horses, and abundance of cattle."

Native Americans confiscated hunters' skins, warned off land surveyors, and pleaded with colonial authorities to

Famous Sons and Daughters: Daniel Boone

Hunter and explorer
(November 2, 1734–September 26, 1820)

Born in Berks County, Pennsylvania, to Quaker pioneers, Daniel Boone is America's best-known frontiersman. After being expelled from the Society of Friends in Pennsylvania, Boone's father relocated to the Yadkin River valley in North Carolina in 1751 or 1752. Soon after, Boone served as a wagon driver in General Edward Braddock's failed campaign to take Fort Duquesne (present-day Pittsburgh) during the French and Indian War.

A little more than a year after his return from the war, he married Rebecca Bryan on August 14, 1756. In the winter of 1768–69, he traveled with his friend John Finley through the Cumberland Gap to hunt in Kentucky. He stayed two years and resolved on his return to North Carolina to resettle his family in Kentucky.

After Native American attacks foiled his initial attempt to found a settlement in Kentucky, Boone signed on with Richard Henderson to negotiate a treaty with the Cherokees that ceded a vast tract of land to Henderson's Transylvania Company in 1775. Henderson then dispatched Boone and a party of 30 to cut a road from the Cumberland Gap to the Kentucky River and establish a fort. Boone did so, but Henderson's bid to hold on to the land ultimately failed.

Boone remained in Kentucky, and in 1778 he and a group of saltmakers from the fort were captured by the Shawnees. After a five-month stay, during which he was adopted as a son by the chief, Black Fish, Boone escaped and returned to Boonesborough. In September, he helped repel the Shawnees' siege of the fort. Suspected of collaboration with the tribe during his captivity, however, he was tried for treason—and acquitted.

From 1779 on, things went badly for Boone. Robbed of his own and some friends' money, with which he intended to buy land, he spent several years paying off the debts. In 1781, during the American Revolution, Boone—serving as a Virginia legislator—was captured and imprisoned by the British. In

August of the same year, Boone was involved in the Kentucky militia's disastrous foray at Blue Licks. He moved two or three times during the 1780s and 1790s, working as a tavernkeeper, government contractor, surveyor, and legislator. By 1798, continual litigation had stripped him of most of his lands; in September 1799, he left for Missouri. He served as magistrate in Missouri, but had similar bad luck holding on to any land.

On March 18, 1813, Rebecca died. Boone followed seven years later. At his request, he was buried next to his wife in Defiance, Missouri. In 1845, the remains of Boone and his wife were dug up, shipped to Kentucky, and reinterred in the Frankfort Cemetery.

The famous frontiersman was saved from obscurity by John Filson, a Pennsylvania schoolteacher transplanted to Kentucky. Filson interviewed Boone in the 1780s, fashioned Boone's remembrances into a narrative, and published it as Boone's memoirs in Filson's 1784 guidebook. The following extract relates Boone's first impressions of Kentucky in 1769.

> [A]fter a long and fatiguing journey, through a mountainous wilderness, in a westward direction, on the seventh day of June following we found ourselves on Red river, where John Finley had formerly been trading with the Indians, and, from the top of an eminence, saw with pleasure the beautiful level of Kentucky....
>
> We found everywhere abundance of wild beasts of all sorts, through this vast forest. The buffalo were more frequent than I have seen cattle in the settlements, browzing on the leaves of the cane, or cropping the herbage on those extensive plains, fearless, because ignorant, of the violence of man. Sometimes we saw hundreds in a drove, and the numbers about the salt springs were amazing. In this forest, the habitation of beasts of every kind natural to America, we practiced hunting with great success....

—from John Filson, *The Discovery, Settlement and Present State of Kentucky* (1784) restrain their citizens from illegally occupying Native land. By the mid-1770s, an undeclared war raged on the frontier. In 1774, the governor of Virginia, Lord Dunmore, decided to end the Native American threat. Dunmore had dispatched parties to Kentucky in 1773 and 1774 to survey land for military warrants. These parties alarmed the Native Americans because they understood that surveys necessarily meant more settlers on their lands. As violence between natives and colonists increased, Dunmore proposed to march 1,000 men to attack the largely Shawnee villages north of the Ohio River. A group of 1,300 frontier militiamen also decided to join Dunmore's expedition.

As the militiamen traveled north to meet Dunmore's soldiers, the Shawnee attacked them where the Kanawha River enters the Ohio, in present-day West Virginia. Although outnumbered, the Shawnee killed or wounded 200 of the frontier soldiers. They suffered heavy losses, however, and rather than pursue the war, they decided to sue for peace. In the resulting treaty, the Shawnee signatories agreed not to hunt anymore south of the Ohio River, so long as the colonists remained south of the river. Lord Dunmore's War opened a window of opportunity for pioneers, and the first permanent colonial settlements took hold in Kentucky.

Although Daniel Boone established Boonesborough in April 1775, the claim of first permanent settlement actually belongs to Harrodsburg. In March 1774, James Harrod, a Pennsylvania-born backwoodsman, led a party of 31 men down the Ohio River to the mouth of the Kentucky River. They then canoed upstream about 100 miles. Going overland a few miles, they made a camp near a spring close to the source of the Salt River in present-day Mercer County. On June 16, 1774, they began laying out claims and building cabins. Lord Dunmore's War persuaded them to abandon their efforts for that year, but they returned to the site on March 15, 1775. Now a state park in Harrodsburg, Old Fort Harrod includes the oldest cemetery west of the Allegheny Mountains.

Boonesborough and Harrodsburg were forts, large and well-fortified for defense against Native American attacks. But in the years after their founding, numerous smaller stations also sprang up. A station meant simply a defensible residential structure, usually two or more cabins in close proximity to each other. By one estimate 187 stations went up in the Bluegrass in the two decades after the founding of the first permanent settlements. In times of trouble, however, families quickly abandoned their stations and moved to the forts for protection.

In April 1780, for example, Squire Boone came with 13 families to Painted Stone Station in Shelby County. Harassed by Native Americans, the settlers lasted barely longer than a year, deciding to evacuate in the fall of 1781. Their evacuation in September, aided by the militia, culminated in a Native American attack known as the Long Run Massacre. Seven settlers were killed before the attack was repulsed. The following day, local militia leader John Floyd led 26 men back to the site to bury the dead and pursue the natives. Encountering a small group near the present-day town of Eastwood, Floyd's men charged straight into an ambush, and the natives killed seventeen of Floyd's company. In 1999, local history buffs staged the first historical reenactment of those events, now performed annually in September at Clear Creek Park in Shelbyville.

The forts, although palisaded and largely impervious to arrows and muskets, had other problems, namely water, food, and sanitation. Forts often depended on an outside source for water, which made them extraordinarily vulnerable in the event of a long siege. The settlers also wasted prodigious amounts of food, to the point of endangering their lives. Within a few weeks of the establishment of Boonesborough, for example, the settlers had killed so many of the numerous buffalo in the area that they soon found themselves journeying 15 or 20 miles to find meat, exposing both hunting parties and the settlement itself to Native American attacks. Finally, unsuited for the number of people that might crowd together in a fort during times of trouble, the forts became a sanitation nightmare. In 1780 one visitor to Harrodsburg wrote that "the whole dirt and filth of the Fort, putrified flesh, dead dogs, horse, cow, hog excrements and human odour all wash into the spring... [making] the most filthy nauseous [sic] potation of the water imaginable."

Fortunately for the settlers, Native American war parties did not favor long sieges. Little glory accrued to warriors who simply waited and starved people out. Quick strikes against backcountry settlements continued to be the natives' main *modus operandi*.

The arrangement worked out at the end of Dunmore's War quickly broke down, as neither side could hold to its promises. Settlers did not stop south of the Ohio but continued to trespass on Native American lands. Likewise, many Shawnee warriors never accepted the abandonment of Kentucky, despite the pleas of more peace-minded leaders. Most disturbing to the pioneers, by 1776 Shawnee and Cherokee warriors—historically at odds with each other—often made common cause against the settlers.

The Native American attacks unsettled the stations, terrified pioneer families, and led to unremitting cycles of retaliatory violence, but they stood no serious chance of dislodging the pioneers. Once gathered in their forts, the settlers could mount an effective resistance. That might have given peace-minded Native American leaders a better shot at persuading their warriors to accept the limitations laid out in the treaty following Dunmore's War, if not for the American Revolution. The Revolution brought a flow of British arms, advice, and encouragement into the country that tipped the balance of power firmly toward the warriors' party.

THE AMERICAN REVOLUTION

The British aimed to divert Patriot arms and attention from the battles in the East by unleashing the Native Americans against the settlements of Kentucky. Shawnee warriors, already angered by pioneer outrages, were not very tightly leashed anyway. The year 1777 saw the most sustained Native American attacks to date against the Kentucky settlements. The Shawnee chief Blackfish led 200 warriors across the Ohio in March and established a base camp on the Licking River. From there, he launched a series of hit-and-run strikes that forced the settlers into their forts and depopulated the country. Settlers virtually abandoned the area north of the Kentucky River, and the total population probably numbered no more than 300. The remaining settlers, desperate for food, wavered in their loyalty to the Patriot cause. Some men even defected to the British side, lured by the generosity offered by British commanders.

Famous Sons and Daughters: George Rogers Clark

Soldier
(November 19, 1752–February 13, 1818)

Born in Virginia, Clark traveled to Kentucky as a soldier and a surveyor. He served as a militia captain in Lord Dunmore's War against the Shawnee in 1774, then returned to his job as surveyor for the Ohio Company in Kentucky. He helped lay out the town of Leesburg, which is now a part of Frankfort, in 1775, and was elected as a delegate from Harrodsburg to Virginia's lower house.

With the outbreak of the American Revolution, Clark concocted his plan to take the British forts in the country north of the Ohio River. After drilling his troops at Corn Island near the Falls of the Ohio, he departed on June 24, 1778. Clark took the forts of Kaskaskia and Vincennes, and in 1880 and 1882 led major assaults against the Shawnees.

After the Revolution, Clark's star tumbled. Virginia awarded him over 18,000 acres of land and 2,193 pounds sterling for his service, but most of the money went to pay off debts incurred during the military campaigns. He laid out the town of Clarksville, Indiana, but the Virginia legislature revoked his right to build the first sawmill. In 1786, he became embroiled in controversy regarding the Spanish conspiracy, during which Spain attempted to woo the West away from the United States. Later he accepted a commission in the French army to attack Spanish-held New Orleans, a commission which the US government viewed in a dim light and forced Clark to resign.

In 1803, Clark resided in Clarksville, where he suffered a stroke in 1809. He then moved to Locust Grove, the estate of his sister, near Louisville, where he died after suffering two additional strokes. His remains were removed from the family cemetery at Locust Grove in 1869 and buried in Cave Hill Cemetery in Louisville.

Peace-minded Shawnee leaders still held out hope that some kind of accommodation might be reached without embroiling their people in the struggle between the English and the Americans. In November 1777, the Shawnee chief Cornstalk journeyed to Fort Randolph, in present-day West Virginia, to negotiate peace with the Americans. Instead, the fort's commander took Cornstalk and his party hostage. Pioneers, outraged by Shawnee attacks on the frontier, broke into the Shawnees' cell a few days later and opened fire. They killed Cornstalk, then mutilated his body. Their actions united the Shawnees in their resistance to American occupation of their country.

In February 1778, Blackfish set out to attack Boonesborough and avenge Cornstalk. On his way, however, he found Boone himself. In early January, Boone had led a 30-man expedition from the fort to the Lower Blue Licks to secure a supply of salt for the settlement. Out hunting in early February, Boone ran into Blackfish's party. "They pursued, and took me; and brought me on the eighth day to the Licks, where twenty seven of my party were," Boone recalled. "I knowing [sic] it was impossible for them to escape, capitulated with the enemy, and, at a distance in their view, gave notice to my men of their situation, with orders not to resist, but surrender themselves captives."

At this point, many of Boone's companions began to question Boone's loyalties. He told the Shawnee that the fort was already on the verge of surrender, but that it would be better to take it in the spring, when the women and children could travel. He promised Blackfish that come spring he would lead the chief to Boonesbrough himself and arrange the fort's surrender. Blackfish agreed and, after much debate, the Shawnee warriors voted on the plan, finally approving it 61 to 59.

The Shawnee marched the captives back to their villages and then on to Detroit, where ten of them were turned over to the British. "During our travels," Boone recalled, "the Indians entertained me well; and their affection for me was so great, that they utterly refused to leave me there [in Detroit] with the others, although the Governor offered them one hundred pounds sterling for me."

Boone returned with his captors to their home village. He said: "I spent my time as comfortably as I could expect;

was adopted, according to their custom, into a family where I became a son, and had a great share in the affection of my new parents, brothers, sisters, and friends." Similar adoptions kept about half the saltmakers in Shawnee hands.

Boone liked leading the Native American life. "I was exceedingly familiar and friendly with them," he described. "I often went a hunting with them, and frequently gained their applause for my activity at our shooting-matches." Blackfish became so trusting of Boone that he even let the pioneer hunt by himself: "I frequently returned with the spoils of the woods, and as often presented some of what I had taken to him, expressive of duty to my sovereign."

Boone's cheerful acquiescence to his "captivity" only led his compatriots to wonder further about his loyalties. When he engineered an escape from his Native American family and showed up back in Boonesborough in June 1778, many settlers suspected he had come to sell out the fort. Boone told them they had it all wrong; his "betrayal" had only been a deception meant to spare the saltmakers' lives and save the fort from imminent attack, but not everyone trusted him.

When Blackfish showed up in September with 350 warriors from several Ohio Valley tribes, he reminded Boone of his promise to give up the fort. Blackfish's promise of good treatment looked better to Boone than the way the settlers had been living, holed up in a fort and fearing the next attack, but he told Blackfish he could not surrender the fort without consulting the other leaders. His fellow settlers derided Boone's confidence in Shawnee promises. When the final vote was taken, Boone joined in the unanimous decision to fight to the death.

The siege of Boonesborough lasted ten days, the longest siege of any Kentucky fort. The "siege" mostly consisted of an exchange of sniper fire, which took 37 Shawnee lives but only two settlers'. Losing their appetite for waiting out the residents, the Shawnee subsequently broke up into small raiding parties, adopting the old strategy of hit-and-run strikes.

Boone, meanwhile, found himself accused of treason and facing trial before a panel of Kentucky militia officers. After hearing Boone's rationale for his actions, the court declared him not guilty and promoted him to major in the militia.

Must-See Sites: Historic State Parks

Fort Boonesborough State Park

Kentucky's homage to Daniel Boone's prominent role in opening the state to American settlement, Fort Boonesborough contains a 180 x 280-foot walled fort, inside of which are the blockhouses built by the settlers to withstand Native American attacks. In pioneer-style log cabins, settlers lived outside the fort walls, but retreated inside the palisades when trouble threatened. Neither fort nor cabins are on their original sites, having been relocated and reconstructed to survive the ravages of modern tourism.

The park contains a museum that documents the history of the fort, with particular attention given to the siege of Boonesborough by the Shawnee in 1778. It is this slice of time that the park hopes to recapture; indeed, with the lessening of the Native American threat in the 1790s, Boonesborough's population declined rapidly. There is also a self-guided walking tour around the park with signposts indicating important events in the life of Boonesborough and the settlement of Kentucky.

To give visitors a more realistic appreciation of life on the Kentucky frontier, the park features regular pioneer craft demonstrations by costumed interpreters from April to October in the cabins outside the fort's walls. These demonstrations cover work-a-day activities like blacksmithing, weaving, soap making, candle making, and so forth.

Fort Boonesborough State Park is located on State Route 388 between Richmond and Winchester. For more information, call (859) 527-3131 or visit parks.ky.gov/stateparks/fb.

Old Fort Harrod State Park

Old Fort Harrod re-creates the settlement founded by James Harrod in 1774, the first permanent European settlement in Kentucky, predating Boonesborough by a year. Like Fort Boonesborough, the buildings of the old fort have been reconstructed and moved from their original site. In Fort Harrod's case, the reconstructed version ended up about one third smaller than the original. Unlike Boonesborough, the early settlement gave rise to a town—Harrodsburg.

Replicas of the thick-walled cabins of early settlers are located inside the fort, as are reconstructed blockhouses—all designed to withstand Native American attacks. As at Fort Boonesborough, costumed interpreters in the cabins demonstrate various pioneer crafts and offer information about pioneer life in the fort from April through October. The first American cemetery west of the Alleghenies is also located on the park grounds.

Located in an old Greek Revival mansion built on the site in the early 1800s by a Harrodsburg resident, the museum at the park focuses more on the Civil War than on the history of the fort or the local area. The park also contains a memorial honoring the marriage of Abraham Lincoln's parents, which occurred in Harrodsburg on June 12, 1806.

Old Fort Harrod State Park is located in Harrodsburg on South College Street. Call (859) 734-3314 or visit parks.ky.gov/stateparks/fh.

Blue Licks Battlefield State Resort Park

Occupying the site of the 1782 defeat of Kentucky forces by a combined British and Native American force, Blue Licks Battlefield remembers this event with a prominent granite shaft bearing the names of the Kentucky militiamen killed in the battle. Some are buried in the nearby cemetery. Re-enactors also converge on the park every August to take part in the Battle of Blue Licks Celebration, re-creating the conflict with period-costumed interpreters.

The park also has a pioneer museum with artifacts of frontier life, as well as prehistoric remains found at the salt licks (like Big Bone Lick, the Blue Licks attracted animals and therefore hunters). The museum does not focus extensively on the battle fought at the site.

Blue Licks had a lively history after the battle. In the mid-1800s, the salt springs became a rather famous "watering place" for wealthy Americans suffering from various ailments. The spa benefited from its location on a major North–South stagecoach line and its proximity to Maysville on the Ohio River. A luxury hotel was built at the springs in 1845, though it burned down in 1862. The salt spring itself went dry in 1896.

The state has emphasized the resort aspects of the park more than the historical aspects, constructing a swimming pool, a lodge, and guest cottages. Blue Licks Battlefield State Resort Park is located on US Highway 68 in Mount Olivet. Call (859) 289-5507 or visit parks.ky.gov/resortparks/bl.

The continued harassment by the Shawnee further demoralized the settlements, but the leaders of the Patriot cause in the East paid little attention. Many feared that the West could not be held. George Rogers Clark, a Virginian who had first come to Kentucky in 1775, thought differently. What was needed, he argued, was an offensive strategy, a plan to take the conflict to the British and the Native Americans rather than waiting hunkered down in the forts. Clark envisioned taking the old French forts back from the British, with his ultimate goal the conquest of Detroit. In 1778, he persuaded Patrick Henry, the revolutionary governor of Virginia, to back his plan.

Clark enlisted less than 200 men for his army, and many of those assumed that Clark merely intended to provide forward defense for the Kentucky settlements. When they discovered his true intentions, a significant number deserted. Clark trained his small detachment for about a month on Corn Island, at the Falls of the Ohio. For this reason he is regarded as the founder of Louisville. He chose to encamp on an island, he said, "to stop the desertion I knew would ensue on the Troops knowing their Destination."

In late June he marched into the Illinois country. Clark's bold campaign proved largely bloodless. He surprised Kaskaskia on July 4 and persuaded the mostly French inhabitants to give up rather than die for the British Crown. He then secured similar surrenders at Cahokia, Vincennes, and other smaller outposts.

With no determined British resistance, the Native Americans became Clark's main concern. He assured them that his invasion was aimed at dislodging the British, not occupying their land. The Illinois tribes, vastly outnumbering the Americans, accepted his assurances and pledged their neutrality. Clark never made it to Detroit, for the British soon reoccupied Vincennes, to which Clark returned in February 1779. After a brief siege, the British commander surrendered.

Clark's campaign helped move the western theater of the American Revolution north of the Ohio, providing some protection for the Kentucky settlements. In addition, militiamen followed Clark's lead in the years after 1778, mounting offensives in Native American country north of the Ohio, where they burned villages and corn crops. These scorched-earth tactics had an impact. In the spring of 1779, around 400 Shawnee warriors and their families left the principal Shawnee town of Chillicothe, migrating west to Missouri. Left behind were a core of Shawnee warriors resolute in their hatred of the Americans.

These warriors, together with those of other Ohio Valley tribes, continued their campaign of harassment in Kentucky. At times they threw in their lot with their British allies; at times they acted independently. In the spring of 1780, local militia leader John Floyd wrote that "hardly one week pass[es] without some one being scalped... and I [have] almost got too cowardly to travel about the woods without company."

When the British decided to retake the western forts in 1780, the tribes combined with the British to field an army of nearly a thousand men. This force took two stations and some small settlements in Kentucky in June, but did not move on to more strategic targets. The tribes were satisfied with their successes, and they soon withdrew from Kentucky.

Clark determined to punish the Native Americans for their incursion. Raising an army of nearly a thousand Kentucky men, he marched to Chillcothe, only to find it largely abandoned. Clark burned the buildings and destroyed the crops, then engaged a large force of Native Americans at Piqua. Cannon fire quickly dissuaded the Native Americans from continuing the fight, and they escaped northward.

But still the raids continued. In the first nine months of 1781, Native Americans killed or captured 131 people around the Falls of the Ohio. Even as the Revolution drew to a close in the East, with British General Charles Cornwallis's surrender at Yorktown in October 1781, it continued in the West. Although the treaty ending the war established the northern boundary of the United States at its present location, the British remained in control of the western forts. They hoped to chisel away at the new American borders and, by continuing to arm the Native Americans in the Ohio country, prevent further American expansion. For their part, the Native American warriors in no way considered the British surrender binding.

Kentuckians christened 1782 the Year of Blood because of repeated attacks. In March, a group of Wyandot warriors

Must-See Sites:
Frazier Historical Arms Museum

Within its overall emphasis on the role of firearms and weaponry in US history, the museum has several exhibits that highlight the bloody contest between Native Americans and frontiersmen for the lands of Kentucky and other places on the frontier. The museum gives full play to the important role played by native people in the French and Indian War, the American Revolution, and the War of 1812, but it also tells the story of the ongoing run-ins between settlers and natives on the frontier.

While it accords prominence to its collection of weaponry, the museum tries to situate the arms in their historical context. Life-size battle-scene dioramas, video presentations, and numerous live-action dramatizations by costumed actors help visitors see how the weapons were used and the role arms technology played in the history of human conflict.

The Frazier is one of the most recent additions to the Louisville museum scene. The 100,000-square-foot, state-of-the-art facility was built to showcase the collection of Louisvillian Owsley Brown Frazier. The museum also has secured a long-term loan of materials from England's Royal Armouries. The second floor, which houses the museum's permanent collection, deals with arms and United States history through the end of the nineteenth century; the third floor transports visitors back to medieval Britain.

The Frazier Historical Arms Museum is located at 829 West Main Street in Louisville. Call (502) 753-5663 or visit www.frazierarmsmuseum.org.

struck a station near Boonesborough, killing two settlers. A pursuing party of frontiersmen overtook the warriors at Little Mountain, near present-day Mount Sterling, and fought a pitched battle in which half the pursuers were killed or wounded. The Wyandots suffered similar losses, but forced the Kentuckians to withdraw.

Such small raids paled next to the major invasion carried out by a combined British/Native American force in August. A force of about 300 warriors from the Shawnee and other

Ohio tribes and 50 British rangers crossed the Ohio and penetrated nearly 100 miles into Kentucky before the frontiersmen knew about it. After brief battles at the Upper Blue Licks and Bryan's Station, near present-day Lexington, the attackers retreated with a party of about 180 Kentucky militiamen, including Daniel Boone, in hot pursuit.

At the crossing of the Licking River known as the Lower Blue Licks, the militia caught up with the invading force. Boone urged caution, but hotter heads prevailed. According to Boone's son Nathan, present at the scene, Major Hugh McGary despised the reluctance of the other officers and urged an immediate attack: "McGary spurred his horse into the water calling out 'All who are not damned cowards follow me, and I'll soon show you the Indians.'" The militia plunged into the crossing and was cut to pieces by native fire. Sixty settlers died in the withering attack, nearly a third of the Kentuckians' force. The survivors, splashing back through the blood-reddened waters of the Licking, fled toward Lexington.

Four days later, Daniel Boone returned to the site with a reinforced burial detail. "I cannot reflect upon this dreadful scene, but sorrow fills my heart," he wrote. "Being reinforced, we returned to bury the dead, and found their bodies strewed everywhere, cut and mangled in a dreadful manner. This mournful scene exhibited a horror almost unparalleled: Some torn and eaten by wild beasts; those in the river eaten by fishes, all in such a putrefied condition that no one could be distinguished from another." The state now commemorates this battle at Blue Licks Battlefield State Resort Park.

Again Clark responded with force, moving his forces north of the Ohio and scattering the Shawnee. Boone, who marched with the expedition, wrote that they found Chillicothe deserted: "We continued our pursuit through five towns on the Miami rivers,... burnt them all to ashes, entirely destroyed their corn, and other fruits, and everywhere spread a scene of desolation in the country." The campaign, Boone said, "in some measure damped the spirits of the Indians, and made them sensible of our superiority."

Doubting this "superiority," Native Americans continued their sporadic raids through the rest of the 1780s. Appeals to the new national government for assistance yielded nothing, and for a while Kentuckians talked of secession from the new republic in the hope of securing greater protection from a European sovereign. Between 1783 and 1789, one federal judge in Kentucky guessed that nearly six hundred Kentuckians lost their lives to Native American attacks, and that upwards of 20,000 horses were stolen.

The Tanner family had direct experience with these attacks. John Tanner was just a boy when, in the early 1780s, his father moved the family to the small community of Elk Horn in the Green River country. Tanner remembered that "Elk Horn was occasionally visited by hostile parties of Shawneese [sic] Indians, who killed some white people, and sometimes killed or drove away cattle and horses." Tanner remembered his uncle gathering together some of the other men to retaliate one evening. They "fired upon a camp of these Indians; he killed one, whose scalp he brought home; all the rest jumped into the river and escaped."

Tanner's family later moved north to the shores of the Ohio, across from the mouth of the Miami River. There, in 1789, nine-year-old John had another run-in with the Shawnee: "I think it was not more than ten days after our arrival, when my father told us in the morning, that from the actions of the horses, he perceived there were Indians lurking about in the woods, and he said to me, 'John, you must not go out of the house to day.'" Left in the house to help his stepmother tend the younger children, John soon grew "impatient of confinement." "I began to pinch my little brother, to make him cry." After a while, his exasperated stepmother took the baby from the boy, and young John made his escape out the cabin door.

Hiding behind a tree to avoid his father's notice, John recalled, "I heard a crackling noise behind me; I looked round, and saw the Indians; almost at the same instant, I was seized by both hands, and dragged off betwixt two." Tanner was later passed from the Shawnee to the Ojibwa people of the Great Lakes region. Like Boone, he was adopted into the tribe, replacing a son who had died. Unlike Boone, Tanner married an Ojibwa woman, and spent much of the next five decades of his life living as an Ojibwa.

Despite experiences like the Tanners', however, the number of settlers in Kentucky increased so rapidly after the Revolution that the Native Americans had no realistic hope of ever taking back their hunting grounds. Continued invasions north of the Ohio by Kentucky militia to burn crops and villages put the native subsistence system under great strain. By 1790, the combined Native American population north of the Ohio was probably one tenth the size of Kentucky's population.

The Native Americans' last hurrah occurred in the 1790s. The new American government, pressured by land-hungry settlers, sent in the army to conquer the natives and bring peace to the frontier north of the Ohio. A multi-tribal confederation defeated the army, which largely consisted of Kentucky and Pennsylvania militiamen, in 1790 and 1791. In the latter battle, the army lost 623 men, nearly half its force, in the worst US defeat ever inflicted by Native Americans.

Americans viewed the defeat as a national disaster and vowed revenge. Three years later, a force of 2,200 regular troops and 1,500 Kentucky militia under General "Mad Anthony" Wayne defeated a combined Native American force at the Battle of Fallen Timbers in present-day Ohio. The defeat at Fallen Timbers and the resulting Treaty of Greenville, in which the assembled tribes gave up most of Ohio and placed themselves under the sovereignty of the United States, finally ended the Native American threat to Kentucky.

"Brother, we have given you a fine land," the Cherokee chief Oconostota supposedly told Boone after the 1775 negotiations at Sycamore Shoals, "but I believe you will have much trouble settling it." The next twenty years proved the chief prescient. The ground of Kentucky had soaked up the blood of both Native Americans and frontiersmen, but there had been other losses, too. Kentucky was no longer the hunters' paradise that had first lured Boone. The ravages of the fur trade and wasteful overhunting by the settlers had depleted the supplies of game. Gone too was the faint hope of working out a way to coexist with the Native Americans as part of a truly diverse society.

What remained was the land and the opportunity to make something of it. With the grim struggle for survival over, settlers set out to take full advantage of the fertile bounty of Kentucky. Doing so would require a new kind of struggle—less bloody perhaps but no less grim. Fought by lawyers instead of riflemen in courtrooms rather than canebrakes, it was a struggle over the shape of the country that Native Americans and frontiersmen had fought and died for.

4

ANTEBELLUM KENTUCKY

K entucky filled up fast. Despite the Native American raids, despite the American Revolution, people came. Writing in 1784, guidebook author John Filson marveled at the "amazingly rapid… settlement in a few years. Numbers are daily arriving, and multitudes expected this Fall; which gives a well grounded expectation that the country will be exceedingly populous in a short time."

When the Shawnee chief Blackfish established his warriors' camp in 1777, he faced 300 or so settlers. By 1790, that number had grown to 73,000. George Rogers Clark's 1778–79 campaign to take the war to the Native American homelands in Ohio triggered a flood of immigrants to Kentucky in 1780 and 1781. Then, after the Revolution ended, thousands of Virginia war veterans holding military land warrants, with which Virginia paid its soldiers, added to the crowds heading to Kentucky. In the ten years between 1790 and 1800, the population tripled to 220,955. Ten years later, it had grown another 84 percent, to 406,509.

Most of these immigrants were native-born, hailing from Virginia predominantly, with Pennsylvania and North Carolina contributing significantly to the streams of the Kentucky-bound. Migrants from slave states brought their slaves with them. In 1790, there were 11,830 enslaved blacks in Kentucky.

During the 1780s and 1790s, more settlers traveled the mountain route to Kentucky, passing through the Cumberland Gap, then down the Ohio River. The overland route was not easy. Wagons could not pass through the Gap until 1796, when the road was finally widened. The Methodist bishop Francis Asbury commented in 1803 on the "almost naked" people "paddling bare-foot and bare-legged along, or labouring up the rocky hills" on their way

63

to Kentucky. The narrowness of the Gap also made it a natural ambush spot for Native American war parties or gangs of outlaws. So settlers gathered at jumping-off points such as Martin's Station before proceeding through the passage.

Moses Austin, the father of renowned Texas pioneer Stephen Austin, passed through the Gap in December 1796 in search for new business opportunities and recorded his observations in his journal:

> I cannot omitt Noticeing the many Distress.d families I pass.d in the Wilderness nor can any thing be more distressing to a man of feeling than to see woman and Children in the Month of Decembr Travelling a Wilderness Through Ice and Snow passing large rivers and Creeks without Shoe or Stocking, and barely as maney raggs as covers their Nakedness, with out money or provisions except what the Wilderness affords…. [T]o say they are poor is but faintly express'g there Situation.

By the turn of the nineteenth century, significant numbers of migrants began floating down the Ohio River to Kentucky. It was just a short 703 miles to the Falls of the Ohio from Pittsburgh, claimed one early travel guide. A trip down the river on a flatboat—a flat-bottomed rectangular wooden boat usually with a shelter of some sort on deck—might take only one or two weeks if conditions were right. Low water, sandbars, river pirates, or Native American raiding parties, however, all could make trips down the river go horribly wrong.

Francis Baily, a touring Englishman, rode the river from Pittsburgh to the Cincinnati area in 1796. He began his journey in November, after an initial delay because of low water. As the weather turned colder in December, Baily and his crew were obliged to put ashore because the river had iced up. On December 21, Baily recorded in his journal that the river had again begun to rise, which broke up the ice but brought a new disaster: "We were awakened out of our sleep with a noise like thunder, and, jumping out of our beds, we found the river was rising, and the ice breaking up. All attempts would be feeble to describe the horrid crashing and tremendous destruction which this event occasioned on the river."

Must-See Sites:
Along Wilderness Road

Cumberland Gap National Historic Park

In 1940, Congress authorized the establishment of this park to preserve and perpetuate the memory of the Gap's significance in the nation's history. If not for this break in the mountains, several more decades doubtless would have passed before any significant settler population made it to Kentucky. As it was, during the 35 years between 1775 and 1810, between 200,000 and 300,000 people passed through the Gap en route to the lands of Kentucky. However, with the development of steamboats and canals during the first third of the nineteenth century, the importance of the Gap as a route for settlers declined.

The park covers 20,000 acres in three states (Kentucky, Virginia, and Tennessee). It is long and narrow, extending some 20 miles astride the top of Cumberland Mountain. More than 14,000 acres of the park are wilderness. The developed part of the park includes a road up to Pinnacle Overlook, where visitors can see into three states, seventy miles of hiking trails, and a Visitor Center.

The Park Service has returned the corridor to its natural topography and rehabilitated the trail of the Wilderness Road, so that visitors can walk the same route as the pioneers and see the country more or less as it appeared in the late eighteenth century. To accomplish these changes, the service has invested over $280 million in creating tunnels through the mountains and relocating two federal highways.

Cumberland Gap National Historic Park is located off US 25E in Bell County along the Kentucky/Virginia border. Call (606) 248-2817 or visit www.nps.gov/cuga.

The Levi Jackson State Park

The Levi Jackson State Park contains another section of the Wilderness Road and part of Boone's Trace—pioneer trails that led settlers to the Bluegrass region—so that travelers can continue to retrace the steps of early pioneer settlers once they had passed through the Cumberland Gap. Visitors can also learn to appreciate the dangers of the journey; the park contains the site of McNitt's defeat, one of the deadliest Native American attacks on settlers in Kentucky history. McNitt's party, numbering about 60 people comprising 21 families, stopped at the site along Boone's Trace en route to the Bluegrass. On the night of October 3, 1786, a combined force of Shawnee and Chickamauga tribesmen attacked the camp, killed 24 of the party, and took between 5 and 10 people captive. The Defeated Camp Burial Ground in the park became the last resting place for some of those killed.

The park also contains the Mountain Life Museum, which is a replica of a 19th-century mountain village. The seven buildings, which were either relocated from different sites or built as replicas by the park, include an old schoolhouse, church, settler's cabin, smokehouse, blacksmith shop, and barn. All the buildings contain pioneer relics—tools, household implements, rifles, farm products, etc.

The park covers 896 acres, with the initial 300 acres donated in 1931 by the Jackson family on the condition that the park be named after their father, an early Laurel County judge. The original intent of the park was "to perpetuate the memory of the pioneers." The Levi Jackson State Park is located in London, Kentucky, at Exit 38 off Interstate 75. Call (606) 878-8000 or visit parks.ky.gov/stateparks/lj.

As the morning dawned, Baily wrote, "a scene the most distressing presented itself to our view. The river was one floating wreck! Nothing could be discerned amidst the vast bodies of floating ice, (some of which were as big as a moderate-sized house) but trees which had been torn up from the banks, and the boats of many a family who had scarcely time to escape unhurt from such an unlooked-for event, and whose whole property (perhaps scraped together to form a settlement in this distant territory) was now floating down, a prey to the desolating flood." Baily did not reach his destination until February 27, 1797.

Ebenezer Stedman, who made the river trip as a seven-year-old with his mother and siblings to join his father in Lexington, by contrast, recalled the overland trip from New Jersey to Pittsburgh as being much more arduous than the flatboat portion of the journey. "Time passed verry pleasant Compared with our trip over the mountains. The Men sung the 'Song of the pleasant Ohio.' No accidents happened." The family landed at Limestone (now Maysville), which Stedman remembered as having no wharf, just "the plain River Bank with a Road Cut in to It. The place was small [with] But Few houses. But it was the Great Landing for all emigrants for Ky."

Whether coming overland or by water, people came to claim a piece of Kentucky for themselves. On his trip through the mountains, Moses Austin took the time to ask his fellow travelers why they were making the journey:

> Ask these Pilgrims what they expect when they git to Kentuckey the answer is land. have you any. No, but I expect I can git it. have you anything to pay for land. No. did you Ever see the Country. No but Every Body says its good land. can any thing be more Absurd than the Conduct of man, here is hundreds Travelling hundreds of Miles, they Know not for what Nor Whither, except its to Kentucky.

So eager were they, one historian writes, that "within a decade after opening Kentucky to settlement, inrushing land claimants had posted claims to more than three times the amount of land available to them in the Kentucky backwoods."

Under the Virginia land system, one could claim land before an official survey had been made. A claimant filed a claim with the county surveyor, noting the natural landmarks that constituted the boundaries of the claim. The county surveyor then supposedly conducted an actual survey, which would adjust the boundaries as necessary and make them official. Then the surveyor would file a plat and field notes with the land office, which would issue a title to the settler.

The land system produced two clear results: immediate revenue for the Virginia treasury, since settlers could buy the right to a piece of land without waiting for an official survey, and lawsuits. Since neither the claimants nor the surveyors were especially well trained at making accurate sightings, the "original surveyors' notes read more nearly like botanical inventories of Kentucky's virgin forests than as foundations for legal instruments," says historian Thomas Clark. The survey method was called "metes and bounds," which meant taking note of prominent natural features for use as reference points. Unfortunately, such reference points as "three oak trees" or "large rock" were not all that helpful. Such "whimsical descriptive writing," continues Clark, "generated murders, hard feelings, family feuds, and lawsuits by the courthouseful."

Lawyers, therefore, figured prominently among those incoming groups of settlers. Henry Clay's mother told him to go to Kentucky because it was good lawyer's country, and he joined the ranks of a burgeoning corps of legal players that would shape the early history of the state. As early as 1786, a French traveler commented that Kentuckians "would hardly know how to buy a piece of land without involving themselves in a lawsuit."

The lawsuits aimed at sorting out the one "true" claim to land that might be claimed by several people. Clay noted a case involving a piece of land that generated 12 overlapping claims. Yet the suits' resolution—if resolved at all during the lifetime of the claimants—rarely satisfied all parties, and the dissatisfaction only generated appeals, countersuits, and charges of fraud, which added to the claimants' legal expenses. "The last Cow and Horse must be sold to maintain the Suit," complained one petition to the Virginia General Assembly. But failing to maintain the suit meant that "the Land upon which we had Hopes of supporting ourselves and Families in peace during the Remainder of our Lives will be wrested from us."

Must-See Sites: Constitution Square State Historic Site

The long and tendentious struggle for Kentucky's separation from Virginia and eventual statehood is retold here. Kentuckians had to hold ten constitutional conventions before they were able to agree on the terms of separation from the Old Dominion and the legal structure of the new state. The whole process—from initial rumblings to actual statehood—took eight years.

Constitution Square holds a replica of the old courthouse, built in 1785, that was home to the Supreme Court of the District of Kentucky and that hosted all those conventions. One of the first things the court did was to order the construction of a jail, a replica of which is also on the square. The jail has nine-inch-thick logs. Also on the square is Grayson's Tavern, still in its original 1785 building, where delegates and politicians met to drink, debate, and discuss the issues of the day, and a replica of the meetinghouse of Kentucky's first Presbyterian congregation, led by the anti-slavery minister David Rice. The original building for the first post office built west of the Appalachians is also still standing on the site.

The Danville/Boyle County Historical Society runs a small museum near the site in the 1816–1817 Watts-Bell House. Constitution Square is located at 134 South Second Street in Danville, the administrative capital of the District of Kentucky when it was still part of Virginia. For more information, call (859) 239-7089, or visit parks.ky.gov/statehistoricsites/cs.

Men ill-equipped to play such a game, like Daniel Boone, found themselves shut out of land ownership. Boone lost all of his land claims to court decisions, and in 1798 left Kentucky for the Missouri frontier, where he died in 1820. His body eventually made it back to Kentucky, however, and the state interred it in the lovely old cemetery in Frankfort, overlooking the Kentucky River.

By 1792, only 17 years after the first permanent settlements appeared, two-thirds of adult white males in Kentucky did not own land. Moses Austin accurately forecasted the fate of many of those he passed on his 1796 journey to Kentucky. Anticipating a "Land of Milk and Honey," Austin wrote, what did they find once "arriv.d at this Heaven in Idea a goodly land I will allow but to them forbiden Land. exausted and worn down with distress and disappointment they are at last Oblig.d to become hewers of wood and Drawers of water." The common folk of Kentucky developed a long repertoire of lawyer jokes in response—a type of self-defense against the legal machinations that rendered so many landless.

In the 1780s, as the number of Kentuckians swelled, they began to consider separating themselves from Virginia. Kentuckians felt outvoted and underrepresented in the Virginia legislature, which they felt would never take their concerns seriously. First among these concerns in the 1780s was defense against the Native Americans. Far removed from the danger, Virginia legislators would never approve the money or manpower necessary to secure Kentucky. Indeed, Virginia required that any militia offensive against Native Americans be pre-approved in Richmond, an administrative scheme that did not appeal to Kentuckians on the front lines.

Second among those concerns was navigation of the Mississippi River, then controlled by the Spanish. Given the difficulties of freighting goods through the Gap, Kentucky's products were only economically viable if they could be shipped downriver through New Orleans. Politicians in Richmond seemed much more concerned with the economic interests of Tidewater planters than with the concerns of Kentucky's backwoodsmen.

Finally there was the simple issue of the services state government provided in return for the taxes Kentuckians paid. Paying the same rates as easterners, Kentuckians got very little back. In 1782, Kentucky did not even have regular mail service. And as the lawsuits proliferated, it became an obnoxious burden to travel to Richmond every time somebody appealed a decision to a higher court.

Even though the agitation commenced in the 1780s, it did not reach culmination until 1792. It took nine statehood conventions before Kentucky and Virginia reached mutually agreeable terms of separation. Some of the delay resulted from unforeseeable circumstances. The fourth convention, for example, could not meet as scheduled because a military expedition against the Native Americans had taken away most of its elected members. By the time it did get around to meeting, the Virginia legislature had called for a fifth convention. Finally, in 1792, Kentucky formally separated from Virginia and entered the Union as the fifteenth state. These political events are commemorated at Constitution Square in Danville, which served as Kentucky's capital city before its separation from Virginia.

Real political disagreements, however, also slowed down the process of achieving statehood. Many of the landless wanted to break up large landholdings and redistribute them. Those fortunate enough, well connected enough, or ruthless enough to possess a large landholding naturally thought redistribution was a bad idea. The state of Virginia also thought it was a bad idea, since many of those large landholders were prominent Virginians. So before agreeing to Kentucky's separation, it made sure that the rights of nonresident landowners were protected.

The new state's constitution, adopted in 1792, created a relatively strong executive branch, a senate chosen by a body of electors, and an independent judiciary—all tools to keep unpleasant popular pressures from gaining control. Those pressures built steadily during the 1790s as the popularly elected lower house of the state legislature began heeding its constituents' calls for land reform. The legislature punished nonresident landowners through the tax system. It ordered landowners who evicted settlers to compensate those settlers for the improvements they had made on the property. It also tried to impeach unpopular judges and decentralize the court system to make the judiciary more responsive to popular pressure. In 1802, it even passed a law that two of the three judges in each circuit court be unschooled in the law, a misguided attempt to ensure that legal decisions rested on common sense rather than lawyers' trickery.

The aspirations of the landless also shaped the land laws passed in 1795 and 1797, aimed at disposing of the unclaimed lands in the state. The area lying south of the Green River, which had originally been reserved for holders of military warrants, still had a good deal of unclaimed acreage. Speculators pressured the legislature for sweetheart deals that would give them rights to vast tracts in the Green River country. What emerged instead were laws allowing those already settled on the land to file preemptive claims at a prefixed price, with fairly generous credit terms. This recognition of "squatters' rights" irritated the large landholders in the Bluegrass, who had argued for higher prices and no credit as a way of boosting state revenues. But the squatters got what they wanted, and by 1800, the Green River counties had a higher percentage of land ownership than the state as a whole.

The ongoing conflict between the landed and the landless resulted in a second constitutional convention in 1799, just seven years after the first charter had been adopted. The new document that emerged democratized the system somewhat, allowing direct popular election of the senate and the governor. And it allowed the legislature more control over the court system. But it fell far short of decreeing a land redistribution or undercutting existing property rights. Opening up the political system, however, quieted the calls for more far-reaching reforms.

A New State in a New Nation

Kentucky's internal problems played out against a national backdrop no less filled with tension. Beginning in George Washington's presidency, the national political elite had begun to cleave into distinct parties, known as the Federalists and the Democratic Republicans. George Washington and John Adams were Federalists; Thomas Jefferson and James Madison were Democratic Republicans. Kentucky politics strongly followed the Democratic Republican line, which favored the western settlements more than the Federalist establishment did. Federalists wanted a strong central government, but westerners wanted more local control. They felt a strong national government would only use its power to benefit established eastern interests.

At about the same time as the 1799 state constitution took effect, Kentuckians found themselves at odds with the national government over the Alien and Sedition Acts. The Acts, passed by the Federalists during a time when war with France was felt to be imminent, harshly punished any dissent from government policies. Kentuckians, who almost always dissented from Federalist policies, felt their freedoms threatened.

Mass protest meetings took place in 1798, when the acts were first passed, and in November of that year the Kentucky legislature passed the famous Kentucky Resolutions, drafted by Jefferson himself. These Resolutions laid out the Democratic Republican political philosophy of state sovereignty and limited national authority as the best guarantors of freedom. A state had the right to pass judgment on federal laws, the resolutions declared, and to declare such laws null and void if the state found them unconstitutional. The resolutions then went on to declare the Alien and Sedition Acts "void and of no force" in Kentucky. Under the philosophy of the Alien and Sedition Acts, the resolutions stated, "no rampart... remains against the passions and the power of a majority of Congress." Ultimately, this states' rights philosophy would be pushed by others to its most extreme limits to justify southern secession during the Civil War.

The war of words over the Alien and Sedition Acts ended, of course, with the election of Jefferson to the presidency in 1800. The offensive acts either expired or were repealed in short order, and Kentuckians celebrated that their man had made it to the highest office. Jefferson delivered the goods for Kentucky in 1803, when he pulled off the Louisiana Purchase. The purchase gave the United States control of the Mississippi River and the port of New Orleans, finally ending Kentuckians' anxiety over market access for their surplus produce.

Still, as a new state in a new nation, Kentucky often considered itself slighted by the national government. Shady characters such as James Wilkinson in the 1780s and Aaron Burr in the early 1800s had tried to capitalize on that feeling to take Kentucky out of the union, but their plans had always foundered on a bedrock of nationalism. For while they often complained about the national government, Kentuckians also hotly resented any imputation on their loyalty or on the country's honor. So when the British navy high-handedly stopped and boarded American ships during England's war with Napoleonic France, many Kentuckians bristled and called for war.

Jefferson disappointed them in that regard, preferring to maintain the country's neutrality. James Madison, who became president after Jefferson, initially followed the

Literary Extracts: John James Audubon

Audubon came to Kentucky in 1807 to open a store in Louisville. The store failed, and Audubon moved to Henderson, Kentucky, in 1810, where he prospered for a time as a merchant. Throughout this time, he pursued his passion for collecting and drawing natural specimens, especially birds, though his great works would not be published until the 1820s, after he had left Kentucky. In the following passage, from his 1826 *Delineations of American Scenery and Character*, Audubon describes his favorable impressions of a young Louisville:

> Louisville in Kentucky has always been a favourite place of mine. The beauty of its situation, on the banks of La Belle Riviere, just at the commencement of the famed rapids, commonly called the Falls of the Ohio, had attracted my notice, and when I removed to it, immediately after my marriage, I found it more agreeable than ever. The prospect from the town is such that it would please even the eye of a Swiss. It extends along the river for seven or eight miles, and is bounded on the opposite side by a fine range of low mountains, known by the name of the Silver Hills. The rumbling sound of the waters, as they tumble over the rock-paved bed of the rapids, is at all times soothing to the ear. Fish and game are abundant. But, above all, the generous hospitality of the inhabitants, and the urbanity of their manners, had induced me to fix upon it as a place of residence....

same course. But in 1812, a group of war-hawk congressmen, led by Kentucky's Henry Clay, made war with Great Britain the price of their support for Madison's reelection bid. After negotiations with England broke down in April, for instance, Clay dashed off a newspaper editorial, proclaiming that "the final step ought to be taken; and that step is WAR.... [A crisis] exists; and it is by open and manly war only that we can get through it with honor and advantage to the country. Our wrongs have been great; our cause is just; and if we are decided and firm; success is inevitable." On June 1, 1812, Kentuckians got their war.

And in the western theater, it truly was their war. Over 25,000 Kentuckians served either as regulars, volunteers, or militiamen. One of them was Jack Birchfield, who told his story to Ebenezer Stedman, who recorded it in his journal. Birchfield volunteered for service in Frankfort and soon thereafter his company marched to Georgetown:

> He Says In goin from Frankfort to Geotown they did not look much like Soldiers, thare ware no 2 dressed alike. Some had on the Big Bell Crown hat, Some Coon Skins Caps, with the tails on, and some might as well have had no hat. And then their dress.... Some had Buxskin pants, Some plad linsy home made. Some Barefooted. All had tomahawks. As Birchfield Said we ware goin to fight indians.

Of the 1,876 Americans killed during the war, about 1,200 were Kentuckians. Most died fighting in the Old Northwest. (The Old Northwest, *a.k.a.* the Northwest Territory, encompassed the present-day states of Ohio, Indiana, Illinois, Michigan, and Wisconsin.) Often they fought against their old enemies, the Shawnees. The Shawnees and several other tribes allied with the British in a last-ditch effort to push back the expanding American frontier. General William Henry Harrison commented on the eagerness of the Kentucky militia in 1813: "It rarely occurs that a general has to complain of the excessive ardor of his men, yet such appears always to be the case whenever the Kentucky militia are engaged."

That "excessive ardor" almost got Jack Birchfield killed in a battle near Fort Meigs, Ohio, in May 1813: "One day we war orderd out of the fort to drive of Some indians that ware getting two near the fort. When we Got to the indians, they Retreated Into the woods and, Contrary to orders, we followed them and when they got us whare they wanted us, then They Commenced on us."

Ordered to retreat, the men broke and ran. "Evry man for himself," remembered Birchfield. "He says he did not hear the Retreat called. He was after Indians." After a near miss, however, Birchfield noticed his compatriots in full retreat "and the indians after them. He said if he Ever had anny wit it was then. He Broke in another direction for the Rivver by himself.... He Said he had alwais Believed he

Could out Run anny Man in franklin County and he thought he was farley Flying as The yells of the indians and death was all around."

Experiences like Birchfield's helped cool Kentucky's war fever. As the hopes for a quick victory evaporated, Kentuckians began to shy away from soldiering. A call for three thousand men in 1813 went unfilled by volunteers, forcing the state governor to authorize a draft. Things did not really pick up until the Battle of the Thames in October 1813 in Upper Canada (present-day Ontario). There, a 5,000-man force made up largely of Kentuckians defeated an army of 1,000 British regulars and 3,000 or so Native American warriors, killing the Shawnees' great leader Tecumseh in the process. It was the last major action of the war in the Northwest, and it helped take away the sting of earlier defeats.

Although Kentuckians fought in the last battle of the war, the Battle of New Orleans, they viewed their part in the war as largely over once the victory in the Northwest was won. Recruitments fell, even as things went badly for the Americans in the east. Finally, on December 14, 1814, the war ended. The treaty ending hostilities settled none of the questions that had caused the war, but that did not really matter to Kentuckians. They celebrated the peace and the American victories, conveniently overlooking the dim spots in the war's history.

KENTUCKY'S RISE TO PROMINENCE

Historians of the national experience refer to a "market revolution" taking place after the War of 1812. Improvements in transportation bound the young nation together as never before, creating a large domestic market for American-made goods. Farmers, who in pioneer days had thought only about subsistence, now thought about bringing their crops to market. Craftsmen who had made products by time-honored hand techniques began to organize workers into factories. And people who had long lived on farms or in rural villages began congregating in growing cities. Kentucky felt the impact of all these changes, and the state's rapid development catapulted it to national prominence during the first half of the nineteenth century.

Transportation had long been a trouble spot for Kentucky. Blocked from eastern markets by the

Appalachians, the state's farmers had always looked downstream to the Mississippi River and New Orleans as the route for their surplus crops. As early as 1787, James Wilkinson had won friends in Kentucky when he shipped two boatloads of produce down the Mississippi and came back with gold in his pocket and riding in a four-wheeled carriage. Of course, he had also promised Spain, who controlled New Orleans at the time, that he could separate Kentucky from the United States, but the treason mattered less than the treasure to Kentuckians of the time.

By the turn of the century, Kentucky's farmers had taken to the rivers themselves in keelboats, braving the currents, the foreign intrigues, and the predations of river pirates to get their products to market. Whiskey was one of the most common of these products. Pioneers easily transported the parts for their small copper stills over the mountains, and farmer/distillers made whiskey out of corn grown on their own and their neighbors' farms. Turning corn into whiskey turned a bulky grain into a marketable product that traveled well over long distances.

By 1820, however, those boatmen had largely vanished from the rivers, replaced by the steamboat. During the second decade of the nineteenth century, the steamboat turned the great rivers of the Midwest into two-way commercial highways. The first regular steamboat made the trip from New Orleans to Louisville in just 25 days in 1817, as opposed to the months it took either laboring upstream in a keelboat or journeying around to the east coast and then coming back to Kentucky overland.

Ebenezer Stedman recalled the wonder that those early steamboats caused among the populace:

> The First appearance of a steam Boat on the Ohio River produced as you may Supose not a little Excitement and admiration. A steam Boat at that Day [the summer of 1817] was to common observers almost as great a wonder as a Flying angel woold Be at presant. The Banks of the River in Some places ware thronged with Spectators gazing in Speachless astonishment at the Puffing and Smoking phenomenon.

The steamboat took its toll on the farmer/distiller. Larger distillers able to produce greater quantities of whiskey emerged during the first third of the nineteenth century, especially in Louisville. Steamboats brought in column stills, expensive copper contraptions four stories high that were capable of producing large amounts of alcohol. Some of these historic old distilleries, dating back to the early nineteenth century, are still in operation and offer tours to visitors. The Maker's Mark distillery in Loretto began operations in 1805; the Labrot and Graham Distillery, a restored 1812 facility, is located in Versailles. The declining economic importance of the farmer/distiller did not mean the end of the old home still, however. Many rural dwellers kept on distilling home brew for their own and their neighbors' consumption well into the 20th century.

As steamboat technology improved, the reach of the market spread. Flat-bottomed, side-wheeled steamboats could negotiate even shallow rivers, where navigation had been thought impossible. One captain boasted he could float his boat in a heavy dew. Such flexibility opened many interior towns to the market economy.

Steamboats fueled demands for "internal improvements" to the rivers to provide locks and dams to tame the rough spots so that boats could get through. Five locks and dams on the Kentucky River, for example, opened up 95 miles of slackwater navigation in December 1842. For today's travelers, the *Dixie Belle*, a sternwheeler that plies the Kentucky River near Harrodsburg, offers seasonal excursions with spectacular views.

The call for internal improvements echoed everywhere in Kentucky in the first half of the nineteenth century. People wanted the rivers dammed, canals dug, and roads built. Internal improvements, a group of Lexington elites declared in 1818, was "a subject intimately connected with the vital interests of this country, as it regards the wealth, union, power, and general prosperity of the states."

Most people wanted the improvements done as cheaply as possible, preferably without raising taxes. The state, therefore, chartered private turnpike companies to build and operate toll roads for wagon traffic. The state could buy stock in the companies, but the companies collected the tolls and maintained the roads. By 1837, the state had invested around $2.5 million in private road companies, outstripping actual private investments by $500,000. The

Skinny-dipping children dive off steamboat

result was 343 miles of stone-surfaced roads and an additional 236 miles under construction. Only 30 miles of road had been built without state help.

The private-toll system had drawbacks, of course. Companies would not touch routes that yielded no promise of profit, and so isolated communities that generated little traffic remained isolated. Sometimes towns and counties followed the state's example, chartering their own companies to build roads for municipal use, but these entities did not have the financial clout of the state government. Finally, toll companies often let tolls rise and maintenance decrease when times got hard.

What ultimately challenged the steamboat was not road traffic, but railroad traffic. The steamboat era peaked in the 1850s, and it was clear to most that the future belonged to railroads. Kentucky used the same financing system for railroads as it used for road building, with the state granting charters to private rail companies. It jumped on the rail bandwagon early, chartering its first railroad, a Lexington-to-Louisville line, in 1831. The line reached Frankfort in 1834, then stalled because of legal challenges, and was not completed until 1851. Investors launched several other ambitious projects, but few were ever realized. The most successful railroad of the period was the Louisville and Nashville, chartered in 1850. Constitutional restrictions on the amount of debt the state government could incur meant that towns and counties along the proposed route ponied up most of the capital. Completed in 1859 at a cost of over $7 million, the L&N made money from the start, cutting the thirty-hour stage journey to Nashville by two-thirds.

Overall, the transportation improvements helped link Kentucky to the nation, but they did little to link together communities within Kentucky. This lapse generally reflected the biases of Kentucky's commercial farmers and merchants. They wanted ways to get their goods to market and to bring in manufactured goods to the local market, but they cared less about linking the Bluegrass to the Pennyroyal or eastern Kentucky with the rest of the state. Thus the entrepôts were relatively well served; the hinterlands were not.

The tight relationship between transportation and commercial development also meant that those with access to adequate transportation embraced the market revolution more readily than those who were more isolated. No area of Kentucky embraced that revolution in the first half of the nineteenth century so readily as the Bluegrass. Hemp and livestock were the mainstays of this commercial agricultural economy.

The favorite animal on the frontier was the hog, because it could be turned loose in the forest to feed and supplied a major portion of a family's meat as wild game disappeared. But in the Bluegrass, farmers enclosed their fields and experimented with selective breeding and blooded stock, particularly of cattle and horses. As a farm product, cattle had the great advantage of being able to walk to market, and large herds passed eastward through the Cumberland Gap, driven to Virginia to meet their doom.

Breeders also experimented with horses, importing blooded stock and breeding selectively for particular characteristics. Kentuckians both loved and needed horses. They needed them for transportation and drayage, but the admiration went beyond that. "A handsome horse is the highest pride of a Kentuckian," one visitor wrote in the early 1830s. The Kentucky Jockey Club opened its doors in 1797, sponsoring horse races and setting up rules for the sport. In 1839, Oakland race course in Louisville held a match race between two of the most famous thoroughbreds in the nation—Wagner, from Louisiana, and Kentucky's own Grey Eagle—for the outlandish prize of $14,000. "The number of ladies in attendance was estimated at nearly eight hundred, while nearly two thousand horsemen were assembled in the field," reported one observer. "The stands, the fences, the trees, the tops of carriages, and every eminence overlooking the course were crowded." Unfortunately for the Kentucky crowd, Wagner defeated Grey Eagle. Nonetheless, a national sports journal opined that "Old Kentuck" was on its way to becoming "the race horse region."

Hemp provided another valuable cash crop. Virginia-born planters distrusted tobacco; they had seen the way it exhausted the soil and fluctuated wildly in price. Kentucky's farmers wanted more stability. They tried cotton, but the climate was too cold. Fortunately for them, as King Cotton expanded its reign across the Deep South,

the demand for rope and bagging material mushroomed. Kentucky-grown hemp filled the bill.

With viable cash crops and transportation to get them to market, all farmers needed to complete the market revolution was goods on which to spend their cash. Those goods came primarily from the eastern states, and the more

Buyers inspect tobacco piled on the auction room floor in a Louisville warehouse, ca. 1928

prosperous Kentucky merchants made one or two trips back east to place orders and settle accounts with their suppliers. The cumbersome triangular trade raised prices by 50 to 100 percent over eastern markets, but the Bluegrass gentry did not seem to mind. "Many a bluegrass farmer... built a pretentious Georgian or Greek Revival house and filled it with handsome furnishings brought from New Orleans and Philadelphia, even France and England," writes historian Thomas Clark.

Increased commerce sparked the growth of commercial cities, particularly Lexington and Louisville. Lexington, in the heart of the Bluegrass region, benefited from the immediate proximity of rich soils and wealthy landowners. But it suffered from its landlocked location. Without easy access to the rivers, getting goods in and out of Lexington remained a costly and troublesome exercise. Nonetheless, the city bloomed into the "Athens of the West" in the early nineteenth century. A public library, several private schools and academies, a seminary turned university, a prominent host of lawyers and public men, and a thriving commercial spirit led many to forecast that Lexington would become the commercial and cultural capital of the west, if not the nation. Someday, the Bluegrass elite dreamed, Philadelphia would be known as the Lexington of the east.

The steamboat and the Falls of the Ohio soon shattered those dreams. Lexington not only lost its prominence in the region to cities like Cincinnati and St. Louis, but it lost its place within the state to Louisville. The Falls—actually just a series of rocky rapids in which the river dropped about twenty feet over a distance of two miles—made Louisville a natural stopping point, where goods had to be offloaded and then transported above the Falls before continuing their journey. By 1820, the steamboat had turned a muddy river village into a thriving commercial town that soon left Lexington in its wake. By 1830, a canal linking Louisville and Portland—the destination at the downstream end of the Falls—further improved Louisville's fortunes.

The city attracted the aspiring young merchant John James Audubon in 1807, though his frequent sojourns in the woods to observe and paint birds would bring him more renown than his retail prowess. "During my residence at Louisville, much of my time was employed in my ever favourite pursuits," Audubon recounted. "I drew and noted the habits of every thing which I procured, and my collection was daily augmenting, as every individual who carried a gun always sent me such birds or quadrupeds as he thought might prove useful to me."

Because it was a river town, Louisville never made the claims to cultural pretension that Lexington made, but it was clear enough where the business of the state was being conducted.

HENRY CLAY AND THE WHIGS

Henry Clay was the most prominent Kentuckian of the antebellum period, and his life in many ways epitomized the changes Kentucky went through during the first half of the nineteenth century. He came looking for opportunity, found it in the state's courtrooms and political battles, passionately pursued commercial farming and economic development, and ceaselessly promoted internal improvements.

Clay came to Kentucky in 1797 with little wealth but a gift for oratory. His lawyering skills found ample play in the land disputes that dominated so many Kentucky court dockets, and he soon established a successful reputation as a litigator. He married well, wedding Lucretia Hart in 1799, which gave him connections to many of the most prominent families in the state.

He built an estate, Ashland, near Lexington, which he turned into a model farm. Visitors can still tour the 18-room mansion and the grounds where Clay grew hemp and some tobacco, and imported Hereford cattle and thoroughbred horses from England to improve his livestock. Like many commercial farmers of his day, he cultivated the image of a leisured country gentleman, spending his profits on opulent furnishings and imported goods, while also bankrolling several commercial and manufacturing ventures. Finally, he promoted western development relentlessly, demanding from political leaders at the state and national levels a governmental commitment to economic development.

Those demands lay at the heart of the political program of the Whigs, a new political party that emerged in the 1820s, and Clay soon rose to a position of leadership within it. In the years after the War of 1812, the Federalists had slowly withered and died, and the United States for a short period became a one-party nation, controlled by the Democratic

Famous Sons and Daughters:
Henry Clay

Senator and political leader
(April 12, 1777–June 29, 1852)

Born in Hanover County, Virginia, Clay moved west to Lexington, Kentucky, in November 1797. His mother and stepfather had earlier settled in Versailles, Kentucky, but young Clay stayed behind to serve as a copyist for a prominent Virginia chancellor. When he was 19, Clay studied law for a year before being licensed to practice law in Virginia. Soon after his removal to Kentucky, he had a thriving legal practice. He married Lucretia Hart on April 11, 1799. She was the daughter of a prominent Lexington merchant.

Clay began his legislative career in 1803, when he was elected to the Kentucky House of Representatives. In 1806, he served a short time in the United States Senate, having been appointed to fill an unexpired term. In 1807, his initial foray in the Senate over, he returned to serve in the Kentucky House, where he was elected speaker in 1808. After being appointed again to the Senate to fill an unexpired term from 1810–1811, he won election to the US House of Representatives. He soon became Speaker of the House, a position he held for the next fourteen years. As a congressman, Clay led the group of "war hawks" that pushed President James Madison to declare war on Great Britain in 1812.

After the war, Clay articulated the political platform known as the "American System," which called for Federal support of internal improvements, high tariffs to protect American industry, and a national bank. Clay engineered the Missouri Compromise in 1820 that allowed the slave state of Missouri to gain admission to the Union, but forbade slavery in lands north of Missouri's southern border.

Clay ran for president in 1824, finishing fourth. With neither John Quincy Adams nor Andrew Jackson, the two front-runners, receiving a majority of electoral votes, the election went to the House of Representatives, where Speaker Clay threw his influence to Adams, who was declared president. Adams appointed Clay secretary of state, which led Jackson's supporters to decry a "corrupt bargain" between Clay and Adams to deny Jackson the presidency. Clay worked for Adams' re-election in 1828, but Jackson won.

Clay won election to the US Senate in 1831, setting his sights on the presidential election of 1832. He led the opposition to Jackson's policies in the legislature, championing measures that Jackson vehemently vetoed—such as rechartering the national bank (the Bank of the United States) and using Federal funds to build a road from Lexington to Maysville. Jackson whipped him at the polls, however, with a 219 to 49 electoral-vote margin.

Jackson's opposition soon formed the Whig Party, and Clay became the party's leader. An advocate of gradual emancipation of slaves and then their colonization in Africa, his reluctance to embrace abolitionism cost him the Whig Party's presidential nomination in 1840. However, Clay looked to 1844 with high hopes, especially after the un-Whiggish John Tyler—the vice president—took over the reins of the presidency following the incumbent's death. With the annexation of Texas—and implicitly the status of slavery—the dominant issue in the 1844 election, Clay's muddled views and widespread electoral fraud by both sides gave the victory to Democrat James K. Polk.

After a brief retirement, Clay returned to the Senate in 1849, helping to piece together the Compromise of 1850, which uneasily preserved the Union even as it dodged the fundamental questions over the future of slavery. Clay died in Washington, DC, on June 29, 1852. He is buried in Lexington Cemetery.

Republicans. Factions soon split the party, however, into Democrats and so-called National Republicans. The latter group morphed into the Whigs in the 1830s. Clay, a Jeffersonian since his entrance into politics, became a National Republican in the 1820s. He ran for president in 1828 as leader of that faction, then ran again on the Whig ticket in 1832. He tried and failed a third time in 1844.

By that time, Clay retained little of Jefferson's agrarianism. He and the Whigs promoted a vision of active governmental assistance in the development of a commercial and industrial economy. That meant support for high tariffs to protect domestic industry from foreign competition, a national bank to stabilize the nation's finances, and federal financing of internal improvements. Clay's "American System" stressed the importance of tying the nation together economically and of using the power of the government to forge those ties. "Of all the modes in which a government can employ its surplus revenue, none is more permanently beneficial than that of internal improvement," Clay proclaimed in an 1818 speech. Clay's national program merely echoed the policies he had championed while a Kentucky state legislator. He had pushed for state government support of road-building and canal-digging, even serving as chairman of the board of the Louisville and Lexington Railroad in the 1830s.

Clay believed that while blood ties between the people of the East and the people of the West might maintain the Union for a while, such ties were bound to weaken over time. The solution, he stated, was to have the "general government penetrate through the intervening mountains by roads, connecting the navigable streams on each side of them.... Could then a better basis for the union, a stronger tie to connect the various parts of the country together, be conceived[?]"

As befit his entrepreneurial outlook, however, Clay was also a wheeler-dealer, a practical politician who swapped backroom favors and negotiated deals with political enemies. His nickname in national political circles was "The Great Compromiser." For some, this showed Clay's fickle adherence to principle. For others, it marked him as a statesman, and many credited Clay with holding the nation together as passions over slavery increased. He engineered the Missouri Compromise of 1820, which papered over the sectional tensions created by the admission of slaveholding Missouri into the Union; the Compromise Tariff of 1833, which reduced tariffs offensive to the South and helped end the nullification crisis in South Carolina; and the Compromise of 1850, which again finessed the issue of slavery as it applied to the territory acquired by the nation in the Mexican War.

The Whigs dominated Kentucky politics during the antebellum era, largely because of Clay. Starting with the election of the National Republican Thomas Metcalfe in 1828, the Whigs elected eight of the next nine governors of

Must-See Sites:
The Kentucky Bourbon Trail

Several bourbon distillers have collaborated on a tourism and marketing initiative to christen this trail. Some of the distilleries date back to the early 1800s, when market-oriented distillers began displacing smaller-scale farmer-distillers. Two distilleries in particular emphasize these historical themes: Makers Mark and Labrot & Graham.

The Makers Mark distillery is the only operating distillery to be designated a National Historic Landmark. The current site began operations as a gristmill and distillery in 1805 and became home to Makers Mark bourbon in 1953. On the site are a master distiller's house that dates from the 1840s. The master distiller lived on site until the advent of refrigeration—allowing climate control during the distilling process—permitted him to live away from the distillery. There is also a toll house, a reminder of the private toll roads that the state used to build transportation infrastructure without burdening taxpayers. Finally there is the Still House, where the actual bourbon-making takes place. Though located on those 1805 foundations, the Still House hides a modern industrial distillery within.

The Labrot & Graham distillery, owned and operated by spirits giant Brown-Forman, also boasts a long history. It sits on the site of an 1812 distillery; Brown-Forman restored the buildings as a showplace for the old methods of making bourbon. Labrot & Graham is thus the oldest and smallest operating distillery in Kentucky, still using traditional copper-pot stills. Labrot & Graham also features a short video on the history of the site and the history of bourbon-making.

All the distilleries on the Bourbon Trail—including Makers Mark and Labrot & Graham—offer tours. Other distilleries on the trail, though not dating back as far as the former two, are Jim Beam's American Outpost in Clermont, Heaven Hill distillery in Bardstown, Four Roses distillery near Lawrenceburg, Austin Nichols distillery near Lawrenceburg, and Buffalo Trace distillery located just north of Frankfort. The Makers Mark facility is located off State Route 52 on Burks Spring Road in Loretto. The phone number is (270) 865-2099. Labrot & Graham is located on McCracken Pike in Versailles. The phone number there is (800) 542-1812. Information on the Bourbon Trail can be found at kybourbon.com.

the state until the slavery issue finally overwhelmed the party in the 1850s. With varying degrees of success, the Whig governors pushed for internal improvements and a more active governmental role in economic development. This finally triggered a taxpayer revolt, culminating in severe restrictions on state indebtedness in the 1850 revision of the state constitution. The Whigs, grasping for a program and a means to deal with slavery, died a slow death in the 1850s, following Clay, who died in 1852, to the grave.

Antebellum Social and Cultural Life

The market revolution, like all revolutions, reverberated throughout society, but its impacts were uneven. In some regions, in some aspects of life, people changed rapidly and noticeably, embracing new ideas and attitudes. In other areas, changes came slowly if at all. Antebellum life in Kentucky was thus a hodgepodge of inherited tradition and brand new patterns.

The gap between rich and poor was the most noticeable change. A market society rewarded some and penalized others, so that from the rough equality and mutualism of the pioneer settlements sprung a highly stratified society of a few large landowners, a bulge of small farmers, and a large class of landless. In Woodford County, in the heart of the Bluegrass, almost half of those on the tax rolls in 1825 owned no property, and another 45 percent owned less than 500 acres. At the top of the pyramid stood 33 households that owned 1,000 or more acres. In the more equitably distributed Green River country, the landless proportion was smaller and the middles bulged.

Not unexpectedly, life on the great plantations differed from life on the small family farms. Plantation grandees in the Bluegrass and the western Pennyroyal aspired to live like the great landowners of Virginia and England. They lived in an aggressively social world, where conviviality and competition among gentlemen provided the spice of life. "What a pleasure we have in raking up money and spending it with our friends," gushed Lexington planter and merchant Thomas Hart. The image of the Kentucky Colonel got its start here.

Some planters turned portions of their estates into private hunting preserves. They dressed in the finest clothes and had dozens of household slaves. They organized fox hunts and horse races, and tried to impress their friends with generosity and ostentation. "We could not invite a friend to dinner, but the table must groan with costly piles of food," observed one plantation matron. In a burst of enthusiasm one night, Henry Clay leaped upon a banquet table and danced its entire 60-foot length, shattering china and crystal the whole way. The next morning, he cheerfully paid the bill for the breakage.

Life on the smaller farms was decidedly more meager. In the eastern mountains and on the less fertile soils of the other regions, clearing trees and planting on steep slopes and in narrow valleys proved difficult, backbreaking work. Labor was scarce, and few small farmers could afford slaves, so farmers and families worked cooperatively to do the heaviest toil. Some idea of the life of these small farmers can be gained at the Mountain Life Museum in the Levi Jackson State Park near London and at the Homeplace, a working nineteenth-century farm, located in the Land Between the Lakes National Recreation Area in western Kentucky.

Ebenezer Stedman, a budding apprentice craftsman, saw firsthand how the family of one backwoods hunter lived while on a journey with his father in 1822. "Soon we saw a little Log Cabbin, on the Side of a hill, one of those primitive Log Cabbins that you have Read about. Mud & Sticks Composed the Chimbly.... On the out-side Thare ware all kinds of Skins Streached to Dry.... Close By The Cabin thare was a Small patch of Corn. On the Side of that was a Rail pen Coverd with Corn Stalks.... In this Rail pen he kept his horse."

Small farmers focused less on the market and more on providing for their families. As opposed to the hemp and blooded cattle of the Bluegrass, smaller farms planted corn and ran hogs loose in the forest. The family with whom Stedman stayed "Raised only Enough Corn For their Bread & often not Enough for That. Then when the Corn gave out they Eat Beach nuts." Butter, eggs, whiskey, or skins might be bartered or sold if the farm produced a surplus, in order to obtain necessaries like salt and metal tools. This most likely meant a trip down the valley to the local general store rather than to one of the burgeoning commercial cities of the

Must-See Sites: Famous Homes

Farmington Mansion

This 14-room Federal-style mansion stands at the center of a hemp plantation owned by John and Lucy Speed. Most of the structure is original, constructed in 1816, and is in excellent condition. A plan drawn up by Thomas Jefferson inspired the design of the house, offering an excellent example of Federal-style architecture. The 18-acre site also includes an elaborate nineteenth-century-style garden, a stone spring house, a barn, cook's quarters and kitchen, a blacksmith shop, and an apple orchard. The Speeds sponsored the Bohemian composer Anton Phillip Heinrich—considered America's first professional composer—and Heinrich wrote some of his best-known works while staying at Farmington.

Farmington tells the story of the rise of a Bluegrass-style gentry on the outskirts of Louisville. John Speed came to Kentucky as a 10-year-old boy with his family. In the 1790s, he operated a salt works in southern Jefferson county, the earnings from which enabled him to purchase the land on which Farmington arose. After his first wife died, Speed married Lucy Gilmer Fry in 1808, the granddaughter of Dr. Thomas Walker, the early explorer of Kentucky. Speed purchased land along Beargrass Creek in 1810 and began building shortly thereafter.

Farmington does not shy away from the ultimate source of its owner's wealth—slave labor. Slaves operated Speed's salt works, doing the heavy labor of hemp cultivation and harvesting, and skilled slave craftsmen participated in the construction of Farmington. Between 45 and 64 slaves worked at Farmington between 1816 and 1840, the year Speed died. Some of his descendants later freed their slaves before and during the Civil War.

Farmington is located just off Interstate 264 on Bardstown Road in Louisville. Call (502) 452-9920 or visit www.historicfarmington.org.

Locust Grove Mansion

A National Historic Landmark, this restored mansion depicts the lifestyle of the rich and connected in early Kentucky. The house, a 1790 Georgian-style mansion, sits on 55 of the original 694 acres owned by William and Lucy Clark Croghan. George Rogers Clark, the Revolutionary general and Lucy Clark Croghan's brother, lived at Locust Grove from 1809 until his death in 1818. While Locust Grove plays up its George Rogers Clark connection, the site really tells a broader story of early Kentucky history and life on the frontier.

The mansion has been restored and interior furnishings made to look as they might have in 1790. The current site also includes a smokehouse and eight other outbuildings, as well as formal gardens.

The Visitor Center has some small exhibits and a short film on the history of the site. Locust Grove also hosts special events—such as a Revolutionary War encampment—at different times during the year.

Locust Grove is located at 561 Blankenbaker Lane—just off River Road—in Louisville. Call (502) 897-9845 or visit www.locustgrove.org.

My Old Kentucky Home State Park

The site of Federal Hill, the park holds the antebellum home of Judge John Rowan. The Rowan plantation supposedly served as the inspiration for Stephen Foster's song "My Old Kentucky Home," which is Kentucky's state song (sung by hundreds of thousands every year before the Kentucky Derby). Costumed guides conduct regular tours of the mansion and gardens.

Rowan served as a judge on the Kentucky Court of Appeals and as a US senator from Kentucky. He was a Federalist, and his political ideology influenced the name of his estate, on which he began construction in 1815. Like Farmington, Locust Grove, and other historic homes of antebellum Kentucky, slaves did much of the work in constructing Federal Hill and making the plantation work. Foster visited Rowan, his cousin, in 1852, and penned the song shortly thereafter. The composer is honored during the summer with nightly performances of "Stephen Foster, The Musical," featuring period costumes, lively choreography, and music from a selection of over 50 Foster compositions. It is the longest-running outdoor drama in the state.

The house pays subtle homage to the 13 original colonies that separated from England during the Revolution. Each side of the house sports 13 windows, the ceilings are 13-feet high, the walls 13-inches thick, and the staircase has 13 steps. The interior decor is designed to appear much as it did at the time of Foster's visit.

My Old Kentucky Home State Park is located on US Highway 150 in Bardstown. Information about the park is available at (502) 348-3502 or (800) 323-7803. Information about "Stephen Foster, The Musical" is available at (502) 348-5971, (800) 626-1563, or at parks.ky.gov/stateparks/mk.

Liberty Hall Historic Site

Overlooking the Kentucky River, this four-acre site contains two examples of antebellum Kentucky architecture. The Federal-style Liberty Hall, a National Historic Landmark, was built in 1796 (although not completed until 1803) and was the home of John Brown; the Greek-Revival Orlando Brown House was built in 1835 and was his son's home. Tours of the houses emphasize the lives and contributions of this prominent Kentucky family.

John Brown was a Virginian who studied law under Thomas

Jefferson. In the early 1780s, he moved to Danville, Kentucky, where he became affiliated with the Political Club, a group that was trying to engineer the separation of Kentucky from Virginia. Brown represented the District of Kentucky as part of the Virginia delegation to the Continental Congress in 1787 and, after ratification of the Constitution, served in the US House of Representatives. He helped shepherd Kentucky to statehood and, soon after the state was admitted to the Union, he was elected its first senator.

Defeated for re-election in 1805, he retired to Liberty Hall and devoted himself to public service and his private business. He owned several hundred acres of land in Kentucky and several thousand in Ohio. Among other things, he helped found the Kentucky Historical Society in 1836.

As he grew older, he divided his estate equally between his two sons, Mason and Orlando. He bequeathed Liberty Hall to the older son, Mason, and offered to build Orlando a home on his side of the property. Kentucky's foremost architect, Gideon Shyrock, designed the Orlando Brown House. The homes are located at 218 Wilkinson Street in Frankfort. Call (502) 227-2560 or visit www.libertyhall.org.

Ashland

The former home of Kentucky's most famous antebellum figure, Henry Clay, Ashland was home to him and his wife Lucretia from 1806 until Clay's death in 1852. At its largest, the estate covered 600 acres, but all but about 20 acres of the surrounding property was sold off in the early 20th century.

The home, a National Historic Landmark, is a two-story brick Italianate structure. It is actually an 1857 reconstruction of the original house, built by Clay's son according to the plan for the original home and close to the original site. The interior is Victorian, according to the decorating tastes of Anne Clay McDowell, Clay's granddaughter, who lived there in the 1880s.

During Clay's time, the estate was a working farm. Clay grew hemp, tobacco, and a variety of other crops. He was an early innovator in stock breeding, importing purebred cattle to improve the bloodlines of his stock. Since Clay was often away for lengthy stays in Washington, DC, management of the estate fell to Lucretia who, with the help of an overseer, supervised the labor done by the family's slaves. At its peak, the estate housed 50 bondsmen.

In addition to the house, there are several outbuildings on the property, including a wash house and privy, a smokehouse, an ice house and dairy cellar, and a gardener's cottage. The cottage is now the site of changing historical and artistic exhibits. Behind the house are Henry Clay Walk and Locust Walk. These are the paths Clay would have trod as he composed his speeches and meditated over the political challenges facing him and the nation.

Ashland is located at the corner of Sycamore Road and Richmond Road in Lexington. Call (859) 266-8581 or visit www.henryclay.org.

Ashland

day. Isolated from transportation, many mountain communities were virtually self-contained, developing their own distinctive customs and distrusting outside influences.

Community life among these small farmers, although no less competitive than the gentlemanly sports of the Bluegrass, partook of the rough-and-tumble of the old backwoodsmen. "Squirrel-barking" (shooting just beneath the animal to send it flying off its perch) and "gander-pulling" (riding at full gallop and trying to rip the head off a live goose tied to a tree) remained popular sports, as they had during the pioneer days.

If economic extravagance set the planters apart from the small farmers and landless men, they all shared a set of ideas about masculinity and a man's place in the world. Whether gentleman or hardscrabble farmer, Kentucky men took the notion of personal honor seriously and were quick to answer perceived insults and slights. The form such answers took, however, differed.

For gentlemen, it took the form of dueling with pistols at ten paces. Henry Clay fought a duel with a political opponent after they exchanged words on the floor of the state legislature in 1809, for example. "I have this moment returned from the field of honor," Clay wrote in a letter. "We had three shots. On the first I grazed him above the navel—he missed me. On the second my damned pistol snapped, and he missed me. On the third I received a flesh wound in the thigh, and owing to my receiving his fire first, &c, I missed him. My wound is in no way serious, as the bone is unhurt, but prudence will require me to remain here some days." So prevalent was dueling among the ruling class that an 1811 law required all officeholders to swear an oath not to participate in duels, although it had little practical effect on the frequency of "affairs of honor."

For those lower on the social scale, "fighting words" meant just that: fighting. And fighting did not mean gentlemanly fighting with prescribed rules of conduct, but eye-gouging, hair-pulling, nose-biting brawls. Prominent rough-and-tumble fighters boasted of their exploits and exaggerated their victories. One Kentuckian, for example, told of an all-day fight with an opponent that finally ended when the Kentuckian's wife arrived to cheer him on to new exertions:

I gathered all the little strength I had, and I socked my thumb in his eye, and with my fingers took a twist on his snot box, and with the other hand, I grabbed him by the back of the head; I then caught his ear in my mouth, gin his head a flirt, and out come his ear by the roots! I then flopped his head over, and caught his other ear in my mouth, and jerked that out in the same way, and it made a hole in his head that I could have rammed my fist through, and I was just goin' to when he hollered 'Nuff!'

Conducting the family's business also formed part and parcel of the notion of manhood. Again, whether planter or small farmer, men viewed dealing with the outside world as part of their role. For the elite, that meant politics and commerce was a man's business. For the small farmer, that meant the local market and the courthouse were male bastions.

With the exception of a few European immigrant families, women did not tend to work in the fields of Kentucky's farms, though part of their responsibilities might include tending the garden, the cow, or the chickens. Ironically, the products of this female labor often provided the main cash crop for small farms, though the earnings would be credited to the husband.

Women stayed at home while their men transacted the family's business. For the small farmer's wife, the work of cooking, cleaning, and manufacturing the family's clothing required almost incessant toil. If she lived on an isolated farmstead, she might go months without seeing anybody outside her immediate family. One French traveler to Kentucky in 1802 met a woman who had not seen anyone but her husband and children for 18 months.

Plantation matrons did not face the problem of isolation. While their husbands ventured out into the political or business world, they were kept busy managing the home front. That could be a complex affair, coordinating the work of dozens of household slaves, receiving and entertaining visitors, and managing the household expenses. Lucretia Clay prided herself on her expert management of Ashland and on being able to greet her returning husband by giving him back the check he had left with her for household expenses. But just like poor

Literary Extracts: Charles Dickens

The famed English novelist came to the United States on a lecture tour and took the opportunity to witness firsthand the transformation of the American wilderness. In 1842, he published his impressions in a travelogue entitled *American Notes: A Journey*. During his sojourn, he stayed one night in Louisville and left the following description of the Falls City:

> There was nothing very interesting in the scenery of this day's journey, which brought us at midnight to Louisville. We slept at the Galt House; a splendid hotel; and were as handsomely lodged as though we had been in Paris, rather than hundreds of miles beyond the Alleghanies....
>
> The interval, after breakfast, we devoted to riding through the town, which is regular and cheerful: the streets being laid out at right angles, and planted with young trees. The buildings are smoky and blackened, from the use of bituminous coal, but an Englishman is well used to that appearance, and indisposed to quarrel with it. There did not appear to be much business stirring; and some unfinished buildings and improvements seemed to intimate that the city had been overbuilt in the ardor of "going ahead," and was suffering under the reaction consequent upon such feverish forcing of its powers....
>
> Here, as elsewhere in these parts, the road was perfectly alive with pigs of all ages; lying about in every direction, fast asleep; or grunting along in quest of hidden dainties.

women, all the work that upper-class women did redounded to the credit of their husbands.

Women, rich or poor, thus shared a common bond: legal submission to their husbands. Courts looked askance at divorce, and women had to prove that they had grounds to end their marriages. A rich woman who entered a marriage with a substantial dowry, however, had family resources to fall back on if her marriage went sour, while a poor woman had bleaker prospects. Widowed or divorced, a practical woman looked for remarriage as soon as she could.

And yet, few Kentucky women were drawn into the women's rights movement that began during the nineteenth century in some other regions of the country. When leaders of the movement came to Louisville to speak, which they did on two occasions, they spoke to mostly male audiences. Not until after the Civil War did the movement for women's rights penetrate very far into Kentucky.

For the vast majority of Kentuckians, male and female, the farm remained the touchstone of their existence. Even as the cities grew, the total urban population remained minuscule compared to the farm population. "The story of the great men of Kentucky in the nineteenth century," writes Thomas Clark, "is largely of men with farm backgrounds." Nonetheless, as Kentucky's commerce with the outside world increased, so did the size of its cities.

The hustle and bustle of Kentucky's cities contrasted with the slower pace of the countryside. Travelers who visited Lexington as early as the 1790s commented on the liveliness of the town, comparing it to Philadelphia (at that time the biggest city in the United States). In addition to merchants' shops and general stores, the cities boasted warehouses, manufacturing facilities, and a host of cultural institutions. By the early nineteenth century, Lexington already had such quintessential urban institutions as a fire and police department. The city recently opened a museum devoted to preserving and honoring Lexington's past.

The urban middle and upper classes organized debating clubs, literary societies, schools, dance academies, and other fashionable establishments. Professional theater groups came to the towns; the renowned "Swedish Nightingale" Jenny Lind performed in Louisville in 1851. The cities also encouraged art and artists. Lexington's elites had their portraits painted by Matthew Harris Jouett, one of the nation's premier portraitists, even though their commissions never paid enough for Jouett to support his family on his Kentucky business alone. They had their horses' portraits painted as well; Edward Troye began his career as the nation's preeminent equine artist after his arrival in Lexington in the 1830s.

The urban population, particularly in Louisville, also became more diverse than the surrounding countryside as the century went on. In 1850, only four percent of the state's population was foreign-born, but half their number resided in Louisville. During the late 1840s and early 1850s, Louisville began attracting larger numbers of German and Irish immigrants. Covington and Newport, northern Kentucky towns just across the Ohio River from Cincinnati, also drew significant numbers of Germans.

As an attraction to boost its declining fortunes in the more recent past, Covington created MainStrasse Village— a restoration of a nineteenth-century German neighborhood. In Louisville, the traditional German neighborhood Butchertown holds an annual Strassenfest in late August to celebrate the city's German cultural heritage.

European immigrants had been present in Kentucky from the start, but the immigrants of the 1840s and 1850s not only came in greater numbers but were different than earlier immigrant groups. The economic refugees from Ireland's Great Potato Famine were poor tenant farmers coming to the cities seeking unskilled labor. The political refugees from Germany's failed 1848 revolution were sympathetic to liberal and radical reforms, and brought those views to America. Perhaps most significant to the predominantly Protestant and native-born population trying to absorb them, most of the newcomers were Catholic.

In the 1850s, the influx of foreign Catholics combined with the declining political fortunes of the Whig party led some former Whigs to embrace anti-immigration. The American Party, more often called the Know-Nothings, was born. (The nickname came from the secrecy of the party's initial gatherings, where members were instructed to say "I know nothing" if asked about the party's doings).

The Know-Nothings hoped to unite native-born Americans and push the increasingly virulent political dispute over slavery into the background. George Prentice, the editor of Louisville's Whig newspaper, the *Journal*, watched his party's decline and then jumped on the anti-immigrant bandwagon: "It is evident that this foreign question is to override all others, even the slavery question, as we see men of the most opposite views on slavery, foregetting their differences and acting together." Know-Nothings campaigned for longer naturalization periods for foreigners and for a ban on Catholics and foreigners holding public office.

Must-See Sites:
The Portland Museum

The museum's permanent exhibit, "Portland: The Land, the River, and Its People," chronicles the life of this once independent town—now an annexed neighborhood of Louisville—and its links to the Ohio River. Portland's fate was intimately linked to the steamboat, and the exhibit tells the story of the steamboating era and the commercial life of the town both before and after the construction of the Louisville and Portland Canal. Through dioramas, artifact displays, and "animatronic" narrators, the exhibit details the rise and fall of the riverboat and of the heavily French immigrant community that found its way to Portland.

The museum also has restored several rooms of an old Portland house to illustrate the daily life of a well-to-do nineteenth-century Portlander. These rooms also house the museum's temporary exhibits. The biggest future project for the museum is a collaboration with the City of Louisville on an urban archaeological park that will uncover the building foundations and the streets of the old Portland Wharf area. The Wharf, cut off from the neighborhood by a flood wall and the construction of Interstate 64, is buried under the riverborne detritus of decades.

The Portland Museum is located 2308 Portland Avenue in western Louisville. Its telephone number is (502) 776-7678.

In Louisville, the party's anti-immigrant rhetoric, aided and abetted by some inflammatory newspaper editorials, set the stage for violence. The Louisville *Daily Courier*, for example, blamed the "infusion of the foreign element" for a decline in observance of the Sabbath. "These make each Sunday a Saturnalia, and with all their might are attempting to Europeanize our population." Prentice, writing in the rival *Journal*, painted an even grimmer picture of foreign political domination. "Their hate knows no bounds.... Their insolence is unbearable. If they had the requisite courage and strength they would drive forth into the wilderness every native that refuses to let them set their feet upon his neck."

Must-See Sites: Lexington History Museum

Opened in October 2003 with the mission of telling the story of Lexington, the museum's inaugural exhibits include "The Athens of the West," which uses a variety of artifacts and memorabilia to recapture the life of the city—among all social classes—during the nineteenth century. Another exhibit, "Racing in the Streets," tracks the development of Lexington's love affair with horse racing. The stumps were not cleared from the mud streets of early Lexington before horse races were being run on the main thoroughfares. The exhibit covers the early days up to the development of the track at Keeneland and other horse facilities in the area.

The late Thomas D. Clark, the dean of modern Kentucky historians, worked forty years to establish a museum devoted to the city's history. He was fortunate enough to see it open before his death in 2005. The museum is housed in the old Fayette County Courthouse, which the courts only vacated in 2001. The museum occupies the main and second floors. Outside, on Courthouse Square, there are numerous sculptures and monuments honoring different aspects of Kentucky's past.

The Lexington History Museum is located 215 West Main Street. Call (859) 254-0530, or visit www.lexingtonhistorymuseum.org.

On August 6, 1855, Louisvillians went to the polls to elect a state governor and members of Congress. Naturalized citizens in heavily German and Irish wards were denied access to the polls by Know-Nothing election workers, tempers flared, and fights broke out among those waiting. As the day wore on, occasional fistfights gave way to a full-blown riot as Know-Nothing mobs stormed the city's East End, pursuing and beating German residents. "From my office I saw many men, Irish and German, beaten in the courthouse yard," prominent Louisvillian James Speed recalled. "It was not fighting man to man, but as many would fall upon a single Irish or German and beat him with sticks or short clubs."

Famous Sons and Daughters: Zachary Taylor

General and US President
(November 24, 1784–July 9, 1850)

Taylor came with his family to Kentucky when he was just eight months old. Springfield, the family's plantation, was located near Louisville. He began his military career in 1808 as a first lieutenant in the Seventh Infantry. He played a key role in the defense of Fort Harrison, Indiana Territory, during the War of 1812, and was promoted to brevet major.

In 1815, he returned to Louisville, where he had purchased a farm on Beargrass Creek, but was soon recalled to active duty. He returned again for a year in 1818, but then spent four years serving in the South. He later became superintendent of recruiting for the army's Western Department, which had headquarters in Cincinnati and later Louisville. Taylor left Louisville for Washington, DC, in 1826, followed by service in the Black Hawk War (1832) and the Second Seminole War (1835–42).

Taylor made his name, however, during the Mexican War (1846–48), where as commander of the Army of the Rio Grande he won victories in several key battles. A national military hero, "Old Rough and Ready" gained the Whig Party's nomination for president in 1848, despite his lack of political experience. He won a close election and was inaugurated on March 5, 1849. He died in office just over a year later, probably from cholera. Initially buried in Washington, his remains were reinterred in the Taylor family cemetery (now part of the Zachary Taylor National Cemetery in Louisville) in November of 1850.

When some immigrant residents began firing shots at the pursuers from their houses, the houses were set afire. The mob ransacked German-owned taverns, beat and shot residents, and torched a German-owned brewery, burning ten German workers to death. The rioters then turned west to the heavily Irish section of the city, setting a row of houses ablaze and shooting residents as they fled. At least 22 people died during "Bloody Monday," although the actual death toll may have been significantly higher. Most of the dead were foreign-born, and the "enormous property damage,… like a gaping wound, still showed two years later," writes one historian of Louisville.

In addition to ethnic diversity and growing cultural sophistication, the cities also bred vice. Louisville in particular became as well known for the rowdiness of its waterfront as for the sophistication of its elites. River boatmen more often found prostitutes, alcohol, and gambling of more interest than the scheduled topic of any particular debating society. The elites looked down on such activities, grand juries occasionally convened to condemn them, but the waterfront made Louisville work, and no one wanted to take the risk that cleaning it up might be bad for business.

The perceived tolerance of such sinful behavior, as well as the perceived increase in the amount of such behavior, caused religious leaders no end of worry. Since very early in the history of Kentucky, preachers had almost uniformly bemoaned the sorry religious state of their parishioners. Everyone seemed consumed with the material world, with getting and having either the means to survival or the keys to prosperity. Lexington and the Bluegrass gentry came in for particularly harsh criticism. Lexington was compared to Sodom, its inhabitants derided for not sharing the religious enthusiasm of their rural neighbors.

That enthusiasm grew to a fever pitch in the early nineteenth century. Already in the late 1790s, Presbyterian preachers had begun holding revivals in the pioneer country south of the Green River. These grew, spread, and attracted attention until, in 1801, they exploded into national prominence at Cane Ridge Presbyterian Church, near the small Bluegrass town of Paris. In August, between 10,000 and 20,000 people converged on the area, seeking divine enlightenment and salvation. It was by far the largest gathering Kentucky had ever seen. The tiny Cane Ridge Meeting House still stands, although it is hard for the modern-day visitor to imagine the crowds and the enthusiasm that engulfed the place two centuries ago.

Although hosted by a Presbyterian church, Baptist and Methodist clergy also participated in the Cane Ridge revival. Several preachers held forth at one time, each speaking to just one portion of the huge crowd. Levi

Hazard

Must-See Sites:
Religious Gathering Places

The Cane Ridge Meeting House

This meeting house hosted the 1801 religious revival that altered the regional and national religious landscape by revving up great enthusiasm for more evangelical denominations, like the Baptists and the Methodists, although Cane Ridge was a Presbyterian church. The Meeting House was built in 1791 by a group of early Scots-Irish settlers from North Carolina, who brought their Presbyterian faith with them to Kentucky. The site's literature claims for the church the title of largest one-room log building in the United States. The old log church is now protected by a limestone superstructure that keeps the weather and the woodpeckers at bay.

Barton Stone, a famed frontier preacher, came to be pastor at Cane Ridge in 1796. Stone was pastor during the great revival five years later. Seeing Presbyterians, Baptists, Methodists, and others all working together to save souls at the revival led Stone to begin a non-sectarian movement among a group of Presbyterian ministers. In 1804, Stone and several other ministers authored a document that gave rise to a movement for Christian unity across denominational lines. Ironically, the movement Stone started morphed into several separate denominations—the Disciples of Christ, the Church of Christ, and the independent Christian Church.

Cane Ridge continued to serve its function as a house of worship until 1921, when the few remaining members of the congregation disbanded. In the 1930s, the Disciples of Christ restored the old meeting house to its original appearance. The meeting house is located nine miles east of Paris, Kentucky, on State Highway 537 in Bourbon County. For information, call (859) 987-5350 or visit www.parisky.com/pages/caneridge.html.

Shaker Village of Pleasant Hill

The site is an outdoor history museum in which 33 original buildings have been preserved from the Shaker village that occupied the site from 1805 until 1910. The Shakers—officially known as the United Society of Believers in Christ's Second Appearing—came to Kentucky in the wake of the Cane Ridge revival. They established Pleasant Hill in 1805 on a plateau above the Kentucky River. The community thrived at first, and by mid-century counted nearly 500 residents and 4,000 acres of land.

As the century wore on, however, the number of Shakers declined. Since they lived a celibate life, they were dependent on new converts to maintain the community and lost many to the cities after the Civil War. By 1910, only a few Shakers survived, and the village was closed. The village passed into private hands, but in 1961 a preservation group began efforts to save the village and its history. Now a National Historic Landmark covering 2,700 acres, Pleasant Hill has become a model of historic preservation. It boasts that all its visitor services are provided in original buildings, unique for a site of its kind.

Costumed interpreters now populate Pleasant Hill, demonstrating Shaker crafts and agricultural practices and describing Shaker life and beliefs. Visitors are free to wander at their own pace through 17 of the buildings on the site. Shaker Village also operates the *Dixie Belle* steamboat, a restored sternwheeler, which offers one-hour excursions on a quietly beautiful stretch of the Kentucky River.

Shaker Village of Pleasant Hill is located off United States Highway 68 near Harrodsburg. Call (859) 734-5411 or (800) 734-5611 or visit www.shakervillageky.org.

The Shaker Museum at South Union

The westernmost such community in the United States, the Shakers at South Union established themselves in 1807—two years after Pleasant Hill—but survived until 1922, making it the last surviving Shaker community in Kentucky. Like Pleasant Hill, the original buildings have been restored and the buildings house various artifacts—mostly domestic items—that illustrate Shaker life.

The Shakers were inveterate journal keepers, and the museum makes ample use of members' journal entries to paint a picture of daily life in the community. Typical journal entries include weather and crop information, the comings and goings of guests, community rules, and disruptions in the community life. For example, although the Shakers were pacifists, they were not exempt from demands from both sides in the Civil War for food and lodging on their grounds.

The museum offers guided tours of the buildings and recently received a Federal grant to expand their facilities. The Shaker Museum is located near Bowling Green on State Highway 1466 just south of the junction of United States Route 68 and Kentucky Route 80. For information, call (270) 542-4167 or (800) 811-8379, or visit www.shakermuseum.com.

Purviance, who attended Cane Ridge and later went on to become a preacher himself, remembered "Presbyterians, Methodists, Baptists, &c., &c., were there, as one mighty spiritual host, assembled together to fight the battles of the Lord…. They preached and prayed and praised together for the salvation of sinners. Their objects and aims were the same; there was no schism."

Day after day it went on, with emotion-filled listeners suddenly seized by convulsions and shouting as they felt the Spirit descend upon them. Purviance described what he called "the falling exercise": "It was no uncommon occurrence for persons while listening to preaching, exhortation, prayer, or singing, to fall from their seat or feet to the ground, and some appeared almost in a lifeless condition; while others would cry to God in the most fervent manner, for mercy to their needy souls." The falling exercise later gave way to "the jerks," Purviance recalled. "Their heads would jerk back suddenly, frequently causing them to give a yelp or make some other involuntary noise…. I have seen heads fly back and forward so quickly that the hair of females would be made to crack like a carriage whip." Many of these converts backslid once they left the revival grounds, but Cane Ridge ignited a spread of evangelical revivalism across the Ohio Valley and the southeast that worked profoundly on the religious culture of the area.

As word of Cane Ridge spread, churches both old and new picked up recruits. Baptists and Methodists gained the most, and Baptists remain the largest denomination in the state. The Shakers, an offshoot of the English Quakers based in upstate New York, sent missionaries to Kentucky in the aftermath of Cane Ridge to look into the possibility of establishing a colony. The Shakers believed that the second coming of Jesus Christ had already occurred, so the colonies they founded were meant to be part of the Kingdom of Heaven on earth. Villagers therefore lived celibate lives, with strict segregation of the sexes, and they lived communally. In 1806, the Shakers found enough enthusiasm to establish the first Shaker community in Kentucky, at Pleasant Hill, near Harrodsburg. The following year, they founded their second community, at South Union, near Bowling Green.

FOUR: ANTEBELLUM KENTUCKY

Although it predated many of the economic changes that came with the market revolution, the evangelical Christianity that came out of the great revivals may have helped people adjust to those changes when they did come. By stressing the equality of all individuals before God, the irrelevance of material rewards in this life, and the availability to everyone of God's gift of salvation, it contrasted sharply with a world in which material rewards counted for a great deal, much was made of social standing, and the path to well-being seemed open only to a select few.

By 1860, Kentucky boasted several nationally prominent men, a thriving economy built on commercial agriculture, cities that were required stops by European visitors on tours of the United States, and a reputation as a civilized society forged from a wild frontier. "Civilization," however, came at a price, as many of the early pioneers could attest. Economic inequality, the sometimes cruel machinations of the legal system, the pretensions of the planters and the isolation of rural communities seemed a far cry from the "good poor man's country" that the first settlers of Kentucky had touted.

5

THE CIVIL WAR

Kentucky's historical sites tend to commemorate and celebrate the pioneer and antebellum periods, when the state rose to national prominence, more than the post-Civil War era, when Kentucky sank into a period of disorder and confusion. The idea that the war put an end to a golden age in Kentucky's history reflects an undimmed ambivalence about the war itself. Kentucky did not want the war to come, tried initially to stay out of it, and as a slaveholding state that stayed in the Union, never quite made up its mind about which side it favored.

As the nation bumped from sectional crisis to sectional crisis in the 1850s, Kentucky watched and wished the divisive issue of slavery would just go away. Slavery had killed the Whigs, and the Know-Nothings had hoped to mobilize resentment against foreigners to counter the contentiousness over slavery. Now Kentuckians witnessed the rise of a new party, the Republicans, whose platform opposed the expansion of slavery outside of the area where it now existed. As slaveholders, Kentuckians disliked this upstart new party, but as heirs to the nationalism of Henry Clay, they also disliked the idea of dissolving the Union. So they waited, and wondered where to place their allegiances.

SLAVERY AND ANTISLAVERY

Slavery came easily to Kentucky. Slaves had been present since the beginning of American settlement. In 1777, for example, the 198 souls who crowded into Fort Harrod to weather attacks by Native Americans included 19 slaves. By 1830, almost a quarter of the total population was black, and the vast majority of those were slaves. By 1860, the proportion of slaves had decreased to just under a fifth of the total population, although the absolute number of slaves had increased to 225,483.

Must-See Sites: The Underground Railroad

The National Underground Railroad Freedom Center

Opened in August 2004 just across the Ohio River from Covington, Kentucky, this $110 million facility seeks to tell the story of slavery and freedom in the United States in a way that connects that story to ongoing issues surrounding freedom today.

The museum's exhibits are spread over three floors and 158,000 square feet. The "Suite for Freedom" explores freedom, slavery, and preconceptions about the underground railroad through a multimedia presentation of images and music. There is also an actual slave pen, removed from a farm in Mason County, Kentucky, and reconstructed inside the museum. The pen was used to warehouse slaves before they were sold South. Another exhibit, aimed at children, uses interactive displays, storytelling, and role-playing to tell the stories of those who fought against slavery. The "From Slavery to Freedom" exhibit shows how the opponents of slavery used the American Revolution's language of freedom. A follow-up exhibit on life after slavery tells of the challenges African Americans continued to face and of their struggles to make their freedom mean more than just the end of bondage.

The National Underground Railroad Freedom Center is located at 50 East Freedom Way on the Ohio River waterfront in Cincinnati, Ohio. Call (513) 333-7500 or (877) 648-4838 or visit www.freedomcenter.org.

The National Underground Railroad Museum

This museum is a local effort to capture the history of slavery and the resistance to slavery around the community of Maysville, Kentucky. The museum is organized around central clusters of artifacts, each sharing a common theme or thread that is important to understanding slavery, the local African American community, the underground railroad, or the opposition to slavery.

Like the Freedom Center, the museum debunks the myth of the underground railroad as a well-oiled locomotive consisting largely of northern white abolitionists helping runaway slaves. Instead, it focuses on the black community itself—the relatively small groups of free blacks in both the North and the South—that played the most important roles in helping runaway slaves find their way to freedom.

The museum also plays up its links to the community outside its walls, noting the presence of safe houses and way stations in the Maysville area. On the Kentucky side of the river, these include the Paxton Inn in Old Washington and Phillip's Folly in downtown Maysville. Across the river in Ripley, Ohio, are the Rankin House and the John Parker House, the old homes of two abolitionists who did serve as "conductors" on the underground railroad.

The National Underground Railroad Museum is located at 115 E. Third Street in Maysville. For information, call (606) 564-6986 or (606) 564-6063 or visit the web at www.coax.net/people/lwf/urmuseum.htm.

Like the ownership of land, the ownership of slaves was wildly unequal. According to the 1850 census, only 28 percent of white families owned at least one slave. Nearly a quarter of slaveowning families owned just one, and just five families owned more than 100 slaves.

As might be expected, the Bluegrass was home to many of the state's big-time slave owners. The population of Woodford County, in the inner Bluegrass, was over half slave by the time of the Civil War. Twenty-one counties (out of 109) had a slave population of 30 percent or higher. Twenty-three counties, on the other hand, had a slave population of 6 percent or less. The cash price of slaves simply made them too costly for the bulk of small farmers to afford.

This pattern of slave ownership had important effects on the lives of slaves. As opposed to the Deep South pattern of gang labor supervised by drivers and overseers, a good many slaves in Kentucky worked alongside their masters in the fields. In addition, because small farmers often planted corn and other subsistence crops rather than strictly cash crops like hemp or cotton, the intensity of a slave's labor varied seasonally. As opposed to so-called "slave crops" like cotton, hemp, and tobacco, which required year-round care and cultivation, corn had defined seasonal periods of intensive labor, namely planting and harvest, and a long period of relative idleness.

Since slaves represented a continuing expense for the slaveowner, however, ways had to be found to keep the bondsmen busy. Kentuckians therefore often hired out their slaves, renting them to neighboring landowners and even factory owners who needed laborers. Slaves also learned crafts and helped with a wide variety of farm chores, including shoemaking, spinning, and carpentry. The result of all these trends was perhaps a slightly higher degree of slave autonomy than on the great plantations, and masters sometimes found themselves negotiating with their slaves rather than simply commanding them. The existence of a long border with the free states to the North may have also contributed to some masters' restraint.

Green County slaveowner Burton Carr, for example, could not keep his slave Frank at home on his isolated farmstead. Instead, Frank demanded to be hired out and expressed his resistance by repeatedly running away from Carr. Finally, Carr gave in. "I have again hired him out to Mr. Blaydes," Carr wrote to his mother back in Virginia. "[H]e wont stay with me & live a lone not Seeing nor hearing from A human mortal at times for A Week or two together."

Overall, therefore, slavery seemed to be a bit milder in Kentucky than in other slaveholding parts of the nation. Such a judgment in no way condones slavery. In the end, a slave worked hard but gained nothing, as all the rewards of the slave's labor accrued to the master. Slaves and masters never occupied equal ground when it came to negotiating the terms of slavery. If that "slightly higher degree of slave autonomy" crossed an unspoken line into insolence, as perceived by the master, the slave could be beaten or whipped with impunity.

Nancy Lowry, for example, described in 1839 the routine beatings of three male slaves on the farm where she grew up. The men had wives on different farms and would often stay longer visiting their wives than their master allowed. The master, Mr. Long, "would tie them up by the wrist, so that their toes would just touch the ground, and then with a cow-hide lay the lash upon the naked back, until he was exhausted, when he would sit down and rest. As soon as he had rested sufficiently, he would ply the cowhide again, thus he would continue until the whole back of the poor victim was lacerated into one uniform coat of blood." All three slaves, Lowry said, "died a premature death, and it was generally believed by his neighbors, that extreme whipping was the cause."

Any judgment about the "mildness" of slavery in Kentucky, therefore, must take such brutality into account. As historian Marion Lucas has written, set against the bedrock fact of lifetime servitude, "statements of degree of harshness pale into insignificance." All such a judgment implies is that if one had to be a slave in antebellum America, it might be better to be a slave in Kentucky than Mississippi.

Unfortunately, many Kentucky slaves ended up in Mississippi and other parts of the Deep South. Just as the spread of cotton culture created a ready market for Kentucky hemp, the increased labor demands of the Cotton Kingdom created a ready market for Kentucky's often underused slaves. And just as the market revolution turned

Literary Extracts:
Alexis de Tocqueville

Alexis de Tocqueville was a young French aristocrat who came to the United States to study the country's prison system. Instead, he took on the far more ambitious project of investigating the nature of American democracy. *Democracy in America*, from which the following extract is taken, remains a classic sociological and political analysis of the American republic:

> The stream that the Indians had named the Ohio, or Beautiful River par excellence, waters one of the most magnificent valleys in which man has ever lived. On both banks of the Ohio stretched undulating ground with soil continually offering the cultivator inexhaustible treasures; on both banks the air is equally healthy and the climate temperate; they both form the frontier of a vast state: that which follows the innumerable windings of the Ohio on the left bank is called Kentucky; the other takes its name from the river itself. There is only one difference between the two states: Kentucky allows slaves, but Ohio refuses to have them....
>
> So the traveler who lets the current carry him down the Ohio till it joins the Mississippi sails, so to say, between freedom and slavery; and he has only to glance around him to see instantly which is best for mankind....
>
> On the left bank of the river the population is sparse; from time to time one sees a troop of slaves loitering through half-deserted fields; the primeval forest is constantly reappearing; one might say that society had gone to sleep; it is nature that seems active and alive, whereas man is idle....
>
> But on the right bank a confused hum proclaims from afar that men are busily at work; fine crops cover the fields; elegant dwellings testify to the taste and industry of the workers; on all sides there is evidence of comfort....
>
> —from *Democracy in America*, 13th ed. (1850)

subsistence farmers into commercial farmers, it turned slaves from simply a labor source into a capital asset. After about 1830, the internal slave trade sent many Kentucky slaves southward, as masters turned human assets into financial ones.

Since Kentucky law did not recognize slave marriage, being sold "down the river" often meant the forcible breakup of families. Eleven-year-old Isaac Johnson, for example, was sold away from his family and then watched his two younger brothers and his mother each get auctioned off to separate owners. "Thus in a very short time, our happy family was scattered, without even the privilege of saying Good by," Isaac later wrote. He never saw any member of his family again. The threat of such sales was the reason a famed slave preacher concluded his marriage ceremonies with "until death or distance do thee part."

The slaves resisted the dehumanization of slavery in several ways. They slowed down their pace of labor, sabotaged machinery or their own bodies, and occasionally resorted to violence to disrupt the efficient workings of the slave system. Many ran away. Some sought permanent refuge from slavery by escaping to the North or to Canada; others used flight merely as "time off" from the demands of the master or to visit family members held in bondage at other locations. Oldham County slaveowner Francis Taliaferro, for example, advertised a $50 reward for the return of his slave Reuben in 1824. "He has a wife at Mr. Fitzhugh Thornton's, in this county," Taliaferro's ad read. "[N]o doubt, [he] will make the principal part of his stay in that neighborhood, being uncommonly fond of his family."

Enslaved blacks also created their own social institutions within the confines of slavery. As Reuben's example attests, despite the tenuousness of slave marriage, it was not uncommon at all for husbands and wives to form strong family bonds. Separate black churches also provided avenues for self-expression that were otherwise unavailable to slaves. First African Baptist Church in Lexington, probably the oldest and most well-known of Kentucky's black churches, was founded by a slave named Peter, who was known to all as "Old Captain" and who pastored the church from its founding in about 1801 until his death in 1823.

If the majority of Kentuckians never owned a slave, a larger majority never actively opposed slavery, either. Most Kentuckians accepted slavery as a legitimate institution and felt the state government had an obligation to protect property, even human property. "If they can by one experiment emancipate our slaves," Lexington elite John Breckinridge complained of those intent on abolishing slavery, "the same principle pursued, will enable them at a second experiment to extinguish our land titles; both are held by rights equally sound."

Kentucky's defenders of slavery resented the abolitionist movement as outsiders meddling in Kentucky affairs. They also resented the accusations of cruelty contained in works such as *Uncle Tom's Cabin* by Harriet Beecher Stowe and *American Slavery As It Is* by Theodore Weld, both of which used observations of slave life in Kentucky to make their case against the institution. As slavery came under political attack during the run-up to the war, ample numbers of Kentuckians defended it.

The house where Harriet Beecher Stowe stayed when preparing material for her book, Uncle Tom's Cabin.

Must-See Sites: Homes from Either Side of the Battle Line

White Hall State Historic Site

White Hall was the estate of Cassius Marcellus Clay, the state's most prominent antislavery advocate. Costumed guides provide regular tours of the house and an overview of Clay's long and stormy career as an emancipationist in a slave state. When he first started publishing his *True American* newspaper in Lexington, for example, he equipped the office with two small cannons and a trap door in the roof (booby trapped with a powder keg), anticipating mob action by his pro-slavery enemies.

In the 1860 election, Clay supported Lincoln and was rewarded by being named minister to Russia. While he was away, his wife Mary Jane supervised the transformation of the house into its current form. White Hall is actually built around and above "Clermont," the smaller, simpler house of Clay's father, built in 1799. Clermont was Georgian and White Hall is Italianate, and the final product blends both architectural styles. The remodeling more than doubled the size of the original house, turning it into a 44-room mansion. White Hall also contained two unique features for its day: indoor plumbing and central heating.

Clay continued to generate controversy long after the slavery question was settled. In 1894, the 84-year-old Clay, divorced from Mary Jane since 1870, married 15-year-old Dora Richardson. An outraged community came to remove the girl from White Hall, and Clay chased them off by firing one of his cannons—filled with nails, tacks, and various other shrapnel—at the posse. Clay became increasingly reclusive, repeatedly threatening to chase off visitors with his trusty artillery, until his death in 1903.

White Hall is located on White Hall State Shrine Road off State Highway 627 in Richmond. Call (859) 623-9178, or visit parks.ky.gov/statehistoricsites/wh.

The Hunt-Morgan House

Home of Confederate cavalry raider John Hunt Morgan, the second floor has been turned into a Civil War museum with an extensive collection of artifacts. The first floor has been restored to its appearance circa 1814, when Morgan's grandfather, John Wesley Hunt, built the house. A Federal-style home historically known as Hopemont, the house contains early Kentucky furnishings, antique porcelain, and various nineteenth-century paintings. The first floor recalls the lifestyle of the antebellum Lexington elite.

In addition to being the home of the "Thunderbolt of the Confederacy," it was also home to Thomas Hunt Morgan, John Hunt's nephew and John Wesley's great grandson. Thomas was a scientist who won the Nobel Prize.

The Hunt-Morgan house is located at 201 North Mill Street in Lexington. Call (859) 253-0362, or visit www.bluegrasstrust.org/historic/morgan.htm.

Of course, antislavery sentiment existed within the state. Just like slavery, it had come with some of the first settlers. In fact, the best chance at eliminating slavery from the state came early, when Presbyterian minister David Rice led a movement to abolish the institution in the 1792 constitutional convention. Rice lost by a vote of 26 to 16, and a constitutional provision legalizing slavery made its way into the final document. Antislavery advocates made another effort when the constitution was revised in 1799 and again failed.

Still, those opposed to slavery kept agitating the issue, eventually getting the legislature to pass a law in 1833 forbidding the importation of slaves solely for the purpose of reselling them southward. Evangelical Christians, influenced by the revivalism of the early nineteenth century, sometimes preached against slavery, but Kentucky's churches eventually made their peace with slavery by declaring it a political issue, not a moral one. Delia Webster and Calvin Fairbank helped slaves escape across the Ohio River, and attracted national attention when the state prosecuted and jailed them for their efforts.

Cassius Marcellus Clay probably holds the title of most notable figure in the annals of antislavery Kentucky. He held rather mild opinions, favoring gradual emancipation rather than immediate abolition, but he defended those opinions avidly. He responded to physical attacks by pro-slave forces with violence of his own, repelling an attack by a hired assassin, for example, with a well-aimed thrust of his Bowie knife. After being told to pipe down by a prominent group of Lexingtonians, he published an open letter that ended: "Go tell your secret conclave of cowardly assassins that C.M. Clay knows his rights and how to defend them." He even wrote a pamphlet on the techniques of knife-fighting (thrust upward, do not strike down, he advised).

Despite the continued agitation of the issue, when a final chance to alter the state's law regarding slavery came along in the constitutional convention of 1850, conservatism reigned. The pro-slavery article from 1799 went into the 1850 constitution virtually unchanged. Kentucky had been wedded to the institution for too long to get rid of it on its own initiative.

A BORDER STATE

Along with Maryland and Missouri, Kentucky occupied the border region between North and South. Kentucky's Virginia heritage, the southern roots of many of the state's settlers, its commercial ties to the South via the Mississippi River, and the institution of slavery all forged a strong bond to the South. But Kentuckians also had ties to the North. A significant number of its settlers hailed from Pennsylvania and Ohio. And although Kentucky's commercial concerns oriented her toward the South, the footsteps of many of her citizens pointed her North. Federal oversight and systematic land surveys in the Old Northwest made land claims there substantially more secure than in Kentucky. Many Kentuckians who had fared poorly in court battles over land—like the young Abraham Lincoln's family—had crossed the Ohio River to try again in the Northwest, leaving relatives and friends in Kentucky. Moreover, rail traffic had begun to weaken the dependence on the river and the resulting southern orientation. Finally, Kentuckians took pride in the nationalism of Henry Clay and in their role in fighting the wars of the nation.

Kentucky showed its indecision in the pivotal presidential election of 1860. It went neither for Abraham Lincoln, the Republican candidate who represented mainly Northern interests, nor for Kentuckian John Breckinridge, who carried the standard for the southern slaveholding wing of the Democratic party. Instead, John Bell, a Tennessean who had withdrawn from the Republican party to form the ad hoc Constitutional Union party, whose sole purpose was to advocate preservation of the Union, carried the state with 45 percent of the vote. Breckinridge took second place with 36 percent. Lincoln pulled less than one percent of the vote, showing the general disdain in which Kentuckians held the Republicans. (The fourth candidate, Illinois Senator Stephen Douglas, polled 18 percent of Kentucky's votes).

A Kentucky physician, Jefferson J. Polk, recounted his mindset during the 1860 election in his autobiography: "The presidential election was held—four candidates, Douglas, Lincoln, Breckinridge, and Bell in the field. The first was the advocate of squatter sovereignty; the second, of

A Kentucky man with his Confederate flag

emancipation; the third, of secession; and the fourth, of the constitution and the enforcement of the laws. I voted for the latter. The result of the election is known to all."

With Lincoln's election, South Carolina seceded. Those hopeful for a compromise turned their eyes to Kentucky, and the state's leaders were actively involved in the four major attempts before Fort Sumter to find a solution. But Henry Clay was dead, and the compromisers who took on his role found it impossible to forge common ground between North and South.

Kentucky Senator John J. Crittenden outlined a set of steps in December 1860 that he thought necessary to keep the Union together. They included reassertion of the line drawn by the Missouri Compromise dividing slave territory from free territory, tougher enforcement of the Fugitive Slave Act, and allowing new states to decide the status of slavery as they entered the Union. In slightly varying form, different forces seeking a compromise put forth the Crittenden proposals. In each case, they were rejected, most often by the Republicans, who saw them quite rightly as an abandonment of their position on the expansion of slavery.

When the war came in April 1861 with South Carolina firing on Fort Sumter, Kentucky declared itself neutral. Lincoln immediately requested 75,000 men to put down the rebellion, four regiments of which were to come from Kentucky. Governor Beriah Magoffin refused. "Kentucky will furnish no troops for the wicked purpose of subduing her sister southern states," he cabled the president.

Within the state, the political parties split into two camps: the Unionists, which joined ex-Whigs and Know-Nothings with Unionist Democrats, and the States' Rightists, who constituted the southern-sympathizing wing of the Democratic party. Neutrality appealed to both sides, since neither could forge a political consensus on the path Kentucky should take. In May 1861, the Kentucky legislature formally declared the neutrality of the state in the conflict. Ardent supporters of both the Confederate cause and the Union cause, impatient with Kentucky's Hamlet act, slipped away to other states to enlist in the armies of their chosen side.

One such ardent supporter of the Confederate cause was Edward O. Guerrant, a schoolteacher in Flat Creek,

Montgomery County. When a friend secured him a position as secretary to a Confederate general, Guerrant "determined... to try my fortunes in a new and unknown field—where honor and patriotism called me though health and friends forbid. I had a fine and flourishing school at Flat Creek.... I had a pleasant boarding house, and every thing that heart could desire—Except the consciousness of not fulfilling my duty to my Country."

Jefferson J. Polk felt his duty lay in exactly the opposite direction: "As soon as it was certain that Mr. Lincoln had been elected, a violent outburst of feeling was manifested in all the slave states.... I wish only to say that I considered it my duty to God and my country to espouse the Union case." At times, his Unionism bred conflicts with his neighbors: "Like others who remained steadfast in their devotion to the government, I too at times was threatened by thoughtless and irresponsible persons of secession proclivities. But none of these things moved me."

At first, both sides respected Kentucky's neutrality. A rash act by either side, it was felt, might easily push the state into the opposing camp. Over the summer of 1861, however, Kentucky's Unionists gained the upper hand politically, winning elections to the national Congress and the state legislature. The Army opened a recruiting station in Garrard County, ignoring the objections of Governor Magoffin about the violation of neutrality. The governor, Lincoln suggested, no longer represented the will of the people.

In September, the state's policy of neutrality crumbled. Both Confederate and Union forces had been eyeing the strategic western portion of the state, where the Cumberland and Tennessee Rivers flowed into the Mississippi. Fearing a Federal takeover of Columbus, on the Mississippi, Confederate troops moved in first. Columbus-Belmont State Park now sits where Confederate artillery once guarded the southward course of the river. Union forces responded to the Confederate move by occupying Paducah and other Ohio River towns. The Confederacy countered by moving troops through the Cumberland Gap into eastern Kentucky.

The state was fast becoming occupied ground and would have to declare its sympathies one way or another. On September 11, 1861, the legislature instructed the

Famous Sons and Daughters:
Abraham Lincoln

US President
(February 12, 1809–April 15, 1865)

Lincoln was born on his father's farm near Hodgenville, Kentucky. His earliest memories were of the nearby family farm on Knob Creek, where the family moved when Lincoln was just two years old. Although they left Kentucky when Lincoln was only seven, he maintained strong ties to the state through friendship and marriage.

Lincoln eventually settled in Springfield, Illinois, to practice law in 1837. He met Kentuckian Mary Todd there, and in 1842 they were married. He returned to Kentucky periodically after his marriage to visit his in-laws in Lexington. His closest friend, Joshua Speed, also came from Kentucky, and Lincoln was occasionally a guest at Farmington, Speed's estate near Louisville.

Lincoln served as an Illinois state militia captain during the brief Black Hawk War in 1832 against the Sac and Fox and in the 1840s as an Illinois state legislator. He won election to the US House of Representatives in 1846, but his opposition to the Mexican War earned him a trip home after one term. He returned to private law practice until his public denunciation of the 1854 Kansas–Nebraska Act and its implications for the spread of slavery brought him back into the national political arena. He ran for the Senate and lost in 1858, although his debates with eventual winner Stephen Douglas gained him national attention. In 1860, the recently formed Republican party, which Lincoln had joined in 1856, nominated him for president.

His election to the presidency precipitated the secession of eleven southern states from the Union, and the preservation of the Union dominated the rest of Lincoln's presidency. He proved an adept wartime president, managing the political and social divisions within the North, relentlessly prosecuting the war against the South, and embracing—albeit reluctantly—the idea of emancipating the slaves. John Wilkes Booth assassinated Lincoln shortly after the main Confederate army surrendered at Appomattox.

Knob Creek Farm, Lincoln's boyhood home

governor to order only the Confederates to withdraw. It rejected a measure calling on both sides to pull back. Kentucky had chosen Union.

FIGHTING THE WAR

The Confederates did not withdraw. Instead, General Albert Sidney Johnston ordered the town of Bowling Green occupied and fortified. Johnston's troops formed a defensive line across the southern portion of the state. He concentrated his forces at certain critical points: Cumberland Gap, Bowling Green, and Columbus. Confederate sympathizers hastily organized a provisional government behind Rebel lines, with Bowling Green as the capital. On November 18, delegates to a state "sovereignty convention" severed their connections with the United States and requested admission to the Confederacy. On December 10, the Confederate government admitted Kentucky.

Meanwhile, federal troops secured a defensive line in the northern portion of the state. Union troops held Paducah and Smithland along the Ohio River in the west. On November 18, they also began constructing Fort Duffield at West Point, a strategic vantage point on the river southwest of Louisville. The present-day site contains one of the largest and best-preserved earthwork forts in Kentucky.

Through the rest of 1861, several small engagements occurred as the underprepared armies began to feel each other out. All over the Green River country, scouting parties from both sides fought skirmishes with each other. One of the most significant of these smaller battles occurred on October 21, when Confederate General Felix Zollicoffer attempted to move into the Bluegrass. Blocked by entrenched Union troops in the Rockcastle Hills, Zollicoffer ordered his men to take Wildcat Mountain. They failed. As Union reinforcements arrived, Zollicoffer withdrew.

The next year, 1862, was the critical year of the war for Kentucky. In three pivotal battles in January and February, the Federals broke the Confederate line and drove them out of Kentucky. The first occurred at Middle Creek in eastern Kentucky on January 10, as Union forces attempted to dislodge Confederate troops. The armies fought to a draw and inflicted only light casualties, but by month's end Confederate General Humphrey Marshall had withdrawn his troops into Virginia and the Union controlled the Big Sandy River valley.

The Confederate line suffered a more serious blow just nine days later. Convinced that the Union would launch an attack somewhere west of Cumberland Gap, Zollicoffer moved his troops to Mill Springs, a small town on the Cumberland River west of London. He crossed his troops over the flooded Cumberland, leaving them with a swollen river at their backs as they faced an advancing Union army. The Confederates attacked on a rainy January 19, hoping to catch the federal army before it could gather all its troops together.

The rain turned the roads to impassable muck and the Confederate assault literally bogged down. The downpour soaked the Rebels' old-time flintlock rifles so they could not

Famous Sons and Daughters:
Mary Todd Lincoln

First Lady (December 13, 1818–July 16, 1882)

The descendant of two prominent Kentucky families, Mary Todd grew up and attended school in Lexington, Kentucky. In 1839, she went to live with her sister in Springfield, Illinois, where she met and married Abraham Lincoln. Although in her domestic duties and life she resembled other American middle-class women, her keen political interests and her ambitions for her husband set her apart. She realized her dream when Lincoln won the presidency in 1860.

She managed the whirl of domestic life and social obligations at the White House, but the Civil War soon made her seem peripheral to her husband's existence. When her son Willie died in 1862, Mary became withdrawn and distraught, seeking comfort through séances that she believed allowed her to communicate with Willie.

After Lincoln's assassination, Mary had to struggle to obtain a pension. She took another severe emotional blow when her son Tad died in 1871, and eventually her son Robert committed her to an insane asylum against her wishes. She successfully fought for her release, which she obtained after just three months. Fearing Robert would try again, she moved to France, where she lived from 1878 to 1882. Deteriorating health forced her back to her sister's home in Springfield, where she died.

fire. The near-sighted Zollicoffer blundered into the Union lines and was shot dead. As the Union troops mounted a bayonet charge, the Confederate line broke and retreated, somehow managing to re-cross the Cumberland that night. The Rebels counted 522 casualties, the Federals 262 in the state's first sizable battle. "The Secessionists will not believe a word of the late battle," noted one pro-Union Lexington diarist, "but put it off by saying that Zollicoffer has whipped [Union General George] Thomas."

With the eastern end of his line crumbling, General Johnston got more bad news in February. Union gunboats under Ulysses S. Grant had come down the Cumberland and Tennessee Rivers to attack Forts Henry and Donelson in Tennessee, critical western anchors of the Confederate line. Fort Henry surrendered on February 6, and Johnston dispatched three of his top generals to Fort Donelson to save it. Rather than attack Grant's undermanned force before it reached the fort, however, the Confederate commander held off, allowing Grant to be reinforced.

"Buena Vista," the summer home of Mary Todd Lincoln's family

February 15 dawned cold and clear as the Union forces attacked. Confederate troops tried to hack an escape route to Nashville through the Union lines, but were called back to their positions. As the battle tilted in Grant's favor, the Confederate generals began to flee. The commander hopped the last steamboat upriver. The second-in-command escaped in a rowboat, leaving the third general the humiliating task of surrendering the fort's 16,000-man garrison to Grant's forces. Famously, he sent a note asking Grant what terms of surrender the Union general would accept. "No terms except unconditional and immediate surrender can be accepted," Grant replied. "I propose to move immediately upon your works."

Johnston realized he could not hold Kentucky. He ordered the evacuation of Bowling Green and Columbus in February and retreated to Nashville, then to Corinth, Mississippi. On April 6, 1862, Johnston was killed at the Battle of Shiloh. Confederate Kentucky's provisional government fled with him, and its leader took a fatal bullet at Shiloh.

The Confederates counterattacked in the summer of 1862. Kentuckian John Hunt Morgan—"the Thunderbolt of the Confederacy"—led the first foray. With 876 cavalrymen, 370 of whom were Kentuckians, Morgan left Knoxville, Tennessee on the symbolic date of July 4 and swept into Kentucky. Five days later, Morgan captured four companies of federal cavalry at Tompkinsville.

With Morgan in the state, Union leaders in Kentucky were in a tizzy. Misled by telegraph dispatches sent by a Morgan sympathizer, their troops blundered about trying to stop the raid. "John Morgan with a large body of cavalry said to be at Glasgow & marching on Lex[ington] expected tonight," Frances Peter, the nineteen-year-old daughter of a Lexington doctor, wrote in her diary in July 1862. "The whole town is in a stir in consequence." On July 16, she wrote that he was only three or four miles away. Rumors swirled, but the anticipated attack on Lexington never came.

Morgan's raid meant that thousands of federal troops needed on the front lines in Tennessee stayed behind in Kentucky, guarding important installations and transportation points. Three hundred and fifty federal troops finally squared off against Morgan in Cynthiana, a town on the Licking River about 25 miles north of Lexington, on July 17. Although the federals repulsed three assaults, a final cavalry charge broke their lines and Morgan's men descended on the town. "The rebels have taken Cynthiana," Frances Peter wrote.

By August 1, Morgan had withdrawn back to Tennessee. During the three-week raid, he had taken 17 towns, captured and paroled 1,200 prisoners, destroyed or appropriated critical war materiel, and stung Union morale, while losing only 90 of his own men. Back in Tennessee, he boasted of his successes and predicted that 25,000 Kentuckians would flock to the Confederate side if the southern army mounted a full-scale invasion of the state.

The Confederate invasion so urgently pressed by Morgan came on August 13, when Major General Edmund Kirby Smith moved through the Cumberland mountains into Kentucky. The original Confederate plan called for Smith's army to join that led by General Braxton Bragg. The combined army would draw the Union forces out of Tennessee and defeat them before reoccupying Kentucky. Smith wanted none of it, especially if it meant ceding command of his army to Bragg. So, pleading a lack of resources in southeastern Kentucky, he marched independently on the Bluegrass.

Smith hoped to attack the Federal army at Richmond before it could be reinforced. Union troops rushed to meet him south of Richmond, where several hours of hard fighting resulted in a collapse of the Union lines. Trying desperately to rally his troops and re-form the line, Union general William "Bull" Nelson marched his big body back and forth in front of his men, telling them that "If they can't hit me, they can't hit nobody." In one of those pitch-perfect moments that occurred with regularity during the Civil War, he was immediately struck twice by Confederate fire. Nelson survived, but his fate foreshadowed that of his troops. The Confederates overran the Union lines, killing, wounding, or capturing over 5,300 Union soldiers, while losing less than 700 of their own.

After Richmond, nothing stood between Smith and the heart of the Bluegrass. He took Lexington on September 2. Frances Peter was unimpressed by both Morgan's cavalrymen and Smith's troops: "A nasty, dirty looking set they were; wore no uniform but were dressed in grey & butternut jeans or anything else they could pick up, but were not quite so dirty and mean looking as Kirby Smith's. They looked like the tag, rag, & bobtail of the earth & as if they hadnt been near water since Fort Sumter fell."

Mean-looking or not, the Confederates took Frankfort on September 3. Kentucky thus enjoys the dubious distinction of

Must-See Sites: Strategic Civil War Strongholds

Columbus-Belmont State Park

Commemorating the early struggle for Kentucky and control of the Mississippi River, Columbus, located at a strategic point for control of the Mississippi, was even mentioned at one time as a potential site for the nation's capital.

In September 1861, while Kentucky was still officially neutral in the war, Confederate General Leonidas Polk camped soldiers and artillery pieces on the high bluffs on both sides of the river. From there he talked of shutting down Union boat traffic at the "Gibraltar of the West." Union forces under General Ulysses S. Grant launched a direct attack on the Confederate position on November 7, 1861, but were beaten back by an artillery barrage and the nearly impregnable fortifications. Instead of a frontal assault, therefore, Grant occupied various upriver towns, occupying the land all around Columbus and outflanking Polk. In February 1862, the Confederate forces withdrew, and federal troops moved into the area, which they used as a supply base for the duration of the war.

The park displays a 60-foot length of the huge chain that once stretched for a mile across the river, placed there by the Confederates to impede Union ship traffic. The Confederate entrenchments along the bluffs have been turned into 2.5 miles of walking trails. And an old farmhouse used as a Civil War hospital is now a small museum. Four galleries house a small collection of Civil War-era artifacts and interpret the events of 1861.

The park is located on State Route 58 in Columbus; for more information, call (270) 677-2327, or visit parks.ky.gov/stateparks/cb.

Fort Duffield

The oldest Union military installation in Kentucky, Fort Duffield contains some of the best-preserved earthworks fortifications in the state. The fort was built on Pearman Hill, a high vantage point overlooking the Salt River, the Ohio River, and West Point, the town where the two rivers merged. The fort was ordered built as Union troops and Confederate troops jockeyed for position during 1861, as Kentucky's neutrality crumbled. General William Sherman dispatched troops to West Point to establish a supply depot; Sherman reasoned that the Ohio River would allow him to provision the depot, while the Salt River would allow him to carry the supplies to his garrisons deeper within the state. He was particularly concerned about supplying the garrison at Elizabethtown, which was charged with protecting the rail line that ran through the town.

To protect the supply depot from attack, Sherman ordered the construction of Fort Duffield, named for the commander of the

Michigan troops stationed in the area. Construction of the earthworks, which are 20–30 feet high and snake 640 feet along the hilltop, began in November of 1861. By December, the fort's soldiers had built cabins just outside the walls and they finished the fort by the beginning of 1862. Ten pieces of artillery were brought into the fort, which eventually housed some 950 soldiers. The fort's active-duty life did not go on for long, however. Fort Duffield was abandoned in early 1862 as Union troops began to push the Confederate forces out of the state.

Fort Duffield is located just off Dixie Highway (US 31W) in West Point, Kentucky. For more information, call (502) 922-4260. Two websites have information on the fort: members.aol.com/FtDuffield/fort.html and www.state.ky.us/agencies/khc/ftduff.htm.

The Camp Nelson Heritage Park

This park honors the many important roles that Camp Nelson, a Union encampment, played during the war. Camp Nelson was an important supply depot for troops deployed in southeastern Kentucky and in Tennessee. It was a staging area for various Federal campaigns into Virginia and Tennessee and a defensive bastion against Confederate cavalry raids into central Kentucky. It was also a recruiting, mustering, and training center for Union troops, especially for the regiments of US Colored Troops raised in Kentucky after 1864, and a refugee camp for the families of those African-American soldiers who fled slavery to accompany their men.

The original camp covered 4,000 acres and contained some 300 buildings and fortifications. It was constructed in June 1863, largely by African-American laborers. Something of an engineering marvel, the camp used a pump house on the Kentucky River, a 500,000 gallon reservoir, and thousands of feet of piping to distribute water throughout the camp and allow indoor plumbing in the hospital and soldiers' home. The camp was closed in June 1866, and all the buildings except the officers' quarters were dismantled and sold. The officers' quarters, nicknamed the White House but officially the 1855 Oliver Perry House, has since been restored and is open for guided tours.

The Heritage Park contains over two miles of interpretive trails, and a restored buggy shed provides an overview of the Camp's history. Also part of the camp's legacy is the Camp Nelson National Cemetery. Begun in 1863 as the cemetery for the camp, it was named a national cemetery in 1868 and the remains of Union war dead buried at Perryville, Richmond, and other Kentucky Civil War sites were dug up and reburied here.

Camp Nelson Heritage Park is located off US 27 about five miles south of Nicholasville. More information is available at (859) 881-5716 or at www.campnelson.org.

being the only Union state to have its capital captured during the Civil War. The Union government fled to Louisville and the Ohio River towns east of Louisville panicked at the prospect of a Confederate takeover.

Smith's superior officer, Braxton Bragg, left Tennessee for Kentucky on August 28 with 22,000 men. Once inside the state, Bragg learned that the invasion had worked the desired effect—Union troops were pulling out of Tennessee. Union General Don Carlos Buell marched from Nashville to Bowling Green, then pushed quickly on to Louisville for reinforcements and supplies. He arrived on September 25.

Bragg, meanwhile, dawdled at the town of Munford-ville, where a vital railroad bridge stood under guard by a detachment of Union troops. On September 14, a brigade of Bragg's army had fought and lost an engagement trying to take the bridge, and now Bragg decided to deploy his whole force against it. After moving his army in, he called for the Union commander's surrender. The commander was at a loss. In desperation, he turned to one of Bragg's own officers for advice. This officer gave him a quick tour of the Confederate lines, revealing just how hopelessly out-numbered the Union detachment was. The Union troops surrendered the next morning.

Having lost the opportunity to engage Buell before he reached Louisville, Bragg marched to Bardstown, some 50 miles south of the city. On October 2, he met with Smith at Lexington, and on October 4 they installed a new Confederate government in Frankfort. The symbolic move had two concrete purposes: to inspire Kentuckians to volunteer for Confederate military service and, if that failed, to allow enforcement of the Confederates' conscription law in Kentucky. Contrary to John Hunt Morgan's predictions and much to Bragg and Smith's disappointment, Kentuckians had not flocked to the Confederates.

Edward Guerrant, marching with the Confederates, wrote in his journal that CSA General William Preston "defined the position of K'y as one of 'General Sympathy & Feeble Resistance!' Tom Marshall said 'did ye never call the spirits from the vasty deep, & they didn't come!' So of K'ys volunteers! God help our native State." Bragg labeled them cowards, but Kentucky's Confederate sympathizers were simply prudent. They wanted to see a few victories before

Literary Extracts: Henry Bibb

Bibb was born a slave in Shelby County, Kentucky, in 1815. Actively resistant to slavery since a young age, Bibb successfully ran away but was recaptured when he returned to try and free his family. Sold south to Louisiana, Bibb again escaped from slavery, eventually making it to Canada. On his journey, he took a steamboat up the Ohio River. The following excerpt from his 1849 autobiography, *The Life and Adventures of Henry Bibb, An American Slave*, tells of his feelings upon seeing Kentucky again:

> When the boat struck the mouth of the river Ohio, and I had once more the pleasure of looking on that lovely stream, my heart leaped up for joy at the glorious prospect that I should again be free. Every revolution of the mighty steam-engine seemed to bring me nearer and nearer the "promised land." Only a few days had elapsed, before I was permitted by the smiles of a good providence, once more to gaze on the green hill-tops and valleys of old Kentucky, the State of my nativity. And notwithstanding I was deeply interested while standing on the deck of the steamer looking at the beauties of nature on either side of the river, as she pressed her way up the stream, my very soul was pained to look upon the slaves in the fields of Kentucky, still toiling under their task-masters without pay. It was on this soil that I first breathed the free air of Heaven, and felt the bitter pangs of slavery—it was here that I first learned to abhor it. It was here I received the first impulse of human rights—it was here that I first entered my protest against the bloody institution of slavery, by running away from it, and declared that I would no longer work for any man as I had done, without wages.

committing their sons to the Confederate cause.

During the installation ceremony for the Confederate state government, the new governor promised the people that the new government was there to stay. Instead, it barely lasted the afternoon. As Union artillery began shelling Frankfort, the Confederates burned the bridges over the Kentucky River and abandoned the capital.

Must-See Sites: Civil War Battlefields

The Mill Springs Battlefield

Mill Springs commemorates the site of a key 1862 Union victory that helped break the Confederate line in Kentucky. Currently, interpretation consists of a 13-stop driving tour (more stops are planned) over a 105-acre section of the battlefield marked off by split-rail fencing. In nearby Zollifcoffer Park stands an obelisk honoring southern valor (part of Kentucky's postwar alignment with the Lost Cause) and a mass grave marker for the Confederate dead. Where individual Confederate soldiers are known to have fallen, the Mill Springs Battlefield Association has erected individual markers.

Just up the road in Nancy, Kentucky, is the site of the Mill Springs National Cemetery, the burial ground for Union troops killed in the battle, and still in use as a veterans' cemetery. Union commander George Thomas laid out the cemetery on a portion of the battlefield shortly after the smoke cleared. Ground has been broken for a 9,000-square-foot battlefield museum, housed on 17 acres near the National Cemetery, expected to be completed in the spring of 2006.

The Mill Springs Battlefield is located on State Route 235 in Somerset. The Mill Springs National Cemetery is located on State Route 80 just up the road in Nancy, Kentucky. The museum will sit just east of the National Cemetery on State Route 80. Information on Mill Springs Battlefield is available at (606) 679-1859, or at www.millsprings.net.

The Battle of Richmond

With the help of the city, local preservationists have mapped a driving tour of the battle, covering eight stops along the battlefield corridor, and there are several other historic sites relating to the battle nearby. Stops on the driving tour include Big Hill, where the initial clash between Federal and Confederate cavalry occurred, and the old Richmond Cemetery, where Union General William Nelson encountered his fleeing and demoralized troops and tried to rally them to resist.

The tour also includes two field-hospital sites; at the Mt. Zion Christian Church, where the Union wounded were treated, it was reported that the surgeons amputated so many limbs that arms and legs were stacked to the level of the window sills.

There is also a Confederate cemetery on the tour. Several graves held unknown soldiers until a researcher discovered the names of the dead in 1972. New markers with these names followed.

Civil War reenactors converge on the site in August to replay the clash. The Battle of Richmond is popular among reenacting enthusiasts because it is played out on a portion of the actual battlefield relatively unchanged since 1862.

A driving-tour map is available at the Richmond Visitors Center at 345 Lancaster Avenue. In addition, the map is available online at www.richmond-ky.com/richmond_battle/default.htm. Additional information can also be obtained by calling (859) 626-8474 or (800) 866-3705.

The Perryville Battlefield State Historic Site

Encompassing 300 acres, the Perryville Battlefield is the site of the largest Civil War clash in Kentucky. More than 6,000 soldiers on both sides were killed or wounded during the battle. The retreat by the Confederate forces ended the South's visions of conquering Kentucky. The battlefield is one of the most unaltered Civil War sites in the nation.

A self-guided walking tour of the battlefield offers interpretation of the events of that October day. Monuments from several states, both North and South, dot the battlefield, honoring the fallen from each state. A museum at the park tells the story of the battle in greater detail, with exhibits of uniforms, weaponry, and medical equipment from the time period. Reenactors also re-create the battle every year on the weekend closest to October 8. The park also offers living history demonstrations throughout the year, as costumed interpreters describe the lives of the soldiers and the surrounding community during the war.

Like many of the sites listed here, Perryville is part of the Civil War Heritage Trail in Central Kentucky. The Heritage Trail offers a week during the summer of coordinated special events at many of the Civil War sites in Kentucky. More information on the Heritage Trail is available at www.kycivilwar.org.

Perryville Battlefield is located on State Highway 1920 off US 150 near the town of Perryville. Park information can be obtained at (859) 332-8631 or at parks.ky.gov/statehistoricsites/pb.

The Union troops wasted little time in Louisville. Having resupplied, Buell sent three columns—about 58,000 men—toward Bragg's position at Bardstown and one column—about 22,000 men—toward Frankfort. As the Union armies marched, Bragg and Smith finally combined their armies at Harrodsburg. On October 7, most of Buell's troops approached Perryville, aiming to secure some desperately needed water from the drought-stricken creeks in the area. The pivotal battle of the Civil War in Kentucky was about to begin.

Learning that the main body of Buell's army was near Perryville but not knowing the number of troops facing him, Bragg ordered an attack on October 8. Bragg waited in Harrodsburg for news of the attack's progress. Hearing nothing, he went to Perryville himself and learned that no attack was under way. Outraged, Bragg again ordered his troops to attack. Finally, at about 2 PM, the Confederates struck against the First Corps of Buell's army. They drove it back over several hours of fighting, virtually destroying some units. Buell, learning of the impending collapse, sent help. As night fell, the exhausted Confederate soldiers, facing fresh troops, stopped their advance. Buell's Third Corps fared better. Attacked by a Confederate brigade on Peters Hill, the Union troops stopped the assault cold.

Over the course of the evening, Bragg learned the true size of the force facing his army. Despite the thrashing administered to Buell's First Corps, Bragg decided the most prudent course was withdrawal to Harrodsburg. So even though the Union lost more men (845 killed and 2,851 wounded versus Bragg's losses of 510 dead and 2,635 wounded), Buell was left holding the field after the battle. Guerrant was devastated. "Long remembered day! Day of blasted hope and ruined fortunes! Day of evil. Dark Day!" he lamented to his journal. "Our army unaided & unassisted by the people of the state they came to deliver, weakened by weary marches, sickness & battle, to 33,000, stands now like a lion at bay, surrounded by 100,000 hungry minions of a ruthless despot."

Intent on saving his army, Bragg did not dally at Harrodsburg, either. "The conflict is unequal—the victory unworthy of the sacrifice of a battle," Guerrant wrote. "The purpose is evacuation by Cumberland Gap!" Buell gave only lukewarm pursuit, annoying his commander-in-chief, who took away his army and sent Buell into premature retirement.

Perryville put permanent end to the dream of a Confederate Kentucky. There would be no further invasions, no more short-lived Confederate governments. The state, recognizing the significance of Perryville, has turned the battlefield into a state historic site covering 300 acres and containing a museum devoted to the battle.

Instead of a Confederate outpost, Kentucky instead became a staging area for the Northern push into the heart of the Confederacy. It thus presented a ripe target for none other than John Hunt Morgan, who made a second raid into the state to disrupt Union supply lines as the Yankees prepared to go after Bragg in Tennessee.

Morgan came in force this time, with 3,100 men behind him. He crossed the Cumberland River on December 22 and stayed in the state twelve days. The "Christmas Raid" destroyed twenty miles of railroad track, three supply depots, and some $2 million of Union supplies. Morgan briefly took Elizabethtown, then rode and fought over 400 miles of central Kentucky. He captured and paroled 1,887 prisoners, while suffering only 26 of his own killed and wounded.

It was a taste of things to come. Confederate raiders continued to invade the state for the rest of the war, but their goal was annoyance, harassment, and troop diversion—not reconquest. Over time ostensible military actions gave way to outright thuggery. Meanwhile, the Union built up its supply stations and recruitment activities. By the end of 1862, Kentucky was clearly under Union occupation.

Union Occupation

The war changed irrevocably on January 1, 1863, when Lincoln issued the Emancipation Proclamation. The Proclamation tied together the preservation of the Union with the abolition of slavery. "The deed is done," complained one Louisville editorialist. "The President is as bad as his promise." Although it raised a storm of protest among Kentuckians, the Proclamation did not free a single slave in Kentucky, for it only declared free slaves in those states currently in rebellion against the United States. Nonetheless, it doomed the peculiar institution in Kentucky. Everyone realized that it would be impossible to maintain slavery in the border states once it was destroyed in the rebellious states.

Slaves themselves helped in the destruction of slavery. They began slipping away to the Union army as soon as the first troops appeared in the state in 1861, where they were put to work as manual laborers. In December 1862, Lincoln decided to enroll black volunteers into the Union army, although he excluded Kentucky from the order for fear of the white reaction. Thousands of black Kentuckians responded anyway, crossing into other states to enlist.

In March 1864, Lincoln finally approved the recruitment of black soldiers inside Kentucky, offering immediate freedom to slaves who enlisted. Elijah Marrs led 27 other slaves on a nighttime march along Shelbyville Road to the Louisville recruiting station in September 1864. "Our arms consisted of twenty-six war clubs and one rusty pistol," Marrs recalled. The small contingent skirted Middletown, "through which the colored people seldom passed with safety," and were inside Union lines shortly after dawn. "By eight o'clock we were at the recruiting office in the city of Louisville…. By twelve o'clock the owner of every man of us was in the city hunting his slaves, but we had all enlisted." By the end of the war, the army enlisted 23,703 black Kentuckians, about 13 percent of the total number of African-American soldiers in the Union armies.

Camp Nelson, founded in 1863, eventually became the state's preeminent African-American recruiting station. Slaves did much of the construction work at Camp Nelson and some of those who had built the place became its first recruits. In all, eight regiments of United States Colored Troops traced their beginnings to Camp Nelson. Three others trained there. Elijah Marrs was part of the 12th US Colored Heavy Artillery. About life at Camp Nelson, he wrote, "I can stand this…. This is better than slavery, though I do march in line at the tap of a drum. I felt freedom in my bones, and when I saw the American eagle with outspread wings, upon the American flag, with the motto E Pluribus Unum, the thought came to me, 'Give me liberty or give me death.'"

Camp Nelson rapidly became not just a military post but a refugee camp. Black recruits often brought their

Famous Sons and Daughters: Jefferson Davis

Soldier and president of the Confederacy
(June 3, 1808–December 6, 1889)

Born at Fairview, Kentucky, the future president of the Confederate States of America lived in Kentucky only two years before his father moved the family to Louisiana and then Mississippi. Davis returned to Kentucky for schooling in his later years, however. He attended St. Thomas of Aquin Catholic School in Springfield, Kentucky, from 1816 until 1818, and studied at Transylvania University in Lexington in 1823–24. Davis went from Transylvania to West Point, from which he graduated a second lieutenant in 1828.

Davis resigned his commission in 1835 and married Sarah Knox Taylor, the daughter of Zachary Taylor, in Louisville that same year. She died of malaria three months later, and Davis lived alone at his plantation in Mississippi for eight years before remarrying.

Davis served in the House of Representatives, fought in the Mexican War, served in the US Senate, and worked as President Franklin Pierce's secretary of war. He was elected to the Senate a second time in 1857, but resigned in 1861 when Mississippi seceded from the Union. He was named president of the Confederacy on February 9, 1861.

When Union forces overran the Confederate capital, Davis tried to flee to Mexico. Apprehended in Georgia, he was imprisoned for two years at Fortress Monroe, Virginia. He eventually settled in Memphis, serving as president of an insurance company, then bought a plantation in Mississippi in 1879. He wrote a two-volume history of the Confederacy. He died in New Orleans on December 6, 1889.

families with them, unwilling to leave them enslaved while they went off to fight. Unfortunately, the army was ill-prepared to handle the influx. In November 1864, the camp commander expelled the refugees by armed force, resulting in the deaths of 102 people, mainly women and children, from exposure and sickness. Higher-ups eventually

Must-See Sites:
The Civil War Museum

The museum focuses on the western theater of the war, with photographs and artifacts from Kentucky, Tennessee, and other states. The story of the western campaigns is told in a straightforward manner in chronological and geographical segments, with an extensive collection of material from both sides in the conflict. The museum also has rooms focusing on different branches of the military: the infantry, the cavalry, and the artillery. The artillery room contains a variety of period pieces, including a howitzer and a portable cannon that could be dismantled and carried on horseback.

The 8,500-square-foot building used to be town's water works and ice house. After a state-financed $450,000 renovation, it was transformed into the fourth-largest Civil War museum in the country. The Civil War Museum is part of Museum Row in Bardstown. Adjacent to the Civil War Museum is a museum dedicated to the history of women in the Civil War, the only one of its kind in the United States. It is located in the historic Wright-Talbott House. Museum Row also includes a Pioneer Village and an American Indian museum.

The Civil War Museum is located at 310 E. Broadway in Bardstown. Call (502) 349-0291 or visit www.bardstown.com/~civilwar.

reversed the order and established a refugee camp as part of Camp Nelson, and an outraged Congress ordered the families of black recruits freed in March 1865.

Still, the refugee camp remained overcrowded and unhealthy. The army shared administration of the camp with the American Missionary Association, and minister John G. Fee did his best to alleviate the suffering, teaching and ministering to the soldiers and their families. "Here are thousands of noble men, made in the image of God, just emerging from the restraints of slavery into the liberties and responsibilities of free men, and of soldiers," Fee wrote. "I find them manifesting an almost universal desire to learn and that they do make rapid progress... I feel that it is blessed to labor with such people." Still, the death rate remained appalling, with between a third and a half of the camp's residents dying.

Federal policies on slavery and black recruitment annoyed white Kentuckians, but the army's wartime administration chafed the state's residents more generally. Union military commanders suspected many Kentuckians of disloyalty and kept a tight grip on the state in the name of rooting out treason. In July 1862 Union military commander Jeremiah Boyle forbade anyone hostile to the Union from running for office, and in 1863 General Ambrose Burnside declared martial law in the state to prevent disloyal Kentuckians from going to the polls. "Less than one half the vote of the State has been polled," the *Lexington Observer* complained. "The voters were intimidated in the first place by the military orders which preceded the placing of the State under martial law." The Peace Democrats in Kentucky, which the *Observer* supported, were branded as disloyal. Under the orders of Union commanders, wrote the *Observer*, "a vote for the 'no more men and no more money' ticket would be regarded as evidence of such [Rebel] sympathy."

When Confederate raiders forayed into the state, Boyle made Confederate sympathizers in the affected counties pay for damages to loyal citizens. Such policies contributed to Kentuckians' continued dislike of Lincoln. In the presidential election of 1864, the state went for Lincoln's opponent, former General George B. McClellan, by a large margin.

Despite the clampdown by the Federals, the raids continued. Morgan returned for a third time in the summer of 1863 to draw forces away from Bragg's army in Tennessee. Encountering a federal garrison at Tebbs Bend on the Green River, Morgan mounted a frontal assault. As his men stumbled through the dense undergrowth toward the well-defended stockade, Union forces cut them to ribbons. Morgan lost 71 men, and he called off the attack after just 30 minutes.

Hard fighting followed at Lebanon on July 5, during which Morgan's men eventually overwhelmed some 450 Union soldiers. Morgan then torched the town. Lexington diarist Francis Peter, who spoke to some of the soldiers who had fought against Morgan, wrote that "it was not until the rebels set fire to the houses [the] men occupied that [they] surrendered. The rebels robbed our men of money (of which they happened to have a good deal having just been paid) watches, boots, hats, in short anything they happened to fancy."

Moving through Bardstown and Garrettsville, the cavalry leader disobeyed Bragg's direct orders and decided to cross the Ohio River. "The emergency," Morgan said, "justified disobedience." Morgan captured Corydon, Indiana, on July 9. His men, beguiled by the prosperity of the Northern towns, helped themselves. "The weather was intensely warm,... yet one man rode for three days with seven pairs of skates slung around his neck; another loaded himself with sleigh bells," wrote one of Morgan's lieutenants. "A large chafing dish, a medium-sized Dutch clock, a green glass decanter with goblets to match,... and a birdcage containing three canaries, were some of the articles that I saw borne off and jealously fondled."

The Union cavalrymen chasing him grew frustrated. "Our pursuit was much retarded by the enemy's burning all the bridges in our front," reported their commander. "He had every advantage. His system of horse-stealing was perfect. He would dispatch men from the head of each regiment, on each side of the road, to go five miles into the country, seizing every horse, and then falling in at the rear of the column."

Morgan then moved his men into Ohio. After a feint at Cincinnati, he began to look for a way back across the Ohio River. By this time, however, the Union troops had him pretty well hemmed in. At Buffington, Union pursuers destroyed his force. They killed and wounded 120 men and took 700 prisoners. They pursued Morgan and the remnant of his command as they tried to reach Pennsylvania, finally taking the fabled leader captive on July 26 and throwing him into the Ohio penitentiary.

Morgan had one last hurrah in him. He escaped from prison in November 1863 and in June 1864 raided Kentucky a fourth time. By now, however, his troops lacked adequate shoes, weapons, and horses. They were an undisciplined lot, and Morgan could not control them. When they reached the town of Mount Sterling on June 8, they looted the town and robbed the bank. Union troops finally met and destroyed Morgan's force near Cynthiana on June 12, one day after the Confederate raiders had

Famous Sons and Daughters: Delia Webster

Antislavery activist
(December 17, 1817–1876)

A Vermont-born teacher and abolitionist, Webster came to Kentucky in 1843 to teach art. With two friends, she founded the Lexington Female Academy to educate the daughters of the Bluegrass elite. On September 28, 1844, she traveled with the abolitionist Calvin Fairbank to northern Kentucky. She later stated that Fairbank left her in Millersville, while he proceeded on to Ohio. Upon their return to Lexington two days later, however, both were arrested and charged with helping three slaves to escape. Found guilty, Webster served two years in the state prison before she was pardoned, over the protests of many slaveholding Kentuckians.

Webster returned to the Northeast and taught for several years in New York before returning to Kentucky in 1854. With financial assistance from abolitionist organizations, she bought a 600-acre farm in Trimble County on the Ohio River. Working the farm with free black labor, she established it as a stop on the underground railroad for slaves escaping to the North. When some local slaves disappeared in the spring of 1854, Webster fled to Indiana to escape arrest. In her absence, the farm was looted.

In 1857, slaveholding Kentuckians blocked her from getting an extension on her loan. To derail foreclosure, a group of Bostonians formed the Webster Kentucky Farm Association to help save the property. Still unpopular with her neighbors after the Civil War, Webster was ordered to leave Kentucky in 1866. In November of that year, $8,000 worth of her property went up in flames after arsonists torched some of her belongings. Over time, the barns, dwelling houses, and the main residence on the farm burned in arson attacks. Unable to pay her debts, Webster finally lost the farm in October 1869. She left Kentucky to teach school in Madison, Indiana, and later died in Jeffersonville.

The memorial at Lincoln's birthplace, Hodgenville

captured some 500-plus Union soldiers. Morgan and a few others escaped back to Virginia, then retreated to Tennessee. On September 4, in Greenville, federal troops gunned him down near his headquarters.

Other Confederate cavalry officers besides Morgan led raids into Kentucky. General Nathan Bedford Forrest led some 2,800 men into Paducah in March 1864 to secure horses and supplies. Forrest's men forced the Union occupiers back into their fort and then, amid shelling by federal gunboats, secured the supplies they needed. Forrest destroyed headquarters buildings, warehouses, and steamboats before he retreated southward. During the retreat, some of Forrest's Kentucky recruits read Unionist newspaper accounts of the battle at Paducah, which boasted that the raiders had missed the finest horses in the town. On April 14, these men returned, beat back the Federal garrison, and found the horses exactly where the newspaper had reported them.

Morgan, Forrest, and other raiders made up regular units in the Confederate army. They had a legitimate wartime role to play behind Union lines, disrupting supplies, diverting troops, and dampening Unionist morale. Other raiders had more tenuous connections to the southern armies—"bushwhackers" operated as independent groups of Confederate guerrillas. There were also similar groups of Unionists, though generally fewer in number. Then there were just plain outlaws, who used the climate of violence to wage their own wars for their own profit. Often the lines between "bushwhackers" and bad men blurred.

William Quantrill was one notorious bushwhacker. He made his name with the infamous 1863 Lawrence Massacre in Kansas, during which his guerrillas killed at least 150 civilians and generally terrorized anti-Confederates during the war. He worked mostly in Missouri, but in January 1865 he led several dozen men into Kentucky. They worked their way eastward, sacking towns, including Hartford, Hustonville, and Danville, while eluding Federal troops. Finally, a leader of Unionist guerrillas caught Quantrill in May near the town of Bloomfield. "The news of his capture will cause great joy throughout the Union," a Louisville newspaper opined. "The inhuman outrages that he committed... are still fresh in the memory of our people." Seriously wounded in the fight, Quantrill died in prison before he could be hanged. (Two of Quantrill's protégés—Frank and Jesse James—revisited the state in later years, allegedly robbing the Russellville bank in 1868, the Columbia bank in 1872, and a pair of stagecoaches in 1880.)

"Sue Mundy," another bushwhacker, had served under John Hunt Morgan as Captain M. Jerome Clarke. After Morgan's death, Clarke adopted his new gender-bending moniker and returned to Kentucky. Mundy waged private war against Union soldiers and sympathizers until finally captured by Federal troops on March 12, 1865. He asked to be treated as a prisoner of war. The Union commander refused and after a brief trial hanged him on March 15.

Lesser lights among the bushwhacking fraternity brought violence to nearly every Kentucky town. One of John Hunt Morgan's men described a Kentucky mountaineer that the Confederate raiders came across during their 1862 foray into the state: "Ill-treatment of his wife and daughter by some soldiers and Home-guards enlisted in his own neighborhood made him relentless in his hatred of all Union men.... The mountains of Kentucky and Tennessee were filled with such men, who murdered every prisoner they took."

During the last year or so of the war, the terror hit floodtide, and Union commanders adopted steadily harsher measures to stop bushwhacking. General Stephen Burbridge, named military commander of Kentucky in February 1864, tried to deter bushwhackers by punishing their relatives. Later, he ordered four Confederate prisoners shot for every Union man killed, leading to the eventual execution of some legitimate prisoners of war. In October he issued a take-no-prisoners order regarding southern guerrillas. Such iron-fisted policies had little effect except to increase alienation among the locals.

PEACE AND FREEDOM

On April 9, 1865, Robert E. Lee surrendered to Ulysses Grant at Appomattox Courthouse. Over the next two months, the various other Confederate commanders laid down their arms as well and the Civil War formally came to an end.

The bushwhackers' raids wound down as the larger Confederate war effort crumbled, but sporadic attacks by disgruntled guerrillas—whether motivated by politics or profit—continued even after the formal end of hostilities. The legacy of the violence lived on as well. The terror and brutality of the irregular war in Kentucky created bitterness and hatred that took years to erase. It showed up in the postwar years of political confusion and social dysfunction.

Peace brought an accounting of the toll of the war. Between 25,000 and 40,000 Kentuckians volunteered for the Confederacy; between 90,000 and 100,000 fought for the Union either as volunteers or conscripts. Of the 140,000 or so who left for war, 30,000 never returned. Of those who did return, many had shattered bodies and traumatized minds.

The wounds ran even deeper than the physical losses, though. As a border state, Kentucky lived the old Civil War cliché about a war between brothers to a greater extent than other places. George Crittenden served as a major general in the Confederate army; his brother Thomas served as a major general for the Union. Two of Robert Breckinridge's sons joined the Union army, two joined the Confederates. Newspaper editor George Prentice was a Unionist, his sons Confederates. The divisions among these prominent antebellum families echoed in families throughout Kentucky as well as in churches, neighborhoods, and communities. Forgiveness—"malice toward none and charity for all," as Lincoln called for in his Second Inaugural Address—came hard.

What had been purchased at such tremendous cost? First, the Union had been preserved and firm limits established on states' rights. Second, and more important, slavery had been abolished. Formal and final emancipation came on December 18, 1865, with the adoption of the Thirteenth Amendment to the Constitution. By that time, almost three-quarters of Kentucky's slaves had already been freed by one mechanism or another. But the Thirteenth Amendment laid the peculiar institution to rest permanently.

6

"Readjustment" and Violence

Most people call the immediate post-Civil-War period in the United States "Reconstruction." The word carries both a physical meaning, in the form of an actual "re-construction" of the war-destroyed South, and a legal meaning, in the form of the Reconstruction Acts passed by Congress during the late 1860s to reintegrate the South into the nation. In Kentucky, people talk about "readjustment." As a member of the winning side, it was not subject to the Reconstruction Acts and the resulting military occupation like the rest of the South. And while its infrastructure had been damaged by the war, the devastation did not compare to that inflicted on the former Confederacy.

But Kentucky did have to readjust to the postwar world. Compared to the antebellum period of rising prosperity and prominence, it had to adjust to a postwar period of lower expectations and slower progress. It had to adjust to a new national and industrial economy that, in the scope of its factories and the reach of its power, isolated, overtook, or destroyed local businesses. And, perhaps most importantly, it had to adjust to the new class of African-American citizens and the new racial realities of a world without slavery. Unfortunately, the state handled few of these imposing challenges with aplomb; conflict, corruption, and violence marked the long period of readjustment.

Embracing the Lost Cause

A Kentucky truism says that the state joined the Confederacy after Appomattox. Despite its sympathies for the South, Kentucky came to espouse the "Lost Cause"— shorthand for the ostensibly noble aim of preserving states' rights and the southern way of life—only after it was lost.

Must-See Sites: Birthplaces of the Civil War Presidents

The Jefferson Davis Monument State Historic Site

This state-sponsored site marks the birthplace of the president of the Confederate States of America. Born on June 3, 1808, Davis only lived in the state two years before his family relocated to Louisiana and then Mississippi. The dominant landmark of the park is a 351-foot concrete obelisk that ranks as the fourth-highest monument in the United States, and speaks to Kentucky's embrace of the Lost Cause in the years after the Civil War.

The initial plans for the monument were laid by the Orphan's Brigade of the Confederate Army, a Kentucky Confederate veterans' organization, in 1907. An offshoot of that organization, the Jefferson Davis Home Association, raised the initial money, selected the site, and chose the design. The obelisk was meant to echo the Washington Monument and claim for Davis a similar stature. Construction began in 1917, but owing to various delays and financing difficulties was not completed until the spring of 1924.

The Jefferson Davis Monument State Historic Site is located on US 68 in Fairview. Call (270) 886-1765 or visit parks.ky.com/statehistoricsites/jd.

The Abraham Lincoln Birthplace National Historic Site

This 116-acre site in Larue County is part of the original 348-acre farm called Sinking Spring, where Abraham Lincoln was born on February 12, 1809. His parents had moved to the area in 1808 and constructed a one-room log cabin, where Lincoln was born. The family only lived here two years before moving about 10 miles northeast to a 230-acre farm in Knob Creek. Kentucky also maintains a state park at Lincoln's Knob Creek home.

The national historic site—established by Congress in 1916—contains a marble and granite memorial reached by a set of 56 steps, one step for each year of Lincoln's life. Inside the memorial is a reconstructed nineteenth-century log cabin, symbolic of the one in which Lincoln was born. The logs used supposedly came from the original Lincoln cabin, which was dismantled prior to 1865 so that the logs could be used on somebody else's house.

The Lincoln birthplace is located on US 31E and State Route 61 about three miles south of Hodgenville. Call (270) 358-3137 or visit www.nps.gov/abli.

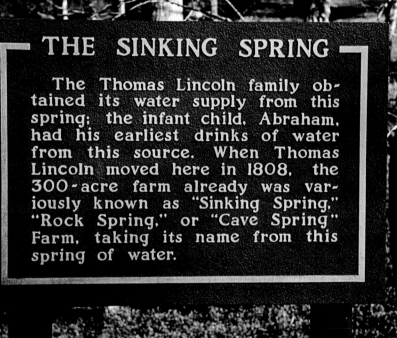

THE SINKING SPRING

The Thomas Lincoln family obtained its water supply from this spring; the infant child, Abraham, had his earliest drinks of water from this source. When Thomas Lincoln moved here in 1808, the 300-acre farm already was variously known as "Sinking Spring," "Rock Spring," or "Cave Spring" Farm, taking its name from this spring of water.

The postwar celebration of the Confederacy shows up in lots of different places—in the numerous memorials in Kentucky towns to their local Confederate war dead, in the prominence of former Confederate officers in postwar business and political life, even in the commemoration of the state's unique status as birthplace of the two opposing wartime presidents, Abraham Lincoln and Jefferson Davis. Lincoln's birthplace near Hodgenville features a relatively modest granite-and-marble memorial containing an early nineteenth-century cabin, which symbolizes Lincoln's humble beginnings but is not the actual cabin of the Lincoln family. The memorial is a national historic site and thus funded by the federal government. The Davis birthplace in Fairview is marked by a soaring 351-foot obelisk that ranks as one of the largest monuments in the United States. It is, appropriately, a state historic site. The dual monuments mark in stone Kentucky's place on the border between North and South, but the different characters of the monuments illustrate where the state's postwar affections lay.

The state found common cause with the former Confederacy in its resistance to African-American civil rights. White Kentuckians had bristled at each of the steps taken toward abolishing slavery during the war. In a fit of pique after the war, the Kentucky House of Representatives refused to ratify the Thirteenth Amendment forbidding slavery. When slavery ended anyway, many of the state's whites could not fathom the idea of allowing the former slaves to move about freely, gather together, and—especially—participate in politics. When blacks held a barn dance in one western Kentucky town, for example, a local minister commented, "This is almost an insult to the moral sense and sentiment of our community."

If forced to accept freedom, Kentucky resolved not to accept equality. Like states across the South, Kentucky enacted laws after the war that sharply restricted African-American rights. They could not vote, serve on juries, or testify in court against whites. When Congress responded by passing the Civil Rights Act of 1866, conferring citizenship upon African Americans, granting them specific legal rights, and allowing federal courts to take jurisdiction of cases when state courts discriminated against blacks, Kentucky dug in its heels. The legislature refused to alter state law to allow African-American the right to testify against whites and the state Supreme Court declared the Civil Rights Act unconstitutional. In January 1867, the state legislature overwhelmingly defeated the Fourteenth Amendment, which put a constitutional stamp on many of the Civil Rights Act's provisions. And when the Fifteenth Amendment, which gave African Americans the right to vote, was proposed in 1869, the legislature took the same course.

In spite of Kentucky's naysaying, the amendments became part of the national Constitution, preventing the state at least momentarily from using the weapon of law against its African-American citizens. White Kentuckians instead directed their wrath directly against black bodies and black aspirations. Some refused to sell land to African Americans or extend credit to them. African-American children were not allowed into the public schools. Some whites threatened violence, and when African Americans made advances anyway, made good on their threats.

Local law enforcement offered African Americans little protection. "The civil laws of the State deprive us of

Literary Extracts: John Fox, Jr.

Born in Bourbon County in 1862, the precocious John Fox, Jr., enrolled in Transylvania College in Lexington at age 14, transferred to Harvard at age 16 and graduated at 19. Despite his erudition, he found his calling among the simple mountain folk of Kentucky. With their culture, speech, and anecdotes as inspiration, he wrote 14 novels and 45 short stories. His novel *The Little Shepherd of Kingdom Come* was the first in American literature to sell one million copies. Fox became a popular speaker, traveling all over the nation to talk about the people of the mountains. The following, from his 1901 collection of essays, *Blue-grass and Rhododendron: Outdoors in Old Kentucky*, describes his overall impression of the Kentucky mountaineer:

> The Kentucky mountaineers are practically valley people. There are the three forks of the Cumberland, the three forks of the Kentucky, and the tributaries of Big Sandy—all with rich river-bottoms. It was natural that these lands should attract a better class of people than the average mountaineer. They did. There were many slaveholders among them—a fact that has never been mentioned, as far as I know, by anybody who has written about the mountaineer. The houses along these rivers are, as a rule, weather-boarded, and one will often find interior decorations, startling in color and puzzling in design, painted all over porch, wall, and ceiling. The people are better fed, better clothed, less lank in figure, more intelligent. They wear less homespun, and their speech, while as archaic as elsewhere, is, I believe, purer. You rarely hear "you uns" and "we uns," and similar untraceable confusions in the Kentucky mountains…. Moreover, the mountaineers who came over from West Virginia and from the southwestern corner of old Virginia were undoubtedly the daring, the hardy, and the strong, for no other kind would have climbed gloomy Black Mountain and the Cumberland Range to fight against beast and savage for their homes.
>
> However, in spite of the general superiority that these facts give him, the Kentucky mountaineer has been more isolated than the mountaineer of any other State. There are regions more remote and more sparsely settled, but nowhere in the southern mountains has so large a body of mountaineers been shut off so completely from the outside world. As a result, he illustrates Mr. Theodore Roosevelt's fine observation that life away from civilization simply emphasizes the natural qualities, good and bad, of the individual. The effect of this truth seem perceptible in that any trait common to the southern mountaineer seems to be intensified in the mountaineer of Kentucky. He is more clannish, prouder, more hospitable, fiercer, more loyal as a friend, more bitter as an enemy, and in simple meanness—when he is mean, mind you—he can out-Herod his race with great ease.

our every right," wrote one freedman living in Owensboro. "Every black man is threatened in the State by every rebel." In 1867, one federal officer wrote from Smithland in the far western portion of the state that "there is quite a bad feeling... between a portion of the white citizens and colored on account of the white people having the colored person arrested for the most trifling offences where there is no such a thing as fining a white man let him do what he will to a colored man."

Outrages occurred with frightening regularity. A Freedmen's Bureau report declared that in 1867, 20 former slaves had been killed, 18 shot, 11 raped, and 270 mistreated in some other form. In the four years between 1867 and 1870, a Frankfort newspaper counted 115 hangings, shootings, and whippings. As under slavery, the slightest breach of the unwritten rules of African-American conduct could bring harsh punishment by whites. When a black woman accidentally brushed against the dress of a county judge's wife on a town street, the judge administered a severe caning to the woman.

Former Union soldiers were especially targeted. In 1868, missionary John Fee wrote from Camp Nelson that "lawless men have recently seized several colored men who were former soldiers and abused them most brutally. The occasion of this is some meetings of the colored people in Union League Meetings. The 'rebs' have resolved to break them up and as a means have commenced a series of brutal whippings and beatings." Historian Marion Lucas wrote that "out in the countryside bands of rogues went from farm to farm beating and robbing black veterans."

The Freedmen's Bureau, the federal agency charged with overseeing the transition of the former slaves to freedom, initially did not extend to Kentucky. But after hearing repeated reports of the treatment given to Kentucky's African Americans, the bureau opened offices in the state in 1866. It provided small amounts of food and clothing, vetted labor contracts, and established a hospital for African Americans, but its schools provided its most lasting legacy. By 1869, when the bureau closed down, 250 schools operated across the state, educating 10,360 African-American citizens. The schools offered just rudimentary learning, but it was the only formal education open to blacks at the time.

Most white Kentuckians hated the bureau. They resented the federal intrusion into Kentucky's internal racial affairs. And they struck back by burning schools, beating teachers, and intimidating students. One historian concluded that Kentucky was "in the forefront in its violent opposition to the activities of the Freedmen's Bureau."

Thomas Noble, head of the bureau's education program in the state, detailed in an 1869 letter the hostility that existed toward the education of African-Americans:

> In Hickman, Fulton County, Miss Jennie Meed (from Ohio) has been insulted many times in the streets and had been threatened with death. One of her pupils has been murdered. At Corydon, the teacher was driven from the town. Schoolhouse burned at Rock Springs. At Cadiz Mr. P.S. Reeves (white) was beaten while trying to organize a school. School burned in Germantown. The Noble Schoolhouse in Shepherdsville burned October 1, 1868. Two churches used as schools in Bullitt County were burned. Schoolhouse at Thompkinsville burned. The teacher in Mayfield was driven from the town. Now in other portions of the United States it is not uncommon for houses to be burned, but the motive is usually gain. The remarkable thing about Kentucky arson is the crime is committed from principle, here education is not believed in and schoolhouses are therefore burned... because instruction is given to ignorant freedmen.

The violence came not just from the spontaneous rage of mobs but also from organized and semi-permanent bands of "Regulators," including the Ku Klux Klan. These groups targeted blacks predominantly, but whites who sympathized with black aspirations also came under attack. Night-riding, terroristic threatening, and the expulsion of entire African-American communities reached epidemic proportions in some rural portions of central Kentucky. Lynch law also prevailed—between 1867 and 1871, over 100 African Americans were lynched across Kentucky.

United States Marshall Willis Russell, who monitored conditions in Owen County, wrote up his observations in an 1874 report: "More than 100 men have been killed, wounded, or driven away from that portion of Owen and Henry Counties lying on the Kentucky River by the Kuklux [sic] in the last three years." Of the residents in the

Fermantown schoolhouse for black children, 1892

counties, Russell wrote, "the majority... are all good citizens, and are at heart opposed to the Kuklux, but they are under a reign of terror, and are really afraid to express their opinions, not knowing what moment they will have to pay the penalty."

By the mid-1870s, some of the racial violence had quieted. With the federal amendments in place, Kentucky had to adjust to postwar reality. In 1872 the state legislature finally passed a bill giving African Americans the same rights as whites in the state's courts. While some localities had fought the implications of the Fifteenth Amendment with lengthy residence requirements for voters or gerrymandered voting districts, eventually African Americans in Kentucky were allowed to vote. White Kentuckians came to realize that since blacks made up only about a sixth of the total

population, their political participation constituted little threat to white control.

But African Americans made other gains as well. By 1876 they sat on federal juries. By 1882 they sat on state juries. The state government ordered the creation of African-American public schools. Louisville had an African-American newspaper. African American lawyers had gained entrance to the bar. African-Americans even held minor political offices in some towns. Racially integrated churches, workplaces, and neighborhoods existed in different locales all across the state.

During the last two decades of the nineteenth century, however, racial lines in Kentucky began to harden anew. As it did across the South, racial segregation began to spread. It crept in piecemeal, locality by locality, law by law. In 1882, for example, the state prison segregated religious services for inmates. Other public institutions began to set up separate departments for blacks. Residential segregation in Kentucky's towns increased; the neighborhoods of California and Smoketown in Louisville, for example, developed into all-black communities by 1900.

Readjustment in Kentucky also meant a drastic political realignment. From its prewar position as a bastion of the Whigs and an opponent of secession, Kentucky moved firmly into the Democratic camp. The racial policies of the Republicans and the continued "oppression" of the South by way of the Reconstruction Acts provided easy targets for Democratic politicians. In the 1868 election for governor, the Democratic candidate polled a remarkable 80 percent of the vote. One politician noted that Kentuckians would not vote for Jesus Christ himself if he ran on the Republican ticket.

Must-See Sites: Homes of the Rich and Not-So-Rich

The Conrad-Caldwell House Museum

Offering a view into the lifestyles of Louisville's commercial and industrial elites during the late nineteenth century, the Conrad-Caldwell house, known as Conrad's Castle, was built for Theophilus Conrad, who made a fortune in the tanning business. It was purchased in 1905, after Conrad's death, by the Caldwell family.

Guided tours of the three-floor, 18-room house show the opulence and modern conveniences that mingled in the lives of the turn-of-the-century rich. The woodwork, fixtures, and stained glass convey the sense of formality that marked upper-class relationships. Modern conveniences include the electric wiring and the gas lighting fixtures.

Outside, the house shows off gargoyles, huge arches, and fleur-de-lis. It is an architectural jewel in a neighborhood full of them. Located on St. James Court in the part of town known as Old Louisville, some of the neighboring homes convey the same sense of Victorian wealth.

The Conrad-Caldwell House is located at 1402 St. James Court in Louisville. Call (502) 636-5023 or visit www.conradcaldwell.org.

The Adsmore Living History Museum

This museum puts a unique twist on the common idea of having costumed interpreters guide tours through historic homes. At Adsmore, the interior decor and the interpretations of events vary with the seasons, and they are based on actual events that affected the family that lived in the home. In the early fall, the theme is an anxious 1906 meeting among the town's business elite to discuss the activities of the Night Riders in the Black Patch War, who have burned one of the town's largest tobacco warehouses. Other events include a wake, a Valentine's Day tea, a child's birthday party, the celebration of an engagement, a return home from a journey, and Christmas. All the events actually took place between the years 1902 and 1907.

Adsmore is a large brick mansion originally built in 1857 by John Higgins. It was purchased by John Parker Smith in 1900, who soon began making improvements—a columned portico, Federal-style architectural flourishes, etc.—until locals began to talk about how Smith always "adds more" to the house. And so the house became known as Adsmore. The furnishings, clothes, and personal items inside the house are original items that actually belonged to the Smith-Garret family, another rare feature among historic homes, which are usually furnished with period antiques but less often with the residents' actual possessions. The last descendant of the Smith-Garret family lived in the house until 1984 and bequeathed the house with all its furnishings to be used as a museum.

The museum site occupies four acres. In addition to the house, the site also features a reconstructed log-house gun shop that was used in the 1840s by the town's first gunsmith. Adsmore is located at 304 North Jefferson Street in Princeton. Call (270) 365-3114, or visit www.princetonkycityhall.com/adsmore.htm

Mountain HomePlace

A living history farm inside the boundaries of Paintsville Lake State Park, the objective of Mountain HomePlace is to recreate the living conditions of an eastern Kentucky mountain farmer of the middle decades of the nineteenth century. The farmhouse dates from the 1860s, and is constructed around the farm's well—a common practice to keep animals and small children out of the water. Corn, sorghums and hay were the primary crops, and Mountain HomePlace continues to grow these crops using traditional farming technologies. Outbuildings include a barn and a hog lot. The site also includes a schoolhouse and a church, some of the principal institutions in a rural community, as well as a blacksmith's shop. In the planning stages is a mule-powered grist mill, which the mountaineers used to grind their corn and their neighbors' corn.

Mountain HomePlace farm is located off State Route 40 in Paintsville Lake State Park in Staffordsville. Call (606) 297-1850, or visit www.mountainhomeplace.com.

The Hensley Settlement

The Hensley Settlement also depicts mountain life, though from a slightly later period than Mountain HomePlace. Sherman Hensley established it about 1904. The settlement sits on an isolated plateau atop Brush Mountain in southeastern Kentucky. At its peak from 1925 to about 1935, it contained about 100 people, living in scattered farmsteads but sharing central community institutions like the school and the church. During the late 1940s and 1950s, the settlement was gradually abandoned, and by 1951 it was deserted. The National Park Service, which manages the site, has since 1965 restored three of the farmsteads, complete with houses, barns, and fenced fields. It has also restored the schoolhouse and located the community's cemetery. As part of its interpretation of the site, the Park Service has also made Hensley Settlement into a working farm with several dozen acres under cultivation.

The Hensley Settlement is located within Cumberland Gap National Historic Park on the Kentucky/Virginia border. For information, call (606) 248-2817 or visit the website at www.nps.gov/cuga.

A Republican newspaper that began publication in 1869 wrote prophetically of the struggle it would have to gain an audience: "Prophecies of evil to our undertaking say that the rebel sentiment of Louisville is so bitter, that she is so dependent on southern trade, and has done so well by being so pronounced in her southern sympathies, that she won't patronize a Republican newspaper."

The Democrats reigned supreme and would hold continual power for the next thirty years. However, despite coming together to win election after election, the Democrats themselves were deeply divided. An old guard trumpeted a conservative agrarian ideology—they wanted low taxes, saw no great need for public education, and routinely attacked the "radicalism" of the Thirteenth, Fourteenth, and Fifteenth Amendments. One former Confederate—a former member of John Hunt Morgan's cavalry—wrote that among "all *true* Democrats,... a large majority of them... say that they will not vote for any man... who has not seen service in the Confederate army."

The other wing of the party, the "New Departure" Democrats, urged the party to put the past behind it, recognize that the amendments were not going away, and forge ahead with the industrial and economic development of the state. They did not accept racial equality, but they did not want to waste time resisting a *fait accompli* and they condemned the violence that poisoned the state's national reputation. "The only difference that exists in the Democratic Party can be stated in a single sentence," editorialized a Louisville newspaper in 1871. "Shall we accept or shall we reject the Fourteenth and Fifteenth Amendments?" Backing the New Departure vision, the newspaper explained that "as we have accepted confiscation in the Thirteenth Amendment, we propose to accept the other two as its logical consequences; to let the whole Negro question go by default; to take the Negro where he stands as a free man, citizen, and voter, and try to improve and utilize him." Overall, the old guard held off the New Departure wing of the party, but not without making some concessions to the modernizers' views.

In some ways, these New Departure Democrats inherited Henry Clay's mantle, constantly urging internal improvements and government activism to develop the economy. Henry Watterson, who took over the editor's

Famous Sons and Daughters: John Marshall Harlan

Supreme Court justice
(June 1, 1833–October 14, 1911)

Named for Chief Justice John Marshall by an ambitious lawyer father, Harlan was born at Harlan Station, Kentucky, just west of Danville. His father moved the family to Frankfort when Harlan was seven years old. He graduated from Centre College in Danville in 1850 and Transylvania University Law School in 1852, returning to Frankfort to practice law.

Harlan was elected Franklin county judge in 1858, and lost a close contest for a US congressional seat the next year. In 1861, he moved to Louisville, opened a law firm, and resigned his judgeship. With the outbreak of the Civil War, Harlan campaigned ardently for the Union cause. In the fall of 1861, he raised a Union regiment, the 10th Kentucky Infantry, and fought in several small battles, earning promotion from colonel to brigadier general. When his father died, however, he resigned his military commission and returned home. He was soon elected attorney general of Kentucky to replace his father, an office he held until 1867.

Harlan had been a slaveholding Whig prior to the war, but he emerged from the conflict a Radical Republican. He ran unsuccessfully for governor in 1871 and 1875, but his efforts helped establish the Republican party's presence in Kentucky. President Rutherford B. Hayes named Harlan to the Supreme Court on December 10, 1877.

Harlan served thirty-four years on the court, and through his frequent and eloquent dissents represented an often solitary progressive voice on a generally conservative court. Particularly galled at the majority's narrow reading of the postwar amendments protecting black civil rights, Harlan railed against decisions that struck down the Federal Civil Rights Act in 1883 and that established the "separate but equal" doctrine of racial segregation in 1896. In these, he probably did not represent the feelings of the majority back in his home state. However, these dissents proved potent precedents for the landmark *Brown v. Board of Education* decision that finally overturned segregation in 1954. A 1972 survey of legal scholars rated Harlan one of the dozen greatest justices of the Supreme Court.

position upon the merger of Louisville's two largest newspapers, the *Courier* and the *Journal*, became a national spokesman for this vision of a "New South." The *Courier-Journal* soon became the leading newspaper in the South.

From his seat in Louisville, it must have appeared to Watterson that his vision of an industrialized and modernized South was coming true. Louisville, long a commercial town, became increasingly industrial in the years after the war. The value of the city's industrial output more than doubled in the twenty years between 1860 and 1880. The number of manufacturing establishments almost tripled in the same two decades. No single industry dominated the city, although the manufacture of steam engines and boilers employed the most workers. "The secret of substantial and steady growth is found in workshops teeming with mechanics and laborers," wrote one observer in 1875, "who are earning money from those living in distant parts of the country."

In 1883, the city celebrated and advertised its remarkable industrial progress by hosting the southern Exposition, a forty-five-acre showcase of the New South's industrial and commercial wares. Watterson's *Courier-Journal* campaigned vigorously for the project. The Exposition offered one of the first public displays of Thomas Edison's new incandescent light bulb. Every evening, 4,600 bulbs, more than in New York City where the new technology had first been installed, lit up the Expo. A million visitors passed through the gates, marveling at the wonders of the industrial age, and the Exposition was so successful that it was held annually for the next four years.

But what held true in Louisville did not hold for the rest of the state. Kentucky remained largely rural and agrarian. It took time for the state to resume the progress it had made in transportation before the war, so many people remained isolated. Many children grew up having never been to a town, not even the local county seat.

The journal entry of one visitor to the mountains in the early twentieth century gives a vivid picture of the traveling conditions:

The old road was washed away so we had to go out of town another way and cross an extra mountain. A mile out, in winding up a steep mountain side, the horses were trying to pull out of a tremendous mud hole, when one of them slipped over the bank and rolled down and over three times. The harness had to be cut off and [only the fact that] the wagon was mired kept it from going over.

A little farther up the road, she commented, "the wagon was fastened on a large rock in the middle of the road and had to be prized off with fence rails."

Isolation bred self-sufficiency and skills extinguished in other parts of the nation by mass production and industry remained alive in Kentucky. Rural Kentuckians made their own soap, spun their own thread, wove their own fabrics, made their own shoes, and butchered their own meat throughout the nineteenth century. "One can yet find a crane swinging in a big stone fireplace, the spinning-wheel and the loom in actual use; sometimes the hominy block that the pioneers borrowed from the Indians, and a hand-mill for grinding corn," wrote John Fox, Jr., a turn-of-the-century Kentucky writer who derived much of his material from his regular visits to the rural isolation of Kentucky's mountains.

The church and the country store offered some relief from the isolation. Both institutions served social purposes well beyond the religious and the retail. Churches offered entertainment in the form of music and formal speaking and the opportunity for fellowship. Fox once described a mountaineer's funeral:

> "A funeral sermon," said the old preacher, "can be the last one you hear, or the fust one that's preached over ye atter death. Maybe I'm a-preachin' my own funeral sermon now." If he was, he did himself justice, for he preached for three solid hours. The audience was invited to stay to dinner. Forty of them accepted—there were just forty there—and dinner was served from two o'clock until six.

Stores served as polling places, post offices, banks, and gossip centers. As roads improved, court day at the county seat might also bring in throngs of local families by the wagon-load. James Lane Allen, another early twentieth-century Kentucky writer, extolled court day as the

Must-See Sites: Penn's Store

Penn Store is the oldest country store in the United States that has been run continuously by the same family. The store has operated on the current site at least since 1845; the Penn family took it over in 1850. It provides a surviving example of one of the main institutions of rural life in Kentucky, the general store—and it still serves the local community. Inside, the store still features glass showcases and counters as per nineteenth-century retail practice. In the ceiling are large spiked nails formerly used to suspend cured meats. It sold food, fabric, shoes, farming implements—anything that might be needed by a rural dweller. As the store claims on its website: "It is not a restored landmark. It is an authentic landmark."

The store served as the local post office for Rollings, Kentucky, during the late nineteenth century. In 1910, the post office was moved to the railroad town of Gravel Switch, so as to be nearer the train. The store also served as a pharmacy during its heyday. Formerly, there were also outbuildings around the store that have since ceased to exist. These included a spirits shop, a storage building, and some houses where members of the Penn family resided. It also included a poultry coop, which housed the fowl that some people brought in to trade for goods.

Currently, the store hosts various events to attract tourists. Local musicians play regularly and once a year the store hosts the Great Outhouse Blowout, a community celebration that honors outdoor plumbing. The store is located off State Route 243 at 257 Penn's Store Road near the town of Gravel Switch. The store's hours are fairly restricted during the winter months (December to April). Call (859) 332-7715 or (859) 332-7706 or visit www.pennsstore.com.

characteristic social institution of the rural Kentuckian: "In the open square around the court-house of the county seat he has had the centre of his public social life, the arena of his passions and amusements, the rallying-point of his political discussions, the market-place of his business transactions."

If they thought about Henry Watterson's vision of the New South at all, many of these rural Kentuckians would doubtless have rejected it. Despite the isolation, despite the poverty, many held to the old Jeffersonian ideal of the independent small farmer, viewing urban industrial society with suspicion. Allen noted the slow penetration into the mountains by "civilization" in the early twentieth century and remarked that the general reaction of mountain people was "to retire at the approach of civilization to remoter regions of the mountains, where they may live without criticism or observation their hereditary, squalid, unambitious, stationary life."

Law and Mob Law

Suspicions of the outside world had been a feature of rural Kentucky life since the antebellum days. Many small farmers had ended up on the wrong end of legal machinations that deprived them of land or made their titles questionable. Lawyers, politicians, judges—"the law"—tended to be viewed not as unbiased public servants but as servants of the wealthy or the well connected.

The war, and the Republican policies that followed the war, did little to ease such suspicions. From the perspective of white Kentuckians, wartime confiscations of property, the abolition of slavery, the enforcement of black civil rights, the Freedmen's Bureau—all these developments had been brought to the state by outsiders clothing themselves in the authority of the law. African-American Kentuckians saw the laws designed to protect them go unenforced and crimes against their persons and property go unpunished. No wonder then that many Kentuckians—both black and white—continued to distrust the law.

Kentucky's political system did little to combat this impression. County-level government exercised most of the functions of government that directly affected citizens and county officials enjoyed a great deal of autonomy in carrying out those duties. As a result, politics was intensely local. Personal loyalties and family relations counted for a great deal. Fox once described the arraignment of a local man for moonshining. The man was unable to make bail, and the judge ordered him imprisoned:

> When the sheriff rose, a huge mountaineer rose, too, in the rear of the court-room and whipped out a big revolver. "You come with me," he said, and the prisoner came, while judge, jury, and sheriff watched him march out. The big fellow took the prisoner through the town and a few hundred yards up a creek. "You go on home,"

he said…. The mountaineer was a United States deputy marshal, but the prisoner was his friend.

In addition, like nineteenth-century American politics generally, corruption suffused the system. Politics ran on the "spoils system," in which the political winner distributed the "spoils" of victory—government contracts, appointive positions, and so forth—to his supporters. The wise use of patronage to reward supporters and punish opponents might not yield effective public administration, but it could keep local political bosses in power for years.

Corruption extended to the voting booth; votes were routinely purchased by political aspirants. One voter from eastern Kentucky remembered selling his vote for four dollars. When he got home, his father scolded him for underselling—the going rate was seven dollars and a half-pint of bourbon. Big-money players could influence such a system easily. The biggest player in late-nineteenth-century Kentucky politics was the Louisville and Nashville Railroad. As it slowly increased its mileage in the state, the railroad strived to keep regulators at bay by buying lawmakers. It put several of them on its payroll as local county attorneys; to others it gave free passes and generous gifts of entertainment and whiskey.

Suspicion of the law and the corruption of politics had long been a part of public life in Kentucky, going back to before the Civil War. In the last decades of the nineteenth century, though, a new element poisoned the political atmosphere further—an overall culture of violence. Fistfights and gunplay accompanied almost every election.

The masculine code of honor, another holdover from the antebellum period, had always provided a ready alternative to a corrupt legal system. But the Civil War's legacy of unregulated guerrilla warfare and the postwar legacy of racial hatred fueled a firestorm of violence in the late nineteenth century. Kentucky's "decades of discord," as one book describes the 1865–1900 period, were hardly unique in this regard; violence flared across the South after the Civil War.

The code of honor continued to influence male actions and attitudes. In 1883, a jury easily acquitted Congressman Phillip B. Thompson, Jr., for murdering a man whom

Literary Extracts: James Lane Allen

Lexington-born novelist James Lane Allen wrote several highly stylized novels in the "genteel" tradition set in Kentucky. He was Kentucky's first nationally prominent author, and he tried hard to capture the accents and mannerisms of his Kentucky characters. His best-known work, *A Kentucky Cardinal*, appeared in 1894, followed by *Aftermath* in 1895 and *The Choir Invisible* two years later. In addition to his fiction, however, he published in 1900 two volumes of sketches of life in his home state entitled *The Blue-Grass Region of Kentucky and Other Kentucky Articles*. In the following, he describes county court day in a rural community:

> It may be that some stranger has sojourned long enough in Kentucky to have grown familiar with the wonted aspects of a county town. He has remarked the easy swing of its daily life: amicable groups of men sitting around the front entrances of the hotels; the few purchasers and promenaders on the uneven brick pavements; the few vehicles of draught and carriage scattered along the level white thoroughfares. All day the subdued murmur of patient local traffic has scarcely drowned the twittering of English sparrows in the maples. Then comes a Monday morning when the whole scene changes. The world has not been dead, but only sleeping. Whence this sudden surging crowd of rural folk—these lowing herds in the streets? Is it some animated pastoral come to town? some joyful public anniversary? some survival in altered guise of the English country fair of mellower times? or a vision of what the little place will be a century hence, when American life shall be packed and agitated and tense all over the land? What a world of homogeneous, good-looking, substantial, reposeful people with honest front and amiable meaning! What bargaining and buying and selling by ever-forming, ever-dissolving groups, with quiet laughter and familiar talk and endless interchange of domestic interrogatories! You descend into the street to study the doings and spectacles from a nearer approach, and stop to ask the meaning of it. Ah! it is county court day in Kentucky; it is the Kentuckians in the market-place.

Thompson claimed had debauched his wife. In a similar 1890 instance, a Louisville jury acquitted a husband who killed his wife and her lover. The code of honor excused such actions as the appropriate responses of offended gentlemen and juries accepted such excuses.

Bands of "Regulators"—organized vigilante groups—

Must-See Sites:
The Hatfield–McCoy Driving Tour

The ten-stop tour takes visitors to several locations where the actual events of America's most famous feud took place. The feud began along the Tug River in eastern Pike County and spilled over into West Virginia, which is one reason the feud attracted so much attention. The interstate nature of the conflict eventually got both state governments, as well as the national government, involved in trying to mete out justice. No historian has ever pinpointed the exact reason that the quarrel between the two clans began except to say that there was an accumulation of grievances both real and imagined. Once violence broke out, however, it proved unstoppable for eight years.

The Pike County tour sticks to those events that transpired in Kentucky. One of the tour stops includes the historic Dils Cemetery where the head of the McCoy clan, Randolph McCoy, is buried along with several members of his infamous family. In addition to the driving tour, the Big Sandy Heritage Museum includes an exhibit on the feud, as well as more general exhibits on Appalachian history and culture. The Big Sandy Heritage Museum is located in Pikeville. For information on the driving tour or the museum, call the Pikeville-Pike County Tourism Commission at (606) 432-5063 or (800) 844-7453. The county's website is www.tourpikecounty.com.

multiplied during these years, inheriting the mantle of the wartime guerrilla groups and the postwar racial enforcers. Regulators operated in various counties throughout the nineteenth century, dispensing their own brand of justice where they thought it needed to counter the ineffectiveness of a corrupt legal system. They administered beatings, expelled those they deemed undesirable from the locale, and sometimes carried out executions—all without the legal niceties of due process, evidence, or possibility of appeal. In the last twenty-five years of the century, at least 166 lynchings occurred. Two-thirds of the victims were black, showing that the line between the "old" racial violence and the "new" regulator violence was blurry at best.

Regulator violence accompanied and encouraged mob violence. Lynch mobs defended their actions as

representative of the will of the community and few
participants in mobs ever faced punishment in a courtroom.
In an 1899 incident in Maysville, for example, a mob took
accused murderer Richard Coleman from the sheriff's
custody. Hundreds watched and helped feed the fire as the
mob burned Coleman alive. The charred corpse was then
dragged through the streets as souvenir seekers cut off
fingers and toes. No one ever faced indictment or trial over
the incident. "The lesson for Kentuckians was that law was
not supreme," concludes one textbook.

Elements of all these strains of violence—electoral
fights, honor killings, and regulator violence—met and
mingled in Kentucky's unique contribution to the
American history of violence: the feud. The various feuds
that erupted in Kentucky—mostly in the eastern
mountains—in the late nineteenth century attracted
national attention, cementing the violent hillbilly stereotype
of Kentucky firmly in the national mind.

Classic feuds involved two or more rival families or
clans battling sporadically over a long period of time in a
deadly circle of violence and revenge. Families invoked the
code of honor to justify killing members of the other side,
some of whom had invariably insulted, hurt, or killed
members of the family. "Each day I shall show my boys the
handkerchief stained with his blood," said one widow,
recalling the death of her husband, "and tell them who
murdered him."

Fox, writing in 1900, claimed to know the petty origins
of one long-lived feud: "About thirty-five years ago two
boys were playing marbles in the road along the
Cumberland River—down in the Kentucky mountains.
One had a patch on the seat of his trousers. The other boy
made fun of it, and the boy with the patch went home and
told his father. Thirty years of local war was the result."

Turning to the law was not only dishonorable but
useless since the law was corrupt—and often in the hands
of the rival clan. Many feuds turned on local politics, with
one side either wrenching power away from the other or
lording power over them. The periodic explosions of
violence that marked feuds often came on or just after
election day. Regulators appeared in feuds also, sometimes
as hired guns for one side or the other, sometimes as part of

a family's effort to short-circuit the corruption of the legal system.

Take the Rowan County War of the 1880s, for instance, which pitted the Martin and Logan families against the Tollivers. Hostilities between the Martins and the Tollivers can be traced back to political disagreements in the 1870s. In 1884, a disputed election led to a gunfight in which one man died and two more were hurt. One of those injured, John Martin, showed up in a saloon several months later, accused Big Floyd Tolliver of the murder, and then killed him. Eight days later, the Tolliver party seized Martin from the authorities, who were holding him for killing Tolliver, and pumped seven bullets into his body.

Tit-for-tat retaliatory violence followed, but the Tollivers were gaining political control of the city of Morehead and the court system. The Logan family got involved when the Tollivers killed Daniel Boone Logan's two cousins after they had surrendered. In June 1887 Logan armed a group of over 100 men, surrounded Morehead, and set fire to the building where the Tollivers had holed up. As the family fled, a hail of bullets cut down their leader and three others. The ringleaders of Logan's army received pardons. In the three years of violent conflict, the feud claimed 20 dead and at least 16 wounded.

The most famous of the feuds—between the Hatfields and the McCoys—gained its notoriety not because it was bloodier or longer-lasting than any of the others, but simply because it attracted the attention of the national media. The McCoys hailed from Pike County, Kentucky; the Hatfields lived across the Tug Fork River in West Virginia. Years of petty difficulties and disagreements had poisoned relations between the two families since the Civil War. On election day in 1882, however, the long-simmering dispute caught fire in a gunfight between a Hatfield and three McCoys. The Hatfield was mortally wounded. The family had no faith that a Kentucky jury would ever punish a McCoy, so they crossed the river and seized the three offending men. They proceeded to tie them to bushes and execute them. One of the victims—a fifteen-year-old McCoy—had his head nearly taken off by a shotgun blast.

Over the next five years, minor incidents of violence occurred between the two families. The Hatfields decided

Famous Sons and Daughters: Henry Watterson

Journalist (February 16, 1840–December 22, 1921)

Henry Watterson cemented his place in the annals of American journalism during his long tenure as editor of the Louisville *Courier-Journal*, which he turned into a newspaper of national prominence. Known most of his life as "Marse Henry," Watterson was born in Washington, DC. In 1856, he began publishing a two-page sheet in his parents' town of McMinnville, Tennessee— *The New Era*—in which he wrote his first editorials, urging support of James Buchanan. The editorial was picked up by other papers and soon Watterson was writing for newspapers in New York and Washington.

With the outbreak of the Civil War, Watterson initially tried to remain neutral but his neutrality, like Kentucky's, crumbled. Unlike Kentucky, Watterson chose the Confederacy, serving in the cavalry under the renowned southern leader Nathan Bedford Forrest. In 1862, Watterson abandoned his military career to return to publishing, this time in Chattanooga. In *The Rebel*, Watterson launched editorial attacks on Lincoln and Northern aggression and praised southern nationalism.

Watterson was no fire-eater, however. He attacked incompetence among Confederate generals and, once the southern cause was lost, he took jobs editing Republican newspapers. In 1868, he was invited to Louisville to take over the nationally known *Journal*. In October 1868, the *Journal*'s rival—the *Louisville Courier*—approached Watterson and his publisher to broach the idea of a merger to form a newspaper that would reach beyond Louisville. The *Courier-Journal* first appeared on November 8, 1868.

As editor of the *Courier-Journal*, Watterson became one of the most influential journalists in the nation, particularly among Democrats. He became an ardent voice for the "New South," a progressive southern vision he shared with Atlantan Henry Grady and other apostles of southern industrialization. Watterson refused to toe the Democratic party line, however, which angered politicians looking for his support. Watterson labeled himself a Jeffersonian Democrat, supporting individual freedom, free trade, isolationism, and nationalism. His critics labeled him as inconsistent.

He broke from his isolationist stance in the run-up to World War I, during which he urged the United States to join the war against Germany. "To Hell with the Hohenzollerns and Hapsburgs," he famously wrote, referring to the German and Austrian royal dynasties. He was awarded a Pulitzer Prize for his editorial efforts. He later broke with Woodrow Wilson over the issue of the League of Nations. When the new publisher of the *Courier-Journal* came out in favor of the League, Watterson retired. He moved to Florida, where he died in 1921. His body was brought back to Louisville and buried in Cave Hill Cemetery.

to strike a more damaging blow on New Year's Day, 1888. They surrounded the McCoy patriarch's home, burned it, and killed one son and a daughter. A Kentucky deputy sheriff led an illegal raid against the Hatfields to apprehend the perpetrators, during which some Hatfields died. The governor of West Virginia protested to the governor of Kentucky and the feud eventually wound up in the US Supreme Court. In 1890, a lawful hanging took place, after which the violence subsided. Between twelve and twenty Hatfields and McCoys died over the eight years of violence.

The feuds gained Kentucky a national reputation for violence. The *New York Times* once referred to the state as "a delightful place to live if one enjoys mobocracy and anarchy." The *Chicago Tribune* in 1885 said Kentucky had failed the test of civilization and sunken into "barbarism." The big-city newspapers relished the chance to tell about the violent squabbles of mountain families to a national audience that craved stories about exotic and unusual phenomena.

Feud violence died down as the nineteenth century waned. It did not go away completely, but a different type of violence arose in the state as the industrializing American economy extended its reach—a violence that gave renewed prominence to issues of social class and economic inequality. The national economy called forth new political forces that superimposed themselves on the old local and family-centered politics of the past.

NEW POLITICAL VOICES

All over America in the last quarter of the nineteenth century, workers and farmers squeezed by the industrializing economy rose up and demanded that politicians pay attention to their problems. In Kentucky, where the violence of the postwar period slowed industrial development, these new voices took somewhat longer to come together and be heard—but they would be heard.

The industrial economy that developed in the United States after the Civil War was truly a national economy. Huge factories commandeered resources from suppliers all over the country and distributed finished products nationwide. Orders and payments were received via a national communications network; raw materials and products traveled on transcontinental railways. Finance and

Must-See Sites: The Kentucky Railway Museum

The museum houses a collection of railroading artifacts and memorabilia in a replica of a small-town train depot in New Haven, Kentucky. The museum is aimed more at train buffs than at an historical explanation of the importance of railroads—particularly the Louisville and Nashville Railroad—in the development of Kentucky. The exhibits show off the technology of nineteenth- and early twentieth-century railroading, with a dining-car exhibit, handcar, a track inspection car, a collection of various steam locomotive whistles, and a ticket office.

The museum has had a peripatetic existence. It got started in 1948 when a group of Louisville railway enthusiasts formed a local chapter of the National Railway Historical Society. During the 1950s they asked the L&N to donate a steam locomotive to form the core of a railway museum. The L&N donated steam locomotive #152, and the Museum leased six acres of land on River Road in Louisville. It first opened its doors in 1958 and grew quickly as other artifacts were donated.

The growth of its collections, plus the fact that the River Road site was subject to periodic flooding, prompted a move to 40 acres of leased land on La Grange Road. When the lease expired in 1993, however, Jefferson County would not renew it, so the museum began a search for a permanent home that it could purchase. When L&N's parent company CSX abandoned the old rail line from Boston to Mount Vernon in central Kentucky, the Museum purchased the 17 miles of track. Two brothers then donated a building and six acres of land in New Haven, where the Museum reopened its doors on July 4, 1990.

The current museum—a replica of the L&N depot—opened in 1995 and covers 5,000 square feet. Museum volunteers also restored the old 152 steam engine until, in 1985, it was able to move again under its own power after a 30-year retirement. The 1905 engine pulling antique passenger coaches now takes visitors on a 22-mile round trip to nearby Boston.

The Kentucky Railway Museum is located at 136 South Main Street in New Haven. Call (502) 549-5470 or (800) 272-0152, or visit www.kyrail.org.

banking grew to be national in scope as well, with New York cementing its position as the financial capital of the nation.

In Kentucky, the Louisville and Nashville Railroad carried the new era on its steel rails. The heyday of the steamboats had passed by the 1870s, and railroad expansion became the rallying cry of every town booster. By 1890, railroad mileage in Kentucky had tripled to 3,000 miles from its 1870 level.

The trains gave more farmers access to regional and national markets, offered salesmen more potential customers, and opened up the possibilities of travel to previously isolated citizens. One resident of the small town of Fidelity recalled the impact the railroad had on his town, even though the town was off the railroad line:

> As long as the railroad kept away from the county seat, that is, until 1891, Fidelity remained much as it had been in pioneer days, a self-sufficient village. Then came the railroad, and gradually the village began to show signs of deteriorating. Proud yet, in spite of being off the railroad, it was lacking in any importance except locally. Some of the citizens moved to the county seat or on to even more remote places.

As the biggest railway in the state, the L&N paid 40 percent of the railroad taxes. It was the state's corporate giant and it aggressively defended its interests in the legislative halls. Although its operational headquarters remained in Louisville, financial control and the makeup of the board of directors passed in the 1880s to New York financiers.

Other signs of the new economy materialized as well. When farmers sold their corn on the market, they competed not just against other Kentuckians but against the vast new grain belt in the Midwest. And prices were set not by local dickering but by far-off commodity markets in Chicago. Tobacco came to be seen as the salvation crop for Kentucky's farmers as the market for hemp dried up, but tobacco growers soon found themselves held virtually captive by the large corporate tobacco trust that organized the purchase of leaf. Even that quintessential Kentucky activity, horse breeding, found itself dependent on outside infusions of wealth from East Coast industrialists to revive its fortunes after the Civil War.

The power held by large corporations finally triggered a farmers' revolt. Almost everything about the new economy annoyed the farmers. They accused the railroads of charging higher rates to short-haul, small-volume growers. They accused buyers, warehousemen, and other "middlemen" of doing no work but manipulating the market to maximize their own profits at the expense of the growers. They accused bankers of charging usurious interest rates to keep farmers perpetually in debt. And they accused politicians of catering to the business and financial classes.

The first formal farmers' organization to give voice to these complaints was the Grange. Grangers first organized in the 1870s. They wanted farmers to form cooperative stores and warehouses to eliminate exploitation by middlemen. By 1875, the Grange counted more than 50,000 members in Kentucky. In the 1880s, new groups such as the Farmers' Alliance took up the agriculturists' cause. By 1891, the alliance claimed some 125,000 members across 88 counties in the state. That same year, farmers disappointed over the conservatism of the state Democratic party formed a third party—the Populists, or People's Party, a year before the Populists were organized at the national level.

These groups had a long wish list of reforms. They wanted tighter regulation of railroads; they wanted farmers' cooperatives to eliminate the middlemen; they wanted—and this became the defining political issue in Kentucky and the nation during the 1890s—more money to be printed. More money would bring inflation, which would raise crop prices and shrink the value of debts owed to bankers. In Kentucky, they also wanted free roads.

Since before the Civil War, the state government had built roads on the cheap by allowing private contractors to build them and then charge tolls to recoup their investment and make a profit. By 1890, over 75 percent of the hard-surfaced roads in the state ran on the toll system. This situation did not mean that they were good roads, merely that they were costly. With the Panic of 1893 triggering a full-blown depression in Kentucky and the nation through most of the 1890s, hard-pressed farmers in Kentucky decided they had paid enough tolls.

Out of Washington, Anderson, and Mercer counties in 1895 sprang the Tollgate War, as masked night riders

Literary Extracts: Robert Penn Warren

The leading light of Kentucky literati, Warren was born into the middle of the Black Patch War in 1905 in the small western Kentucky town of Guthrie, Kentucky. In his 1939 novel, *Night Rider*, from which the following excerpt is drawn, Warren told the story of the conflict that marked his childhood:

> "Look," she had whispered, pointing. He had slipped out of the bed and gone to the window. The night had been unusually dark, the dark mass of the earth scarcely darker than the sky. But a patch of flame had been on the horizon, a single center of rich, cherry-colored glow fading outward and upward into the enormous hollow of darkness. A dog had barked very faintly, very far off.
>
> Lucille Christian had come to stand beside him. "What is it?" she had whispered....
>
> He had told her he did not know what the patch of flame on the horizon was; but he did know. He knew that it was a burning tobacco barn. It was a barn belonging to some man who, after receiving warnings, had not listed his crop with the Association. He knew that a band of men from some other locality, Band Number Six, he remembered, Mr. Burden's band from over in Hunter County, had picked up its guide, a mounted man waiting in the shadows by the roadside at an appointed place, and had been led to that spot where the flames now made that little center of rosy light against the black sky. And he knew that some other night, soon, he himself would stand and watch men apply the match and then would mount and ride away, the hoofs of the horses drumming the frosty earth and the flames climbing the sky behind him. He knew, because that was the way it had already been.

terrorized gatekeepers, attacked road companies, and burned tollgates. The raiders warned a Mercer County gatekeeper that his house would be destroyed by "fire and Denamite" if he collected any more tolls: "We want a Free Road and are agoing to have it, if we have to Kill and Burn up everything." One gatekeeper, defending his home against a night-rider assault, took a shotgun blast full in the face, dying in his wife's arms. The revolt soon spread to other counties. Attempts to prosecute the raiders in court generally failed out of witnesses' fear of the raiders' wrath or sympathy for their goals. The violence largely succeeded; by the turn of the century, most of Kentucky's roads were free and public. Of course, that still did not mean they were good roads, only that they were in the care of local county politicians.

As farmers waged the Tollgate War, the farmers' political movement sputtered and stalled. They had seen some of their reforms enacted with early attempts at railroad regulation and the control of corporate trusts, but fear of agrarian "radicalism" and the destabilizing effects of inflating the money supply had kept anti-inflationary "sound-money" politicians in power. Nationally, some of the farmers' outrage eased as crop prices emerged from the trough of the depression. In western Kentucky, though, farmers still felt hard pressed. With no explicit agrarian political movement to take up their cause, they turned, again, to violence.

The so-called Black Patch War pitted western Kentucky tobacco growers against the power of the American Tobacco Company. Kentucky's farmers had fallen hard for tobacco after the Civil War, particularly for the recently discovered variety called burley tobacco. Burley, the tobacco of choice among Central Kentucky farmers, could be harvested earlier and air-cured in barns, as opposed to the dark-fired tobacco cured by hickory smoke that tobacco growers in the western part of the state cultivated. Burley promised high returns on small plots, and farmers searching for a cash-crop alternative to hemp embraced it avidly. Scott County farmers, for example, grew 43,000 pounds of tobacco in 1880 and 3.5 million pounds in 1889.

As more farmers converted their fields to tobacco, however, the price plummeted. From the 1870s to 1894, prices fell by 50 percent to 6.6 cents per pound. Prices fell further as the American Tobacco Company perfected its virtual monopoly on tobacco purchasing. Farmers had to accept the trust's price, which soon fell below the farmers' cost of production. The Black Patch War resulted from this economic squeeze. "A farmer... might decline a most unreasonable offer for his tobacco," wrote John Miller, a western Kentucky lawyer, in his memoir about the Black Patch War, "and wait for the buyer's competitor; but such competition would not come. Another buyer might come, but it would be merely to say he could offer no more. The producer was at the mercy of the speculator."

Initially the farmers' answer to their problem echoed the earlier answers of the Grangers and the Farmers' Alliance. Growers needed to cooperate in reducing production and holding their crop off the market until prices rose. To organize such cooperation, western growers founded the Planters' Protective Association in 1904 in Guthrie. Farmers in central Kentucky formed the Burley Tobacco Society to achieve the same ends. The turn to violence came when some farmers cheated, selling their crop to the trust even as their neighbors held crops off the market. These non-cooperative farmers—labeled Hillbillies by their enemies—soon became the targets of violence, especially in western Kentucky.

Organized groups of masked night riders, known as the Silent Brigade, patrolled the counties of western Kentucky to punish the recalcitrants. Warnings to join the cooperative came first, then came crop burnings and finally beatings. Some Hillbillies were killed for their refusal. The war between farmers spread to engulf the towns too. Bands of night riders numbering in the hundreds invaded Princeton, Hopkinsville, Russellville, Eddyville, and other places, targeting trust tobacco. They burned warehouses and threatened county officials who tried to enforce the law. The war divided sympathies across the tobacco counties—some saw it as a people's war against a corrupt corporate system; others decried the violence against their neighbors. Everyone armed themselves for protection.

Miller, who sympathized with the growers but disapproved of their recourse to violence, wrote that "anyone who bought or sold tobacco independently of the Association was doomed. The Trust left the independent buyer's purchased tobacco to rot on his hands. The Night Rider burnt his warehouse and his purchase with it, and whipped him, and if he resisted, slew him. To destroy the warehouses, the great receiving plants of the Trust, would leave all tobacco raisers to sell to the Association or lose their crops. Hence to burn a Trust warehouse was a noble act."

With more than 60,000 tobacco growers organized in the two farmers' organizations and some 10,000 in the night riders, few county politicians dared stand up to oppose the violence. "A circuit judge," Miller relates in his memoir, "in private conversation with me, defended the worst of the Night Rider outrages and cited the Boston Tea Party as a justifying precedent."

The night riders waged their campaigns with the tacit approval of the authorities from 1905 to 1909 and, as in the Tollgate War, violence succeeded relatively well. Virtually a whole year's crop was held off the market, and the pooling of crops by growers in the cooperatives helped boost prices moderately. Other actions helped to end the war too. The state governor sent in several companies of state militia to the affected counties, which quieted the violence somewhat. And in 1911, the American Tobacco Company was found guilty of violating the antitrust laws of the United States.

The victory proved short-lived, however. As prices rose, the Planters' Protective Association and the Burley Tobacco Society collapsed. A long-term solution to agriculturists' problems awaited a later generation.

In a rural state like Kentucky, the problems of the farmers loomed larger than those of the working class, but industrial workers also felt squeezed by the new corporate economy. Labor unrest rocked Kentucky's industrial establishments—as it did across America—through the last quarter of the nineteenth century. Workers had fewer victories than farmers, but their protests caused a great deal of hand wringing by officials because they generally occurred in the state's urban-industrial heart: Louisville.

The first sign of labor trouble came with the Great Railroad Strike of 1877. Railroad workers all across the country protested dramatic cuts in wages, resulting in violence and property destruction totaling some $10 million nationwide. In Louisville, workers on the L&N threatened to strike if their pay was not restored. When management gave in, it inspired other workers, primarily in the construction trades, to strike for wage increases. Construction work on the city's sewer lines ground to a halt. On July 24, a group of some 2,000 workers protested at the county courthouse and then shouted down Louisville's mayor when he tried to address them. That evening, a smaller group of 600 or so roamed the city's streets, breaking windows and damaging buildings. As the symbol of the new economy, the L&N came in for special targeting. The mob smashed every single window in the L&N Depot.

Corporate spokesmen, the newspapers, and city politicans were quick to blame the violence on the shiftless element in Louisville, not "honest workmen." The *Courier-Journal* said the disturbances were caused by "a body of thieves and thugs" who needed to be controlled with "powder and bullets." The mayor called the riot the work of "brutes lower than those of the animal creation." And Allan Pinkerton of the famed Pinkerton Detective Agency, said the mob consisted of "Negroes, half-grown rowdy boys, and dirty, disgusting tramps, and many communists." While all recognized that industrial workmen suffered with low wages and long hours, none thought the outbreak of window-breaking represented any serious claim of dissatisfaction by the working class.

However, a weeklong burst of strike activity among workers followed the civil disturbance of July 24. On July 30 Louisville's workers organized a local branch of the national Workingmen's Party and proceeded to elect five of Louisville's seven representatives to the state legislature. Other workers' organizations followed. By 1880, the Knights of Labor had organized 36 assemblies in Louisville. The decline of the Knights in the late 1880s persuaded many Louisville workers to shift their allegiances to the recently formed American Federation of Labor. The AFL accepted the basic premises of industrial capitalism and focused on better conditions, shorter hours, and higher pay. The organization mustered enough support to hold a large May Day parade in 1890 attended by AFL head Samuel Gompers himself.

"We want eight hours and nothing less," Gompers told workers. "We have been accused of being selfish, and it has been said that we will want more.... We do want more.... You ask a workingman, who is getting two dollars a day, and he will say he wants ten cents more. Ask a man who gets five dollars a day and he will want fifty cents more. [W]e shall never cease to demand more until we have received the results of our labor."

As they did all over the country, workers also came together in numerous strikes. Louisville saw 140 different labor strikes between 1880 and 1900, mostly aimed at gaining

Must-See Sites: The Pennyroyal Area Museum

With exhibits that cover the history of the entire nine-county Pennyroyal district, this museum pays particular attention to the importance of agriculture in southwestern Kentucky and includes exhibits on the reign of tobacco—both dark-fired and burley varieties—as the main cash crop in the area. (It has recently been supplanted by soybeans.) Exhibits also give attention to the plight of the farmers and the violence of the Black Patch War. The night riders invaded the town of Hopkinsville in 1907 and burned three tobacco warehouses. Each year, the museum hosts a reenactment of the event in September, in which visitors ride in a wagon retracing the route of the raiders.

The museum also has a railroad exhibit, pointing out the importance of the L&N, which served the Pennyroyal area from 1879 to 1971, operating several small branch lines that eased the isolation of the area's rural inhabitants. Other exhibits focus on the Civil War and the culture of southwestern Kentucky, with displays on toys, clothing, and other memorabilia.

The museum is located in Hopkinsville at 217 East 9th Street. Call (270) 887-4270, or visit members.hopkinsville.net/museum.

---

higher wages for workers. Few such efforts succeeded. A two-month strike in the wake of the 1893 depression, which left some 10,000 unemployed in the city, failed to better labor's situation appreciably. Even their failures, however, helped workers see their common interests and labor increasingly began to vote as a bloc in the city.

Insurgent farmers and organized workers sent shivers through the state's Democratic party. The last thing the fragile coalition of traditionalist and New Departure Democrats needed were new factions threatening to bolt and form their own parties. In 1891, farmers had made good on such threats with the organization of the People's Party, which had drawn votes away from the Democrats. In 1895, with the state and country in an economic depression, with Populists and organized farmers splitting the Democrats on the issue of inflating the currency, and with an unpopular Democratic governor in the statehouse,

Republicans finally ended their thirty-year drought and elected William O. Bradley governor. Adding insult to injury, Louisville's voters gave Republicans control of the city council. When the Democratic mayor died mid-term in 1896, the council chose his successor and the city had its first Republican mayor.

Both Republican victories would soon be overturned. Louisville's Democratic machine engineered a victory for its mayoral candidate in 1897 and state Democratic leader William Goebel propelled himself to the governorship in 1899. But an era of real two-party competition had begun both in the state and in Louisville. Republicans won four of the next nine governor's races and the state went for William McKinley in the 1896 race for president, the first time a Republican had ever won the state. Democrats still held the advantage, however, in county politics and the state legislature.

William Goebel's rise to power illustrated the political ramifications of the new industrial economy. Goebel made blatant appeals to those hurt by the economic transformation. He campaigned as a reformer, advocating greater civil rights for blacks and women, tighter government control over the railroads, more rights for workers, and restrictions on toll roads. He especially targeted the powerful L&N Railroad. "I believe that the railroad corporations should have a bit in their mouths and the Democratic party should hold the bridle," he said in one campaign speech. In another, he phrased the question as "whether the L&N is the servant or the master of the people." Hailed by many as a champion of the common man, he was denounced by an equal number as a demagogue.

Indeed, Goebel's career summed up all the tensions in Kentucky life during the last years of the nineteenth century. As the son of German immigrants whose father had fought for the Union in the Civil War, his background evoked the social tensions in the state. As leader of a group of younger Democrats disillusioned with the party's old-guard leadership, his career evoked the political tensions. And as a champion of the working classes who called for greater controls on corporations, his political positions evoked the economic tensions. "He was the best loved and the best hated man in Kentucky," wrote one contemporary.

Goebel's ruthless ambition and hostility to opponents also fit the state's violent political climate. Goebel had few friends and did not enjoy the meet-and-greet of politics. He craved power and devoted his time to engineering political strategies to help him achieve that power. As a result, he antagonized people. One of his worst enemies, a former Confederate in the Democratic party, drew a pistol on him on a street in Covington in 1895. Goebel shot him dead and went free on a plea of self-defense.

In 1899, Goebel set his sights on the governorship. He faced off against Republican William Taylor, the state's attorney general and the candidate favored by the L&N. Urey Woodson, a Democratic party chairman who worked with Goebel and later wrote an admiring biography of him, declared that the L&N "spared no money in attempting to organize the State to defeat Goebel. Some newspapers were bought outright; others were subsidized to carry on the anti-Goebel war. Many impecunious politicians… were paid liberally to go out and make speeches against Goebel." Goebel himself remarked during a campaign speech that "the only real candidates are the Louisville and Nashville Company and the person who address [sic] you."

In an election marked by widespread fraud, corruption, and intimidation of voters, Taylor edged Goebel by just over 3,000 votes. Taylor was inaugurated in December 1899, but Goebel did not give up. Democrats, who made up a majority in the legislature, convened an investigative committee to examine fraud in the election. Republicans feared Goebel was engineering a coup. If the committee invalidated just a few thousand ballots, Goebel would be declared the winner. "It was apparent to Taylor's adherents that the committee would decide in favor of Goebel," wrote journalist Irvin S. Cobb in a 1928 reminiscence. "On January 19, 1900, a force of more than 1,500 armed mountaineers arrived in Frankfort, the capital, and took possession of the town."

Cobb, who was covering the story for a Louisville newspaper, recalled that

on January 30, 1900, at 11:16 o'clock in the morning, Goebel, accompanied by two guards, walked up St.

Oldest-known photograph of the state capitol in Frankfort, 1859

Clair Street and entered the gate leading up to the Capitol. He was walking toward the center building on the Capitol grounds. Half way on the grounds to the Capitol building was a small fountain. It had been cold, and the water from the fountain was frozen. As Goebel and the guards neared the fountain they passed a little to one side to avoid stepping into the half frozen mud. As they made the turn five shots were fired from a window on the lower floor of the executive building…. As I looked out the window I saw Goebel drop. It afterward developed that had Goebel not turned as he neared the fountain he probably would have been shot through the heart and been killed instantly.

Instead, Goebel lingered for four days, fighting for his life in a Frankfort hotel. The Republican administration declared a state of emergency. Taylor called out the militia and the legislature evacuated Frankfort for more Republican-friendly confines, all justified in the name of public safety. Democrats, forbidden to meet in the state capitol, convened privately in a hotel and voted to accept the investigative committee's report on the election. They promptly threw out the requisite number of votes and declared the wounded Goebel, fighting for his life in a Frankfort hotel, governor. Goebel promptly recalled the militia and ordered the legislature back to Frankfort. Republicans decried the stealing of the election and for a tense few days Democratic-controlled militia units faced off against Republican-controlled militia units.

On February 3, 1900, Goebel made history and earned Kentucky another dubious distinction—the only state to have a governor die in office because of an assassination. He had served three days.

Tensions eased after his death and the threat of armed conflict decreased, but the political circus that surrounded the eventual apprehension of the suspects, their trials, appeals, and retrials (one defendant had three trials, another had four) did nothing to build public confidence in the law or foster bipartisan cooperation. The whole legal process was so tainted by party bias that it remains unclear to this day who actually killed Goebel.

Goebel's violent death capped Kentucky's decades of discord. Lawmakers in the first two decades of the new century did enact some economic and political reforms, but Goebel's fate sent a message to aspiring reformers. Go easy, it said, and watch whose ox gets gored.

7

REFORM AND RESISTANCE

Kentucky limped into the twentieth century carrying the burdens of its factional politics, its reputation for violence, and its second-class status in the new industrial economy. In the years before World War I, however, a national tide of reformist energy—labeled Progressivism—rolled over the state. This tide hardly washed Kentucky clean of corruption or of the exploitation of labor or of violence, but it did produce a series of economic and political reforms that took aim at some of the worst abuses. Kentucky's brand of progressivism also included a strong strain of social control and racism. Segregation increased steadily through the first decades of the new century, and prohibition dominated political discourse.

The reformist tide and a spate of economic and cultural changes that followed World War I modernized a nineteenth-century Kentucky strongly bound to its rural roots and cultural traditions. In the 1920s, however, an anti-modernist backlash began that attacked this slide toward modernism, lest it destroy the state's soul.

PROGRESSIVE ISSUES

Academic historians have built careers defining Progressivism. The term eludes precise meaning because so many reform movements, often with conflicting goals, took hold during the so-called Progressive Era (1900–1920). The reform movements dragged different cross-sections of people behind them; people who were allies in one movement often found themselves at loggerheads over a different issue. Sometimes the movements worked within political party lines; other times they cut across those lines. The most general conclusions about Progressivism stress two issues. First, the pressure for reform grew out of a widespread recognition that the industrial transformation of the national economy had

Famous Sons and Daughters:
Cora Wilson Stewart

Educator (January 17, 1875–December 2, 1958)

A schoolteacher and school superintendent, Stewart was born and raised in Rowan County, Kentucky. She gained national prominence for her work in adult education, particularly her efforts to combat illiteracy. She organized her first "moonlight school" to teach adults how to read in Morehead, Kentucky, in 1911. In 1929, President Herbert Hoover named her chair of the National Advisory Committee on Illiteracy. She received numerous prizes and awards for her educational achievements. She moved to Arkansas in 1936 and then to North Carolina, where she died in Tryon.

caused a variety of social problems that needed to be addressed. Second, government intervention in some form was needed to address those problems.

In Kentucky, the hot Progressive issue for the first twenty years of the new century was prohibition. To jaded post modern eyes, this seems silly. Surely there were bigger fish to fry than drinking. But to early twentieth-century progressives, prohibition struck at the root of many social problems. Poverty would be lessened if workmen did not drink away their wages. Workplaces would be safer if the saloons that provided free lunches were shut down. And political corruption could end if the liquor trusts that controlled the industry and the saloons controlled by political bosses were eliminated. Add to these arguments Kentucky's strong inheritance of evangelical religion, and prohibition became a social improvement with widespread support, despite the prodigious amounts of bourbon produced in the state.

The movement to restrict alcohol had its roots in the 1870s. In fact, in 1874 the state legislature had passed a "local-option" law that allowed towns and cities to vote themselves dry. But the dawning of the twentieth century saw effective political organizations mustered against the evils of drinking. These groups—the Order of Good Templars, the

Women's Christian Temperance Union, the Anti-Saloon League—knew how to practice modern politics. They organized grassroots protests, published newsletters, pamphlets, and leaflets by the ream, and backed political candidates who supported their issues. The WCTU alone had 300 chapters across Kentucky. These groups helped get a county-option law passed in 1906, and by 1907 95 of the state's 119 counties had voted themselves dry.

The movement for statewide prohibition came next. Both Democrats and Republicans found themselves torn by wet and dry factions within their parties. During the 1908 campaign for US Senate, for example, one Democrat wrote that his party's "dry" nominee, John Crepps Wickliffe Beckham, "would sell out the world to go to the Senate. This house is full of squirming cowardly prohibitionists just like him. They keep full of booze and introduce bills to punish the man who sells it to them…. Beckham is the worst type of the demogogue and agitator. Some day they will learn that you can not make men sober by statute."

Ironically, it was a "wet" Democratic governor who finally called a statewide election on a proposed prohibition amendment to the state constitution in 1919. The voters supported the amendment by a 10,000-vote margin, and Kentucky went dry a year before the country as a whole did.

The other major social "reform" of Kentucky's Progressive Era was racial segregation. The blame for this cannot be laid entirely at the door of reformers, for entrenched political leaders often played the race card to gain white votes when they felt threatened by political reform. "All we have got to do is to raise the cry of nigger," one Democratic politician stated. "[T]hat means a gain of 25,000 votes for the state ticket." But equal rights for blacks never ranked very high on the Progressive agenda in Kentucky and so most of the so-called reformers either helped—or did nothing to stop—segregation's spread.

In other parts of the South, Progressive forces were out front on taking the right to vote away from African Americans, alleging it was a means to clean up politics by preventing office-seekers from duping ignorant voters with booze and bribery. Kentucky never took part. In Kentucky segregation was less a political "reform" and more a brand of social engineering.

Fears of racial mixing led to the passage of segregation ordinances from the 1890s through the 1920s. African Americans lost the right to sit on state juries—a right they had gained only a few years before. In 1892, state law segregated railroad cars. In 1903, the town of Henderson segregated its previously integrated municipal parks. In 1904, the state's Day Law banned racial integration in higher education, targeting Berea College, the only remaining biracial college in the South. After 1911, the Kentucky Derby—in which African-American jockeys had ridden more than half of the winning horses—banned black riders. Lexington in 1916 and Louisville in 1924 created parks for African Americans instead of allowing both races to use municipal recreation facilities.

By the mid-1920s, segregationists had succeeded—almost all public facilities had separate accommodations for blacks and whites. "Through a veil I could perceive the forbidden city, the Louisville where white folks lived," wrote one African-American observer of the early twentieth century. "On my side of the view everything was black: The homes, the people, the churches, the school, the Negro park…. I knew there were two Louisvilles and in America, two Americas. I knew also which of the Americas was mine."

The African-American community fought back against the hardening of the color line. Against arguments that they should just accept their "place" in society, one African-American newspaper thundered that "to submit to a degradation without serious objection is worse than cowardly; it is unmanly and ignoble and any race that would do so without exhausting every means of moral and legal protest is unworthy of the name of civilized."

African Americans challenged the Day Law all the way to the US Supreme Court, but in 1908 the court turned down their appeal. "The state court determines the extent and limitations of powers conferred by the State on its corporations," the court wrote. Further, state policy in Kentucky was to "preserve race identity, the purity of blood, and prevent an amalgamation of the races," so the Day Law was therefore constitutional.

A Louisville chapter of the National Association for the Advancement of Colored People (NAACP) formed to fight a municipal ordinance forbidding blacks from moving into

Famous Sons and Daughters: Elizabeth Madox Roberts

Author
(October 30, 1881–March 13, 1941)

Born in Perryville, Kentucky, Roberts spent her childhood in Springfield, which she always regarded as her home. She got a late start as an author due to recurring illnesses that slowed her education. After teaching school in Kentucky, she finally graduated in 1921 from the University of Chicago, where her writing talents were recognized and lauded. After graduation, she returned home to Springfield to write.

Roberts is primarily a southern regionalist, and her writing faithfully captures the lives and language of Kentucky's rural folk. Her novel *The Time of Man*, published in 1926, brought her international recognition, and *The Great Meadow* (1930) is held to be one of the finest historical novels of frontier Kentucky. Despite her regionalism, Roberts was hailed during her lifetime as one of the greatest contemporary American authors.

Plagued by various ailments throughout her life, Roberts was diagnosed with Hodgkin's disease in 1936. She died five years later. She is buried in Springfield.

housing on a predominantly white block. A test case of the new ordinance progressed all the way (again) to the Supreme Court, which declared the law an unconstitutional infringement on property rights. "Supreme Court annuls segregation ordinance," Louisville's African-American newspaper headlined. "Unanimous decision made public— Great for civil rights." It *was* an important victory that carried broad implications for other cities around the country, but it was a rare victory—one of only a handful of successful challenges to the new segregationist order.

Although segregation did not extend to Kentucky's voting booths, other reforms did target the political arena. Reformers wanted to diminish the power of political bosses—those who dispensed the spoils of politics in return for votes—and enhance the power of ordinary citizens. Given the influence of reform-minded agrarians in the

Must-See Sites:
Educational Frontrunners

Berea College

Located in the Appalachian mountains, Berea College was racially integrated from its founding in 1855 by abolitionist missionary John G. Fee. It was intended to serve the underprivileged youth of the state, including African Americans and poor Appalachian whites. In the early twentieth century, the college fought a losing battle against the hardening of racial lines in Kentucky as legislators targeted the institution's interracial philosophy by passing the Day Law, which mandated segregation in higher education. The college challenged the law all the way to the Supreme Court, but eventually lost its appeal. The college's African-Americans students were forced to transfer to black colleges in other states, or to the State Normal School in Frankfort, the only African-American institution of higher education in Kentucky.

Even before the Day Law passed, Berea had already begun to place greater emphasis on the education of poor Appalachian whites. Although the state Supreme Court declared the Day Law unconstitutional in 1955, African Americans currently make up only about 10 percent of the student body, whereas they were often a majority during the nineteenth century.

Berea continues to offer quality higher education to the youth of the mountains and its curriculum remains heavily grounded in Appalachian culture. In the interest of providing educational access, the college offers tuition-free education to students from Appalachia. The town of Berea itself has become an entrepôt for Appalachian arts, crafts, and music. Tours of the historic campus are available. Call (859) 986-9358 or (800) 366-9358 or visit www.berea.edu.

The Pine Mountain Settlement School and the Hindman Settlement School

Both schools represent the continuing legacy of the Progressive Era rural settlement house movement, designed to bring education and uplift to the poor and forgotten of the industrial era. Hindman, the oldest and most successful rural settlement school, was founded in 1902 by Katherine Pettit and May Stone. Pine Mountain got started in 1912, after William Creech, an old mountaineer, heard about Pettit's work at Hindman and recruited her to start a school on land that he donated for the purpose.

The purpose of the settlement schools was both to teach mountain folk the essentials of literacy and science, but also to keep them in touch with their cultural heritage. In that way, the rural settlements echoed the broad objectives of the more famous urban settlement houses in the immigrant communities of the industrial cities. In its ideal form, the settlement movement aimed at a partnership between an isolated local community and the wider world of Progressive America.

Both schools had to change their focus as railroads and highways diminished the isolation of rural communities. As public schools took up the primary educational burden, Pine Mountain positioned itself as an environmental education center for groups of adults and schoolchildren from around the region. Hindman has focused on providing services for disabled and dyslexic children. Both schools continue to serve as community gathering places and as promoters and protectors of Appalachian arts and culture.

Pine Mountain Settlement School is located on Highway 510 in the community of Pine Mountain in southeastern Kentucky. Information on Pine Mountain's programs is available at (606) 558-3571 or at www.pinemountainsettlementschool.com. Hindman Settlement School is located 145 miles southeast of Lexington off Kentucky Highway 160 from Kentucky Highway 80 East. Call (606) 785-5475, or visit www.hindmansettlement.org.

state's Democratic party, Democrats tended to champion political reform more often than Republicans.

Alben Barkley, a Democrat from western Kentucky who was elected to Congress and later became vice president, described in his memoirs his childhood understanding of the workings of the spoils system in the small town where he came of age: "As a boy, I began to notice that when a Republican administration came in, Mr. Rodam Peck, who ran the village blacksmith shop and one of the two general stores, became postmaster. When the Democrats returned, Mr. John Lowe, of the family which ran the other general store, automatically recaptured the job." The observation, Barkley recalled, was "the beginning of my education in practical politics."

The extent of corruption in Louisville's municipal politics led to early movements to clean up the city.

Reformers within the city's Democratic party increasingly challenged the political bosses, succeeding in 1882 in getting the state to remove control of the police from the mayor and the city council (putting political supporters on the force had been a preferred tactic of urban politicians). In 1884, reform forces enacted a voter registration law aimed at abuses such as multiple voting and voting by the dead and other ineligible people. Blatant bribery in the 1887 election for mayor led to the reformers' crowning achievement in 1888— the adoption of the secret ballot. Although long advocated nationally, Louisville became one of the first cities to adopt printed ballots. Previously, voters had simply told a tally clerk their choice. Vote-buyers within earshot could thus easily ensure that the votes they paid for were actually delivered.

The secret ballot did not end corruption, as the pivotal 1905 mayoral election proved. Fearing a reformist alliance of Republicans and progressive Democrats, Louisville's political bosses pulled out all the stops to win. Police harassed supporters of the reformist candidate, ballot boxes mysteriously vanished, and in some precincts voting records showed people arriving to vote in precise alphabetical order. "What happened!" the *Louisville Herald* editorialized after the election. "With a boldness unparalleled even in the history of Louisville, hired robbers, the commonest type of manhood, went into your polling places, stole from the law's receptacle the ballots you had cast, and carried them away as so much junk."

Reformists challenged the election in court and won; the boss-supported victors in the 1905 election were removed from office, and the state governor selected a young Progressive prohibitionist, Robert Worth Bingham, to serve as interim mayor. Bingham served only four months, but he undertook reform with typical Progressive energy. He shook up the police force, enforced the Sunday-closing law for the city's saloons, attacked the Red Light district, and ensured a clean election when his interim term ended. He failed to dislodge the bosses, however, and their candidate returned to power in 1909.

Statewide, other Progressive reformers worked to lessen the influence of the political bosses and to root corruption out of the political system. As in Louisville, their

Famous Sons and Daughters: Madeline Breckenridge

Reformer and suffragist
(May 20, 1872–November 25, 1920)

Born Madeline McDowell in Franklin County, Kentucky, she was Henry Clay's great-granddaughter and at age 10 moved with her family into Clay's estate, Ashland, near Lexington. She attended schools in Lexington and in Connecticut, and devoted herself to intellectual pursuits after tuberculosis forced the amputation of part of her leg, curtailing her outdoor activities. She began writing book reviews for the *Lexington Herald* and in 1898 married Desha Breckenridge, the *Herald*'s editor.

By the turn of the century, she had immersed herself in various Progressive reform projects, helping to establish a settlement school in eastern Kentucky, introducing the methods of "scientific" charity to Lexington relief agencies, and leading the charge for civic improvements in the city. Through her sister-in-law Sophonisba Breckenridge, she developed contacts in the Chicago social-work community, even getting the renowned urban reformer Jane Addams to speak in Lexington. As leader of Lexington's influential Civic League, Breckenridge pushed issues such as technical education, compulsory school attendance, child labor legislation, and a separate juvenile court system.

She came to the movement for women's suffrage via these other reform movements, realizing that without the vote, women could never get the politicians to heed their calls for social reform. She lobbied the legislature hard for a bill granting women the right to vote in school elections, which became law in 1912. Success there led her to press for full female suffrage, and she led the Kentucky Equal Rights Association from 1912 to 1915 and in 1919–1920. She became a nationally known advocate for the women's right to vote and went on various speaking tours as vice president of the National American Women Suffrage Association from 1913 to 1915. Breckinridge avidly supported the Nineteenth Amendment and her intense lobbying on its behalf helped push the state legislature into ratifying it.

After passage of the amendment in 1920, she laid plans to transform the Kentucky Equal Rights Association into the League of Women Voters. Felled by a stroke before the transformation was completed, she died in Lexington. She is buried in Lexington Cemetery.

overall goal remained elusive even as they enjoyed some successes. Kentucky's Progressive congressmen and senators supported political reforms at the national level, such as the election of senators by popular vote, that took some power out of the hands of the bosses. Governor James McCreary, although beholden to the bosses for his election, also heeded the call for political reform, mandating primary elections in the state rather than allowing party leaders to choose candidates. And when western Kentuckian A.O. Stanley reached the governor's chair in 1915, Progressivism hit its peak in the state. Stanley got a Corrupt Practices Act passed, punishing bribery, kickbacks, and other political shenanigans. He also championed a bill forbidding railroads from giving free passes to public officials, a key tactic used by the L&N to curry favor with politicians. "The L&N, by making liberal use of railroad funds (and also scattering passes like peanuts among legislators and politicians)," Barkley recalled, "had a virtual strangle hold on state politics."

Perhaps the most contentious political reform of the period was the question of giving women the right to vote. Henry Watterson, for example, derided the leaders of the women's movement as "Crazyjanes." Watterson wrote that "all of them are politicians. They aim to improve the condition of women by politics, and think that women's votes would help vastly in doing so. They take no account of the evil conditions and ghastly failure of politics everywhere. That is man's imperfect work, they say."

Indeed, women seeking the vote turned the old argument about politics and public life being too unseemly for females on its head; if politics was unseemly, corrupt, violent, and contentious, that was because women had been excluded. Given women's "gentler nature," they could clean up politics if offered the chance. Women also argued that since public policies regarding drinking, education, child labor, and a host of other issues affected family life, they had to participate in those decisions as the national guardians of the family. "No woman will acknowledge that she has not a moral right to her children, and a moral responsibility for their education and training," wrote a Kentucky suffragist in 1917. "Now it is impossible for women to fulfill this responsibility without a participation in politics." Finally, there was the simple issue of justice; women were sick of being treated as second-class citizens.

All these arguments began to carry more weight during the Progressive Era, although like most reforms the initial impulse came earlier. The Kentucky Woman Suffrage Association organized in 1881, the first group of its kind in the South. In 1888, it changed its name to the Kentucky Equal Rights Association (KERA) and championed a broader agenda. Soon after, laws discriminating against women began to fall. In 1894, the state enacted a married-women's property rights bill, allowing married women to own property and enter into contracts on their own behalf. In 1900, it passed a law allowing working women to keep their wages; previously, women's wages became the husband's property. In 1910, the state raised the age of consent for marriage to sixteen years old from the previous twelve years old.

The vote came more slowly. In 1912, the legislature allowed literate women to vote on school matters, but suffrage activists failed to amend the state constitution so that women could vote in all elections statewide. KERA leader Madge Breckinridge, a great-granddaughter of Henry Clay, organized protest marches and used her sharp wit to poke fun at Kentucky's male politicians in her campaign to gain the vote. "Kentucky women are not idiots," she once said, "even though they are related to Kentucky men." Finally, with President Woodrow Wilson supporting an amendment to the federal Constitution, Kentucky's legislators responded. They ratified the Nineteenth Amendment in January 1920, and Kentucky women voted for the first time in the November elections of that year. Suffrage leader Madge Breckenridge rewrote the state song—"My Old Kentucky Home"—to celebrate the event. The final chorus of the new version went: "Weep no more, my lady, Oh weep no more today/ For we'll vote one vote for the old Kentucky home/ The old Kentucky home, far away."

Progressive thinkers liked to see connections between things, especially between economics and politics. They believed that reforming abuses in one area would lead to the reform of abuses in other areas. Given the influence of large corporations on the state's politics, the urge to rein in

Must-See Sites: The Louisville Palace

A surviving cinema treasure from the golden age of the movies, the Louisville Palace opened as the Loew's State Theater in 1928, designed by renowned movie theater architect John Eberson. It featured a Spanish baroque style, with lots of fountains, statues, and tapestries to create opulence. A night sky with electric twinkling lights was painted on the ceiling. During its prime, it was considered the finest theater in the South. After its heyday, it went through a series of financial troubles and several renovations, including closing off the balcony and renaming the smaller space the Penthouse Theater. After several bankruptcy filings and changes of ownership, it reopened as the Louisville Palace in 1998.

The Palace currently serves as a concert venue, but many of the original architectural flourishes are still intact. In addition, since 1998 the Palace has shown a series of classic movies on summer weekends on its large movie screen, approximating the moviegoing experience of bygone days. Ongoing restoration work aims to bring the Palace as close to its original look as possible, so long as it does not interfere with its function as an entertainment venue.

The Louisville Palace is located at 625 South Fourth Street in Louisville. Call (502) 583-4555, or visit www.louisvillepalace.com.

the trusts ran strong in Kentucky's Progressive ranks. The state created numerous regulatory agencies during this time to control corporate power. Prior to becoming governor, A.O. Stanley had taken on the tobacco, steel, and railroad giants as a congressman from western Kentucky. He sympathized with the night riders in the Black Patch War and their efforts to break the hold of the tobacco trust. As governor, he got a state antitrust law passed.

Progressives also believed that curbing corporate political power would allow politicians to address workers' concerns about safety and work hours. Workers, seeing their interests advanced by the government, would not turn to violence and would instead support reformist politicians, thus further reducing corporate influence on politics.

Various Progressive reforms advanced labor's interests. The state passed an eight-hour workday for laborers on public works early in the century, for instance, although

Literary Extracts: Jesse Stuart

Jesse Stuart was a keen observer of life in the Kentucky mountains where he was raised. In the excerpt below from his 1974 story "Thirty-Two Votes Before Breakfast," he takes a humorous dig at the way politics worked in the small rural communities he knew so well. The narrator in the story has been paid ten dollars by the political worker Silas Devers to transport Al Caney to the polls early in the morning. The election is a contest between two rival families, the Greenoughs and the Dinwiddies:

Just before we got to Blackoak, Mr. Devers got out his notebook and looked at the name again.

"Remember, Al, your name is Casper Higgins, and you live on Sand Suck, if anybody questions you," Mr. Devers instructed Al. "Can you remember?"

"Sure can, Silas," Al Caney said.

When we drove up to the Blackoak school, there was a light in the windows. The polls had opened. But I didn't see a crowd hangin' on the outside like we always saw in Blake County on election days.

"My name's Casper Higgins, and I live on Sand Suck," Al Caney said when he got out of the car.

"That's right, Al," Mr. Devers said, as he rolled out like a big barrel.

Just to see what happened, I got out and went in too.

"We don't vote here," Mr. Devers told one of the election judges. "We're bringin' a man here to vote."

"Name, please?" one of the women clerks asked.

"Casper Higgins," Al said.

"Casper Higgins?" the clerk repeated. "Ain't he dead?"

"Dead! Am I dead?" Al asked. "I hope to tell you I'm not. Isn't my name on the record?"

"It's been marked out," she said.

"Mark it back in," Al said. "I'm goin' to vote! How dare you mark it out!"

"Well, if he's not dead," one of the judges said, "he's entitled to vote same as any taxpayer!"

See, we had two Greenough judges at each precinct, and the Dinwiddies had one. Our county judge was a Greenough, and he appointed the election judges.

"You see I'm not dead," Al complained, as if he were mad as a wet hen.

"Let 'im vote," the second judge said.

Mr. Devers seemed pleased. I saw him wink at one of the judges as Al went into the booth, a place surrounded by bed sheets, to vote.

Just as soon as Al had voted, we hurried out the Blackoak schoolhouse, and were on our way.

"You did fine, Al," Mr. Devers said, reaching him two brand-new one-dollar bills. "Smooth talk."...

"To Plum Forks, next, Mr. Devers?" I said.

"That's right," he said. "Step on the gas."

other workers were not included. Reformers also moved against child labor, which they felt undermined family life, undercut wages for adult male workers, and jeopardized the lives and health of the coming generation. Farm families had long relied on the labor of their youngest members to help make ends meet, and many families took advantage of the opportunity to bring cash wages into the household when factories offered employment to children. In 1902, lawmakers banned industrial employment for anyone under fourteen years of age unless they had parental consent. Parents evidently gave their consent in droves; a factory inspector found 40 children employed in one factory, all with signed permits, working 12-hour days for 23 cents per day soon after the law was passed.

Reformers steadily gave more teeth to the law. In 1906, they raised the employment age to 16 and limited children to 10-hour days and 60-hour weeks. In 1914, the state banned children under 14 from working during school hours. The same law reduced a child's work week to a maximum of six eight-hour days. Kentucky thus gave its children some of the strongest legal protections in the nation at that time; lax enforcement, however, led to frequent abuses of the child-labor statutes.

Progressives also addressed public education. Political corruption existed not just because of corporations and political bosses but also because of uneducated citizens, who sold their votes and voted as their bosses told them because they did not know any better. Reform the schools and educate the citizenry and there would be a more independent electorate, a more democratic state, and a more productive work force. Between 1907 and 1930, education in Kentucky thus underwent a wave of reform that corrected many of the state's historic educational failings.

Kentucky's public education system, never strong before the Civil War, came out of the war in tatters. Over the next 40 years, legislators did little significant to rebuild it. In 1905, the superintendent of public instruction declared that Kentucky's barns were more comfortable than its schoolhouses. The one major reform the legislature made came only under duress—it allowed African Americans to be educated, albeit in a system of underfunded, segregated, and poorly equipped schools. In

Must-See Sites:
The Kentucky Derby Museum

The museum honors and celebrates Louisville's signature sporting event, the Kentucky Derby, held every year on the first Saturday in May. The Derby became the premier event in American thoroughbred racing in the early twentieth century thanks to the new mass media of the era and non-stop promotion of the event by Churchill Downs executive Matt Winn. With three floors and over 55,000 square feet of space, the Derby Museum covers the whole history of the race, with available recordings of most of the races in the modern era. It also includes exhibits on thoroughbred breeding and training, the language and technology of parimutuel betting, and African-American jockeys, who were excluded from riding in the Derby in the early 1900s.

The centerpiece of the museum is regular presentation of the high-definition multimedia video "The Greatest Race." Through sound and image, the presentation tries to capture all that occurs on Derby Day, from the horses to the trainers to the spectators to the race itself. The museum also offers guided tours that take visitors outside, onto the grounds of Churchill Downs, where they can visit the Winner's Circle, see the finish line, and walk the Backside—the stable area and the infield.

The Derby Museum is located next to Gate 1 of Churchill Downs at 704 Central Avenue in Louisville. For information, call (502) 637-1111 or visit www.derbymuseum.org.

the early twentieth century, however, Progressivism came to the state's educational system. Calls for reform spurred legislators into action, especially as other southern states bolstered their public education systems.

In 1906, the state chartered two regional normal schools for teacher training at Richmond (which eventually became Eastern Kentucky University) and Bowling Green (which eventually became Western Kentucky University). Murray State University and Morehead State also got their start as normal schools, created in 1922. In 1908, the pace of reform increased. One act required a public high school in each county and enacted a minimum school tax. Another bill abolished the previous school district system (in which

Famous Sons and Daughters: Lionel Hampton

Musician
(April 20, 1909–August 31, 2002)

The master of the vibraphone, jazz giant Lionel Hampton was born in Louisville, and Kentucky claims him as a native son. He only lived in the Falls City briefly, however, before he and his mother moved first to Birmingham, Alabama, and then, in about 1916, to Chicago. Hampton first began playing the drums at the Holy Rosary Academy in Kenosha, Wisconsin. By the late 1920s, he was in California, and in 1930 Louis Armstrong hired him as a drummer for a gig at a Los Angeles nightclub. Impressed, Armstrong invited Hampton to record with him and got him playing the vibraphone.

In 1936, Hampton joined the Benny Goodman quartet, one of the first racially integrated jazz groups. The group's success made Hampton a big name in the Swing Era, and in 1940 he formed the Lionel Hampton Orchestra. Over the years, the group proved consistently popular and an important incubator of jazz talent.

Hampton received a large number of prestigious musical awards, even having the Music School at the University of Idaho named after him in 1987. He is honored in the Kentucky Music Museum and received the Governor's Lifetime Achievement Award from Kentucky.

100 school-age children constituted a district, giving Kentucky 9,500 districts by 1907) and made the county the basic unit. Reformers blanketed the state giving speeches in support of education and urging greater taxpayer support for schools. Local funding leaped dramatically as speakers harangued over 60,000 people in the so-called Whirlwind Campaigns of 1908 and 1909.

Taking their cue from the settlement houses founded among immigrant communities in large cities, other Progressive reformers brought rural settlement schools to the Appalachians. Using private funds and staffed largely by middle- and upper-class women who felt a missionary calling, the settlement schools offered literacy training and vocational and industrial education to mountain people out of reach of the public schools.

Katherine Pettit and May Stone founded the first such school, Hindman Settlement School in Knott County in 1902. They chose Hindman, they later said, because of the appeal of one old mountaineer. The old man told them that "when he was a lad, hoeing corn on the steep hillsides… oftentimes when he came to the end of the row, he used to look up the creek and down the creek and wonder if anybody would ever come and 'larn' him anything. He said 'Nobody ever came and nobody ever went out,' and he just grew up without knowing anything, but he wanted the 'younguns' that were there now to have their chance."

Hindman's co-founder Pettit moved on to help establish the Pine Mountain Settlement School in Harlan County, which began operations in 1911. Caney Junior College in Knott County opened in 1923, evolving out of a rural community center founded by Alice Lloyd, a reformer from Boston. In all, some 200 missionary and settlement schools were established in Appalachia between 1875 and 1920.

Adult education also attracted reformers' attention. In 1910, 12.1 percent of adult Kentuckians—about 200,000 people—were illiterate. In 1911 Rowan County educator Cora Wilson Stewart organized "moonlight schools" to teach people to read at night. "Illiterates, more than any other class, are chained to labor by day," Stewart wrote. But night school also had its problems: "Bad roads with innumerable gullies, high hills and unbridged streams were obstacles to overcome. Besides the county had been, at one time, a feud county and the people were not accustomed to venturing out much after night. It was decided to have the schools on moonlight nights, and let the moon light them on their way to school."

The moonlight schools enjoyed remarkable success, although Stewart tended to exaggerate just how much success. In 1914 she received $5,000 from the state and established the Kentucky Illiteracy Commission. During its six-year existence, the Commission published textbooks and taught reading to hundreds of people, but the illiteracy rate remained stubbornly high—8.4 percent of Kentuckians could not read in 1920. The small schoolhouse where Stewart initiated her moonlight-school campaign still stands. It is located in Morehead near the Rowan County Library.

Like many Progressive reforms, the frenzied efforts to fix education yielded solid gains but did not usher in an educational millennium. Kentucky increased its per-pupil spending by 238 percent between 1900 and 1920, but found its standing in the region and the nation declining. From fourth in the South in per-pupil spending in 1900, the state fell to eleventh in 1920. While its spending had been half the national average in 1900, it had fallen to one third by 1920. Kentucky was pedaling furiously but still falling behind. Those disappointing results sapped the political will to enact further significant reforms for decades to come.

Progressivism came to Kentucky like a shy suitor—late, a little bumbling, and overly cautious—but it did come. Despite the cautionary legacy left by the assassination of Goebel, Progressivism left its mark; Kentucky in 1920 looked substantially different from Kentucky in 1900. Women were voting; alcohol was legally forbidden; more children were out of fields and factories and in school; corporations faced at least a semblance of public regulation. On the bleaker side, the state's African-American population led more constricted public lives—sequestered in separate and unequal schools, libraries, housing, hotels, and train cars—because of changes made during this period.

Assaults on Provincialism

Progressive reformers had changed the look of the state, but deeper cultural continuities remained. Despite all the talk of modernity and progress, Kentucky remained a largely rural and agricultural state; much of its population dwelled in relative isolation and a contented provincialism. No phalanx of do-gooders from Frankfort or Louisville or Boston had changed that. But greater change was coming in the form of a wartime mobilization and a decade of disconcerting confrontation with modernist culture.

Kentuckians embraced neutrality when World War I broke out in Europe in 1914. The war brought prosperity to the state's farmers and coal operators as wartime supply disruptions and overseas demand boosted prices. When the United States did enter the conflict in April 1917, Kentuckians embraced the war with equal fervor. "To Hell with the Hohenzollerns and Hapsburgs," Henry Watterson trumpeted. Anti-German sentiment swelled, and several prominent German immigrant institutions in Louisville became circumspect about their origins. The German Insurance Company, for example, became the Liberty Insurance Company. "The time has passed when 'America' will be known as a nation composed of all nationalities," noted the company in justifying the name change. "We are 'Americans' to the core."

More than 84,000 soldiers from Kentucky fought in the war. Just under 13,000 of these were African Americans, serving in segregated units. Some 2,400 Kentuckians died in the conflict, a third killed in action, the other two thirds from accident or disease. This wartime mobilization helped break down Kentucky's provincialism. Rural boys who had never been out of their home county shipped out to different states for training and all the way overseas to fight. They came back with a greater appreciation for the wider world. "I would not take a thousand dollars," wrote one soldier from Burkesville, "for what I have seen and learned during war."

For the first time in national history, the Army did not group soldiers by state units, so Kentucky boys rubbed shoulders with other southerners, with Westerners, and even with Yankees. The nation also came to Kentucky. Camp (later Fort) Knox just south of Louisville opened during World War I as a training ground for artillery; Camp Zachary Taylor on the outskirts of Louisville oversaw the training and distribution of some 125,000 troops from Kentucky, Indiana, and Illinois during the war years.

Louisville's municipal leaders had campaigned hard for Camp Zachary Taylor. To seal the deal, however, the Army wanted Louisville cleaned up. It feared the offerings of Louisville's red-light district and did not want the debauching of untutored rural boys to take place on its watch. In 40 years of service, one army officer told city officials, he "had never seen a city anywhere in the world where vice is more open than it is in your city." The Army's clean-up campaign fit right into the plans of Louisville's cadres of Progressive reformers. Along Louisville's notorious West Green Street, reformers shuttered the houses of ill repute in 1917, rechristening the avenue Liberty Street.

Must-See Sites: Kentucky Music

The International Bluegrass Music Museum

The Bluegrass Museum keeps alive the memory of the musical pioneers who invented the bluegrass genre, which was exported from Kentucky to the rest of the nation through radio and other mass media. Most prominent, of course, is Bill Monroe—who was born in Rosine, Kentucky—who singlehandedly gave rise to bluegrass in the early twentieth century. The Kentucky legislature has named Monroe's "Blue Moon of Kentucky" an official state song.

The Museum houses interpretive exhibits, posters, costumes, instruments, and other memorabilia from Bluegrass musicians. It also has a Hall of Honor, to which it adds new inductees every year. The first group, in 1991, included Monroe and two of his early bandmates, Lester Flatt and Earl Scruggs, who later left Monroe for a successful career as a bluegrass tandem. Finally, the museum is also behind a video oral history project featuring over 200 surviving members of the bluegrass pioneer generation. The taped interviews will be housed at the museum.

The museum also celebrates bluegrass as a folk music, a "front-porch" music, and not just as an established musical genre. To that end, it offers jam sessions on the first and third Saturdays of each month, and fosters the teaching and learning of Bluegrass by interested visitors.

The museum is located in RiverPark Center in Owensboro, 117 Daviess Street. Call (270) 926-7891, or visit www.bluegrass museum.org.

The Country Music Highway

Officially designated one of America's Byways by the United States Department of Transportation, the highway is United States Route 23 running through Kentucky from the Ohio border to the Virginia line. It earned the name Country Music Highway because of the number of country-music entertainers that hail from towns along the Route 23 corridor. It was during the early twentieth century that "mountain music" first moved from being largely a homegrown affair to being broadcast, recorded, and marketed to a national audience.

The most notable among the early stars was Loretta Lynn, who actually started singing by mimicking songs she heard on the radio. Lynn's hometown of Butcher Holler is off Route 23 south of Paintsville, and the old frame house where she grew up still stands. Members of Lynn's family generally escort visitors on tours of the house.

Famous Sons and Daughters: Bill Monroe

Musician
(September 13, 1911–September 9, 1996)

Monroe grew up to be "the father of bluegrass music," although his birthplace and childhood home in the western Kentucky town of Rosine lies far from both the Bluegrass and the eastern Kentucky mountains most frequently associated with that type of music. Monroe learned to play the mandolin from his uncle, and during the 1920s teamed with his brother Charlie to form the Monroe Brothers. They first performed on radio shows in North Carolina in 1927. In the mountains of North Carolina, rather than Kentucky, Monroe absorbed the influence of mountain music on his own style, which was not christened "bluegrass" until the 1950s.

In 1938, Bill and Charlie split up, and Bill went on to form the Bluegrass Boys. The band joined Nashville's WSM radio station in 1939 and toured throughout the South during the 1940s. During his long career, Monroe sold more than 25 million records, and as producer, mentor, and teacher, influenced many well-known country and bluegrass musicians. A member of the Grand Ole Opry, the Country Music Hall of Fame, and the Rock and Roll Hall of Fame, Monroe suffered a stroke in 1996 and died four days shy of his 85th birthday.

religious leaders found their authority undercut by a national culture that celebrated consumerism, fashion, and the "good life." David Wark Griffith, a Kentuckian from Oldham County, was one of the first to realize the storytelling potential of motion pictures. In the late 1910s, he used innovative camera and staging techniques to tell long dramatic stories, paving the way for the movies' heyday in the 1920s.

Opulent movie palaces such as the Rialto in Louisville—which opened in 1921 at a cost of $1 million and featured marble staircases and imported crystal chandeliers—showed the movies had definitely come of age. Loew's State Theater opened in Louisville in 1928 with a Spanish baroque design that featured fountains, statues, and make-believe stars twinkling in a ceilinged sky. After suffering through tough times in the 1980s and 1990s, the theater has reopened as the Louisville Palace, offering a living memory of cinema's golden age. Less grand but certainly as influential were the movie houses in Kentucky's smaller cities and towns.

One image repeatedly presented in the new media was that of the "new woman." Having gained her political independence with the vote, the "new woman" sought her social and emotional independence. Frank talk (for the 1920s) of female sexuality, new female fashions, and a vision of female independence percolated into Kentucky, although the urban areas saw more actual "new women" than the rural areas. Still, wherever they appeared, they generally caused a stir. One Kentucky woman recalled the negative comments her mother received when she began wearing pants and riding astride horses (rather than sidesaddle) in the 1920s.

While the movies brought Hollywood to Kentucky, radio took some of Kentucky out to the nation. Radio's voracious quest for content gave a jump start to college sports in the state and brought national prominence to the Kentucky Derby. Under the leadership of executive Matt Winn, Churchill Downs came back from near-bankruptcy to become the premier racetrack in the country, with the Derby as its signature race. After Regret became the first filly to win the race in 1915, her owner proclaimed the Derby "the greatest race in America at the present time,… I don't care whether she [Regret] ever starts again." In 1985, the race got its own museum, located right next to Churchill Downs, which depicts the whole history of the "most exciting two minutes in sports," which has become the Derby's tagline.

Radio also featured nationally syndicated music shows, which mined the rural areas and the ethnic groups of America for talent. Traditional folk music that had only ever been performed live for family, church, and community gatherings was recorded and disseminated nationwide. Blues artists such as Sarah Martin and Sylvester Weaver emerged from Louisville's African-American community to become national stars. Bluegrass music, a form largely invented by Rosine, Kentucky-born Bill Monroe, and so-called hillbilly music gained national audiences through live radio shows such as WLS Chicago's "National Barn Dance," Nashville's Grand Ole Opry, and Kentucky's own "Renfro Valley Barn Dance." As one Kentuckian put it, "I'd rather listen to [bluegrass artists] Flatt and Scruggs than to Beethoven, and that doesn't mean I'm uncultured. That means I just got different taste."

The impact of the automobile and mass media came together spectacularly in the saga of Floyd Collins, an obscure spelunker who got trapped underground in 1925. The automobile carried the seeds of Collins' adventure. Touring motorists brought money into cash-strapped rural economies and Collins, a dirt farmer in real life, dreamed of finding a rival to Mammoth Cave—a popular tourist destination since the 1890s—to siphon off some of that tourist money into his own pocket. Fortune-hunters like Collins found Colossal Caverns, Salts Cave, Great Onyx Cave, among others. In fact, Collins and his father owned Crystal Cave.

Like other cave owners, Collins tried various tricks to lure tourists away from Mammoth Cave, including changing the road signs and using "cappers," men who jumped on the running boards of Mammoth-bound cars to disparage the big cave and talk up alternative cave destinations. One study estimated that during the 1920s around a third of tourists aiming for Mammoth Cave got diverted before they arrived. The tricks never turned Crystal Cave into a money maker, but Collins had high hopes for Sand Cave, which he discovered in January 1925. Its entrance was just off the road from Cave City on the way to Mammoth. Collins even believed—rightly, as it eventually turned out—that the cave might be connected to Mammoth, thus giving him control over a more accessible entrance to the big cave. The site of Sand Cave is currently within the boundaries of Mammoth Cave National Park.

Dreaming of his fortune, Collins became trapped in Sand Cave on January 30. For the next two weeks, Collins' entrapment and the rescue attempts became the focus of the national media. It was the third biggest news story of the period between the world wars, surpassed only by coverage of Lindbergh's flight across the Atlantic and the later kidnapping of the Lindbergh baby. Newspaper, film, and radio crews invaded this rural section of central Kentucky to bring the nation the Collins story. Soon a circus atmosphere

Must-See Sites: The Robert Penn Warren Birthplace Museum

The museum is located in the small frame house in Guthrie, Kentucky, where Warren spent his early years. He lived 16 years in Guthrie before enrolling at Vanderbilt University and beginning his literary career. His formative experiences in western Kentucky provided him with material for his writing and a frame of reference for confronting the changes in the modern world.

The house itself went through several owners after Warren's family moved out. Finally, a group of local residents purchased it with the idea of preserving it as an homage to the writer. The museum houses photographs, books, and other items relating to Warren's life and work. Given that the Guthrie house is a small museum facing the inevitable difficulties of dramatizing a writer's life, many of the museum's visitors are Warren devotees making a pilgrimage to the site of his birth. His parents are buried in the Guthrie cemetery and, while Penn Warren is not, the city has erected a small memorial marker at the gravesite.

The museum is located at the corner of Third and Cherry Streets in Guthrie. Call (270) 483-2683, or visit www.robertpenn warren.com/birthpla.htm.

developed, with local hawkers selling hamburgers, balloons, and Collins souvenirs to the assembled mass. Collins died underground and the outsiders packed up and left, but the spectacle demonstrated in dramatic fashion the erosion of rural Kentucky's isolation.

Many of the images retailed by the mass media in the 1920s showed a world where traditional values held little sway, where the old moral guidelines were being questioned. These changes had a chilling effect on Progressivism, which had built its reform momentum on a moral critique of the industrial world. The public's impatience with Progressive sermonizing came clear in the racetrack issue that dominated political discussions in the mid-1920s.

Progressives and prohibitionists from the prewar period came together in the 1920s in an effort to close down horse racing and pari-mutuel betting in Kentucky, which they accused of buying legislative favors, corrupting youth, and generally promoting vice. "Like most Kentuckians, I am proud of our state's tradition in the breeding of thoroughbred horses, and I get a thrill out of attending the Kentucky Derby," Alben Barkley, at the time an anti-racing Democratic candidate for governor, wrote in his memoirs. "However, I felt strongly that the influence exerted at that time by the Kentucky Jockey Club was an unhealthy thing, and that it should be eradicated." As the reformers began their attack on the tracks, organizers of the Derby floated the idea of moving the race to Chicago.

The issue split the state Democratic party severely, culminating in the 1927 gubernatorial election. Democratic nominee J.C.W. Beckham supported the anti-racing movement and had fought a heated primary battle with pro-racing forces in his own party. So disgusted was the losing Democratic faction with Beckham that they turned out for the Republican candidate. When the results came in, every Democratic candidate but Beckham won. Moral reform was dead. As one newspaper editorialized, "evidently a majority of the voters in Kentucky prefer the Derby to the Democratic party."

The public also turned on Prohibition, which had earlier been embraced with relative enthusiasm, in another example of the waning attractiveness of the Progressives' moral vision. In the late 1920s, the Hearst newspapers ran a nationwide essay contest, asking readers to reflect on the Prohibition experiment. One essayist, Dr. Garfield Howard of Gatliff, Kentucky, reflected the growing disenchantment in the state: "The law prohibiting murder does not prevent murder. Neither does the fear of a literal hell produce Christians. The prohibition law is the greatest enemy to temperance. In fact it prohibits nothing but temperance. It causes wholesale intemperance."

Federal prosecutors had vowed at the beginning of the decade to make Louisville "whiskey-proof"; a decade later, one officer marveled at the sheer variety of alcoholic beverages found during a raid on one Louisville club. Stories circulated about the best places to get liquor. One hotel bell captain would supposedly stop the elevator between floors to transact business with thirsty customers. Paducah humorist Irvin S. Cobb once remarked that Prohibition enforcement was so tough in Kentucky that "a thirsty stranger may have to walk all of a half a block to find a place where he can get a drink."

Prohibition gutted the state's distilling industry—Louisville alone lost 8,000 jobs when the distilleries closed—but the long Kentucky tradition of moonshining took on new prominence. One Clinton county man, for example, remembered how his father turned to moonshining after taking the family's tobacco harvest to the warehouse to sell and discovering that after a year of labor in the fields, he owed the warehouse twenty cents. The corn whiskey they sold, on the other hand, "sold for thirty-two dollars [which was] more money than they had worked out in the three years before." This family stopped selling liquor once they got back on their financial feet, but others did not and federal and local agents had regular gun battles with Kentucky's home distillers during the 1920s, enhancing the state's violent reputation.

Just like other industries in the state, moonshining soon became a big business with extensive outside capital and control. Distillers on Golden Pond, between the Tennessee and Cumberland Rivers, supplied Chicago's gangland rum-runners and earned their corn liquor a national reputation. The western Kentucky backcountry and extensive waterways made transportation of the hooch and evasion of law enforcement relatively simple.

The energy behind reform also petered away because of the continued power of the political bosses. Far from democratizing the system, it seemed as if the political reforms of the previous decade had only empowered the bosses further. In 1912, for example, the state had finally taken charge of the public roads directly through the creation of a state highway department—a classic Progressive reform. But the department soon became the plaything of the bosses. The construction and maintenance of highways yielded an almost endless supply of money and jobs—from weed-cutter to construction foreman—to dole out to political supporters. The highway department was, the *Courier-Journal* editorialized, a "bold, imperious machine, manned by politicians, dictating policies of government, commanding the fear of the electorate that want roads."

The continued power of the bosses became clear when Governor Flem Sampson fired political boss Ben Johnson from his post as state highway commissioner in 1929 in an effort to seize control of the department. Johnson took revenge. Using his strong alliances in the legislature, Johnson had lawmakers render Sampson politically impotent by reducing the governor's appointment powers. Soon afterward, the legislature gave Johnson back his job as head of the highway department.

ANTI-MODERNISM

While the bosses thus made their peace with 1920s Progressivism, many Kentucky traditionalists went to war with 1920s cultural modernism. Bethel Woman's College in Hopkinsville, for example, expelled a fashionable young student who bobbed her hair. The traditionalist backlash drew strength from the growing fundamentalist religious movement of the 1920s. As mainstream Protestant denominations embraced a more liberal theology toward the end of the nineteenth century, fundamentalists began stressing the inerrancy of the Bible as the literal Word of God. When fundamentalists looked about them in the 1920s, they saw disrespect for biblical values everywhere and a corrupt society that celebrated sin. The anxious formed purity leagues to denounce dancing, gambling, and the movies. Their denunciations echoed from the pulpits of the more conservative ministers, sometimes dividing congregations against themselves. With Prohibition in force, said Kentucky-born Baptist minister William Bell Riley, the next challenge was to take on "the new infidelity, known as modernism."

One development above all galvanized fundamentalist opposition: the scientific theory of evolution. Evolution surely showed the depravity of modern science, since it denied the biblical account of creation. Riley called it "propaganda of infidelity, palmed off in the name of science." Kentucky became the first state where fundamentalism displayed enough power to mount a serious legal challenge to the teaching of evolution in the schools. In 1921, legislators introduced bills banning the teaching of "Darwinism, Atheism, Agnosticism, or the Theory of Evolution." The lower house deadlocked 41–41 on the bill when it came to a vote in March 1922, sparking a frenzied search by both sides for a tie-breaking vote. Eventually, the bill's opponents prevailed 42–41 and the anti-evolutionists went down to defeat. Critical to the bill's demise had been testimony by leading liberal clergy from Louisville showing the differences of religious opinion on Darwinism.

The anti-evolutionists did not give up. Kentucky Wesleyan College suspended a teacher in 1923 for supporting evolution, and fundamentalist forces introduced new bills in 1926 and 1928. These last efforts lacked legislative support, however, and the anti-evolution movement sputtered and faded by the end of the decade.

The Ku Klux Klan offered another avenue for the traditionalist attack on modernism. The modern Klan, reborn in 1915 on a hilltop in Georgia, came to Kentucky in the early 1920s. In some ways, Kentucky offered little to get the Klansmen's juices flowing. African Americans were already being kept "in their place" thanks to the spreading web of segregationist legislation. Jews, Catholics, and foreign-born immigrants—whom the modern Klan also targeted as undesirable—represented less than ten percent of the adult population and were scarce outside Louisville. Still, as many as 30,000 Kentuckians joined the Klan's ranks during the 1920s, drawn to its anti-modernist message that white Protestant Anglo-Saxons were losing control of the nation. Various towns across the state "whitened" themselves by driving off their black populations by force or various other means of intimidation.

Like the anti-evolution movement, the Klan sputtered and faded by the end of the decade. Again, leading public figures found the courage to speak out against the movement, contributing to its demise. In Lexington, Owensboro, Louisville, Hopkinsville, and other locales, county and municipal officials either spoke out against the Klan or forbade them to meet on public property. The Lexington *Herald*, the voice of Progressivism in the state, wrote that "there is no place in America for a secret organization of this kind."

Anxiety about the modernist age dawning in Kentucky did not limit itself to religious hardliners and redneck yahoos. Many felt that as the new age came on something else irretrievable might be slipping away. The 1920s saw a resurgence of serious literary output by Kentucky authors that subtly portrayed the conflict between living folk traditions and the alienation and anonymity of modern mass society.

Literary Extracts: Robert Penn Warren

One of the most prominent American writers, Warren was born on April 24, 1905, and grew up in Guthrie, Kentucky. He attended Vanderbilt University, where he fell in with the group known as the Fugitives and later the southern Agrarians. His academic career began at Louisiana State University in 1934 and culminated with his retirement from the Yale English Department in 1973.

His writings are voluminous and of all types: essays, criticism, and drama, as well as fiction and poetry. An incomplete list of his most famous works includes *All the King's Men* (1946), *Night Rider* (1939), and *Now and Then: Poems 1976–1978* (1979). He won the Pulitzer Prize three times, and is the only writer to win for both fiction and poetry. He was the nation's first poet laureate and received dozens of other awards.

Warren wrote until the very end of his life. One of his most remarkable feats was to improve the quality of his poetry steadily as he got older, and his poetic output outstripped his other writings in his later years. He died on September 15, 1989, and was buried in Stratton, Vermont.

Warren wrote a memoir about his father toward the end of his life. In the following excerpt from his 1988 *Portrait of a Father*, he tells of his father's move from Tennessee to Guthrie, Kentucky, where Warren would later be born. In it, he captures the encroachment of modern life on the small towns of rural Kentucky in the early twentieth century:

> Since my father had not felt himself "established," he had put aside earlier ambitions… to move to a new town which had great promise, a few miles away up in Kentucky. There everything seemed promising….
>
> So there came Guthrie, on the edge of a region called Pondy Woods, with good farm country to back it on three sides. It was a brilliant idea, too, to name the town Guthrie, for a Mr. Guthrie who is said to have been the president, or something important, of the railroad. But the idea did not pay off. The ungrateful Mr. Guthrie never gave the town a railroad "roundhouse," and only a generation later did the town get a "creosote plant" for treating cross ties….
>
> A large hotel was built at the new railroad station, with a newsstand where later you could come by the *New Republic* or *Poetry* magazine, if you were that ilk of traveler….
>
> The hotel has long since been demolished. Some of the stores on Main Street are abandoned. A big highway two miles off had skipped the town, and businesses that catered to that heavy traffic had moved toward customers. Some of the more pretentious residences, well and solidly built, are sometimes empty. The automobile and the good road have been hard on many of the old "market towns."

Kentucky had produced a crop of nationally renowned authors during the previous generation, but these writers had mostly produced sentimental stories with a Victorian sensibility. James Lane Allen of Lexington published *The Choir Invisible* in 1897 dealing with a man overcoming his forbidden desire for a married woman during Kentucky's frontier period. John Fox Jr. wrote *The Little Shepherd of Kingdom Come* in 1903 about a mountain orphan adopted by an aristocratic Lexington family; he sees the family torn apart by the Civil War but then rejoined in a postwar reconciliation. *The Little Shepherd* sold more than a million copies and was the basis for several motion pictures. Annie Fellows Johnston's wildly popular *Little Colonel* series explored the same themes of wartime loss and postwar healing.

The writers who emerged in the 1920s covered somewhat different territory, although again firmly anchored in a Kentucky landscape and history. Almost all of them hailed from rural areas or small towns and their work focused on agrarian themes. Elizabeth Madox Roberts, one of the most celebrated of these writers at the time, wrote *The Time of Man* in 1926, which focused on the strength and dignity of rural people as they confronted the challenges presented by the outside world. "Again and again... she returned... to Kentucky," wrote a literary acquaintance. "It evidently underlay the outbranching experience, folded shadowily into the typical scenes of an author's life—an immense territorial ghost."

Robert Penn Warren, Kentucky's most prominent man of letters, touched on similar themes in his early work. Born in Guthrie in western Kentucky in 1905, Warren went to Vanderbilt University and became part of the southern Agrarian literary movement fronted by John Crowe Ransome. The group disparaged the vision of a modern progressive-industrial utopia produced by leftist writers of the era and advocated by champions of the New South. Instead, they stressed the local and the regional and the value of a life rooted in a particular landscape. For this they were labeled Agrarians—they celebrated the "simplicity and cultural integrity of the husbandman's world view," in the words of one literary historian. Warren's writings—short stories, novels, poems, and criticism—eventually ranged far beyond the concerns of the Agrarians, but frequently relied on Kentucky settings to explore larger themes. He remains the only writer to have won a Pulitzer Prize for both fiction and poetry. His boyhood home in Guthrie has been turned into a museum honoring his literary contributions.

Somewhat later, during the 1930s, another group of writers came out of rural Kentucky—this time out of Appalachia. Jesse Stuart, born in 1906 in Greenup County, published his first collection of poems in 1934 and his first collection of short stories in 1936. Stuart too had come under the influence of the Agrarians, heeding the advice of his Agrarian mentor Donald Davidson—"Stick to your hills, Jesse, and write about the people you know." Stuart's work painted vivid portraits of the mountain people of W-Hollow, and he returned to them again and again for material. Stuart quickly became the most popular Kentucky author in his home state.

Another Appalachian-born writer—Wayne County's Harriette L. Simpson Arnow—won a National Book Award in 1954 for *The Dollmaker*, which again addressed the conflict between modern industrial civilization and the traditional values of rural America. The heroine of the novel moves from Kentucky to Detroit (echoing Simpson's real-life migration from Kentucky to Michigan), where she fights in vain against the dehumanization of the modern world.

These writers all gave voice to the widely felt cultural anxieties of the 1920s, rooted in the new century's increasing pace of change. Kentuckians had seen modern America and come away with a deeply felt ambivalence. It was an ambivalence that would not change much as the earth-shaking events of the next two decades unfolded.

8

DEPRESSION AND DELIVERANCE

The Great Depression began in Kentucky—as it did in most other agricultural states—well before the stock market crash of October 1929. Farmers saw crop values tumble after World War I, led by a collapse in tobacco prices, and by 1928 Kentucky stood near the bottom of the national rankings for farm income. A severe drought in 1930 only added to the farmers' misery as they watched their crops literally wither on the vine.

As the rest of the national economy followed the agricultural economy into ruin during the early 1930s, traditionalists ran out of answers. The scope of the crisis outstripped the resources of the family, the community, the county—the traditional circles of help Kentuckians relied upon. "The people are going to starve to death," one Kentuckian lamented, "unless something is done soon." Federal action in the form of the New Deal, welcomed initially as salvation from starvation, became accepted and expected. When World War II ratcheted up the federal presence dramatically, it brought the state out of Depression and into a postwar period that posed new challenges to Kentucky's traditions of localism.

COMING HOME TO KENTUCKY

During the 1930s, Kentucky's population grew faster than the national average—the first time that had happened since before the Civil War. Given the poverty and hard times in the state, this seems odd. But people found rural poverty somewhat easier to bear than urban poverty. Many Kentuckians who had migrated during the 1920s to the cities within the state and beyond—to the industrial cities of the South, the Midwest, and the East—came back to crowd in with their families as those urban economies went bust in the 1930s. At the very least, the rural farmstead allowed people to scrounge subsistence from the land. By 1940, in fact, fewer Kentuckians lived in the state's urban areas than in 1930.

What they found when they came back was not pretty. Debt-ridden farmers saw the value of their holdings drop by nearly a third between 1930 and 1935. A medical worker in the mountains in 1931 described an "acute famine" in the communities around her. Even as people came back to their rural homes, others picked up and left, tramping the state in search of jobs.

Years later, William Collins recalled his experiences in a memoir:

> During the 1920s, my family and I lived in Ashland, Kentucky. I was a salesman for a retail furniture store at a salary of $250 per month. Like most young men, I spent my income without saving part of it for rainy days. We bought a home on the installment plan to be paid for at the rate of $50 per month. Everything went fine until July, 1929, when public works came to a standstill. Sales dropped to less than enough gross to pay overhead expenses. I was without a paycheck within a few weeks. Fortunately, I received $250 for turning my mortgage over to someone else. We stored our furniture and made a beeline for relatives and friends in Casey and Adair Counties in south-central Kentucky. Not realizing conditions were nationwide, I spent my scant savings in search of employment and returned to my family without a job or money.
>
> I was desperate and so were my family and relatives. I had only one way out of an oncoming tragedy, and to it I went; not through pride, but because it was the only avenue of escape. I had bought a 34-acre ridge farm, when I was teaching school, and for some unexplainable reason, I was still in possession of it. Imagine a man, wife, and three children moving to a hill farm without money, livestock, furniture or chickens, and adjusting from a $3,000-yearly salary standard of living, to the hardships and drawbacks this last chance had to offer. It looked pretty gloomy, but we were among friends and relatives. Embarrassing as it was, we accepted their hospitality with outstretched arms. A relative loaned me a cow and the use of his team and tools for farm and garden use. A few chickens were obtained from neighbors, and we made, bought, and

Literary Extracts:
The Federal Writers' Project

One of the ways the New Deal put people to work was to commission writers to produce guides to each state's history and culture. The Federal Writers' Project eventually produced such guides for every state in the union, many of which were quite insightful about the local culture. In the following excerpt, the Kentucky guidebook's author takes a shot at generalizing about Kentuckians:

> The rural Kentuckian, whether clad in faded overalls or imported woolens, is an individualist. The rustic lolling at the street corners of towns and villages may give every evidence of being lost or out of place; but try to get the better of him in a trade and often he will prove master of the situation. He may be ragged, dirty, and ignorant, but he is still endowed with something of the unawed self-reliance and resourceful wit of the pioneer.
>
> Wherever a Kentuckian may be, he is more than willing to boast of the beauties and virtues of his native State. He believes without reservation that Kentucky is the garden spot of the world, and is ready to dispute with anyone who questions the claim.
>
> —from *The WPA Guide to Kentucky* (1939).

borrowed enough furniture to sparsely furnish our four-room framed house. This was not a second honeymoon, but the best that circumstances had to offer.

When family resources were exhausted, many of the destitute crowded the relief rolls across the state, but the old county-based system of poor relief soon broke down. Under that system, the county court magistrates reviewed each request for aid each month. With limited resources—one study found that county aid budgets averaged about nine cents per person—the county bosses picked and chose among claimants based on favoritism, politics, family connections, and a host of other factors unrelated to actual need. "Things don't look good," one small-town attorney wrote. "There is no employment and times are extremely hard.... The people feel that there is something radically wrong. In fact, we all know there is something wrong."

The situation in the cities was not much better. In Danville, a quarter of the population survived on local charity in 1932, compared to five percent five years earlier. In Louisville, the state's major industrial center, almost a quarter of white workers and over a third of black workers were unemployed in 1932, and countless more had their wages and hours cut back. The city's meager work-relief program employed just over 2,000 people out of more than 11,000 who signed up. The jobs paid just 30 cents an hour for odd jobs three days a week

Bank failures aggravated the situation further, as people's "rainy day" savings vanished. Between 1930 and 1932, about one of every four banks in the state failed, including the South's largest bank, the BancoKentucky. When BancoKentucky went under in 1930, it took several other financial institutions with it, including two African-American savings banks that had deposited their funds there. Depositors' money remained locked up as the banking system reorganized, and even when banks reopened in the late 1930s, they generally returned only about 60 cents on the dollar to account holders.

By 1932, writer Robert Penn Warren observed that people thought that "things lay beyond any individual effort to change them." The depth of the crisis had overwhelmed efforts at self-help and self-reliance. Something else needed to be done. "You had to have action," Warren wrote, "or die." The election of Franklin Delano Roosevelt to the presidency in 1932 promised some action.

THE NEW DEAL

Roosevelt's election came with a bewildering array of programs. One of the president's primary goals in the early days of his first administration was simply to get money into the hands of people who needed it. In May 1933 Congress created the Federal Emergency Relief Administration, and Roosevelt put his pal Harry Hopkins in charge of it. In two hours, Hopkins spent $5 million, offering it to states in the form of matching grants for direct relief to the poor. With the infusion of federal aid, whole counties in Kentucky went on relief—over 85 percent of families in Morgan County went on the dole when federal funds became available, 68 percent in Magoffin County. Counties across the state saw similar percentages.

Other programs aimed to put the unemployed back to work by putting them on the federal payroll. The Civilian Conservation Corps enlisted 80,000 young Kentuckians at $1 a day to work in the state's forests on erosion-prevention projects, reforestation, and trail- and cabin-building. The Works Progress Administration (WPA), created in 1935, employed 60,000 people in Kentucky by Christmas 1935. One woman later recalled that her parents "didn't make enough to make a living on the farm, and my father went to work with the WPA. It embarrassed him and humiliated him." But Elsie Welte of Newport told WPA interviewers, "We believe in WPA." She had gotten a job with a WPA sewing center, making clothes for the needy. "It sure did help because the bills were really getting ahead of us.... With this money we are started to get on our feet."

WPA workers constructed schools, post offices, parks, community centers, and a host of other public buildings. Their legacy is seen all over the state—in Morgan County's high school, in Cadiz's old post office (now an art museum), in the administration building at Louisville's municipal airport Bowman Field, and in the Jefferson County Fiscal Court building in downtown Louisville.

The WPA put librarians to work by funding "pack horse librarians," who brought books on horseback to remote areas in Kentucky's Cumberland Mountains. It put artists to work painting murals on post office walls. It put academics to work conducting the first systematic archaeological digs in the state, which employed hundreds of fieldworkers. As one study of Kentucky archaeology summarized, "WPA relief labor had a revolutionary effect on Kentucky archaeology."

WPA jobs saved many people from starvation and despair, but as federal programs reached into the fastnesses of Appalachia, the Pennyroyal, and the Jackson Purchase, the traditional isolation of Kentucky's rural communities eroded further. The grander public-works projects undertaken by the Public Works Administration, the Rural Electrification Administration, and especially the Tennessee Valley Authority worked toward the same end. The TVA's damming of the Kentucky River in the western part of the

Must-See Sites: New Deal Parks & Forests

Kentucky Dam Village State Resort Park

The Kentucky Dam illustrates the increasing role played by the federal government in the Kentucky economy during the 1930s. The Tennessee Valley Authority (TVA), created by President Roosevelt in 1933 to manage the flood plain of the Tennessee River, worked as an overarching economic development agency, transforming rural economies all along the drainage of the Tennessee. The Kentucky Dam impounds the Tennessee River to create Kentucky Lake. Linked by canal to neighboring Lake Barkley, which was created when the Army Corps of Engineers dammed the Cumberland River in the 1960s, the two lakes together make up one of the largest manmade bodies of water in the world.

Construction began on the 206-foot-tall Kentucky Dam in 1938, and it opened in 1944. To house the workers at the site, the TVA built a small village with cottages, a hospital, and several other buildings. These were sold, along with the surrounding acreage, to the state after the completion of the dam, and form the nucleus of the present-day state park. Many of the cottages now available for overnight stays were originally TVA worker cottages, and the Village Green Lodge is housed in the old hospital building.

Kentucky Dam Village State Resort Park is located on US Highway 641 in the western Kentucky town of Gilbertsville, on the edge of the Land Between the Lakes National Recreation Area. Call (270) 362-4271 or visit parks.ky.gov/resortparks/kd.

The Daniel Boone National Forest

Established by President Roosevelt in 1937 as the Cumberland National Forest (it was renamed the Daniel Boone in 1966), the Forest covers over 706,000 acres in a long, narrow strip along the Cumberland Plateau stretching north from the Tennessee border almost to Ohio. The purpose of the national forest is resource conservation and management, rather than recreational development, but the forest attracts over five million visitors annually. The Daniel Boone is one of the most heavily utilized national forests in the South.

The national forest was established to protect the wide swaths of mountain land that had been subject to uncontrolled logging and mining during the first three decades of the twentieth century. The goal was to prevent further depletion of the region's natural resources and move toward a policy of sustainable yield, meaning that logging and other extractive activities are tightly controlled by the federal government. A reminder of the earlier era of exploitation can be found in the remains of the Barren Fork coal camp, located within the national forest.

The Daniel Boone contains a large number of natural attractions, including dozens of natural arches, Red River Gorge, and the 269-mile Sheltowee Trace trail. It also contains several prehistoric archaeological sites within its boundaries. For more information, call (859) 745-3100 or visit www.southernregion.fs.fed.us/boone.

state, completed in 1945, infused millions of dollars of federal money into the region during construction, provided cheap hydroelectric power to rural communities, and transformed the area into a tourists' paradise.

The New Deal also attempted to tackle the problems of farmers by controlling overproduction. The 1934 Tobacco Control Act offered farmers a federally subsidized floor under tobacco prices if they agreed to mandatory production quotas. The state's farmers signed on to the program, and in 1936 the tobacco harvest fell by 28 percent and income rose by several million dollars. The various federal price-support programs gave needed stability to the state's agriculture, but smaller farmers benefited less than neighbors with larger landholdings. In addition, federal controls called for the killing of livestock to limit production, which naturally raised the ire of people who were starving.

In the short story "Appalachian Patriarch," Kentucky author Jesse Stuart captured the attitude of one mountain farmer who participated in the government program. "I ust to farm these hills. But life is easier now. I 'signed up,'" says Uncle Peter. "I get paid fer not raisin' tobacco. I get paid fer not raisin' corn. I get paid fer not raisin' cane. I get paid to let these old hills take a rest and to take a rest myself. I get paid fer not raisin' hogs. I'm gettin' money fer th' things I have done. I'm takin' it easy."

The federal government also attempted to transform the economic base of rural areas by putting huge swaths of land under federal management through the creation of Daniel Boone National Forest and Mammoth Cave National Park. The Boone National Forest, created in 1937, includes over 706,000 acres in 21 different counties running almost the entire length of the state. The creation of Mammoth Cave National Park in 1941 transformed what had long been a profit-oriented tourist attraction into a 50,000-acre government site.

Looking back in the 1950s, Alben Barkley, Kentucky's senior senator and Democratic majority leader during the Roosevelt years, wrote that

> ... contemporary partisans may criticize shrilly; they may yap and bark and snap at the heels of a giant figure of a

new and stronger social system that came into being under twenty years of Democratic administration. However, I do not think that any administration or any political party will have the nerve to attempt to repeal the fundamental laws passed under Roosevelt and Truman which are now an inseparable part of our way of life.

Federal programs made local governments more dependent on federal largesse, but the New Deal did not obliterate the petty politics of local power bosses. Distribution of federal relief—whether in the form of money or jobs—remained in the hands of county magistrates, who still often heeded the call of party politics and racial bias when determining who qualified.

Roosevelt used New Deal programs to bolster the fortunes of the Democratic party and the fortunes of New Dealers within the party. In Kentucky, the 1938 Democratic primary for US senator, for example, pitted Democratic Governor "Happy" Chandler against incumbent Senator and friend of FDR Alben Barkley. Chandler had state patronage—some of it federally funded—to dole out to supporters, but Barkley had the president and the federal relief agencies campaigning on his side. Barkley won easily.

Barkley later wrote that he "did not appreciate... the introduction of untrue charges that my election had been influenced through improper activities by WPA workers." But journalist Thomas L. Stokes won a Pulitzer Prize for a series of articles that demonstrated that "the WPA... was deep in politics" in Kentucky. WPA offices distributed Barkley campaign literature, and federal officials solicited campaign funds from government employees. In fact, such activities eventually led Congress to forbid political work by federal agencies and employees.

New Deal politics worked wondrously for the state's Democrats. Starting with Roosevelt's landslide in 1932, the state's voters would choose Democrats in almost every state election for the next sixty years. FDR himself carried the state by commanding margins all four times he ran. The New Deal brought change to the party's make-up, however. The black community, which had favored Republicans since the Civil War, gradually abandoned the party of Lincoln for the party of Roosevelt. And eastern mountaineers, who had supported Republicans often out of pro-Unionist sympathies handed down from the Civil War era, shifted to Democratic ranks once the federal government backed their battles to unionize the coal mines.

"Bloody Harlan" and Unionization

The unionization of the American work force following the passage of the Wagner Act in 1935 stands as one of the most significant social changes brought about by government policy during the New Deal years. The Wagner Act gave workers the legal right to join unions and bargain collectively, required employers to recognize such actions by their workers, and created the National Labor Relations Board to make sure both sides acted in good faith. By abandoning the traditional anti-union stance of business leaders, the federal government clearly threw in its lot with the labor movement's long and often bloody struggle to gain collective bargaining rights.

The eastern coal fields of Kentucky offered many examples of that struggle. Between 1880 and 1900, over a third of the 223 labor strikes that occurred in Kentucky took place in the coal regions. Workers campaigned for higher wages, increased mine safety, and union recognition. They met fierce resistance from employers.

The eastern coal fields rose to prominence in the early part of the twentieth century. Until 1912, western Kentucky produced more coal than the eastern part of the state. Promoters had long known about the coal deposits in Appalachia, but rugged terrain, poor transportation and unrelenting violence had prevented exploitation of the deposits. What was mined was generally for household use; small community-owned mines dotted the mountainsides. Some 60 percent of the coal mined in the state in 1900 was burned in Kentucky rather than sold outside the state.

Enter John C. Calhoun Mayo, the man whom Appalachian writer Harry Caudill declared had the greatest impact on the economic life of Kentucky. Born in 1864 in Pike County, Mayo first became a schoolteacher and then a businessman. He traveled throughout eastern Kentucky, chatting up landowners and persuading them to sign broad-form deeds. These gave Mayo the right—for about a dollar per acre—to mine the land. Mountaineers, enticed by the prospect of hard currency, signed over

hundreds of thousands of acres. Mayo promptly formed mining companies of his own and sold off rights to other companies, becoming fabulously wealthy in the process. The eastern coalfield was born.

Boom towns followed, most often built and dominated by the coal companies. Rural residents, amazed by the modern amenities—movie theaters, electricity, libraries, schools—flocked to the towns and then into the mines. The transformation of a rural community could occur with lightning speed; the town of Jenkins in Letcher County bloomed in a few days where previously a single cabin had stood. Harlan County saw its population mushroom to 65,000 in the two decades before 1930. Adding to the sense of dramatic change was an influx of immigrants and blacks

United Mine Workers, Local no. 806, ca. 1913

to a previously racially homogenous region, looking for new opportunities in the mines. "I didn't have any choice," one worker said. "I had a family. They had to eat. There wasn't anything else to do."

Management of the towns varied from the paternalistic to the tyrannical. In the most extreme cases, companies dictated how workers voted, where they lived, and how much they paid for goods in the high-priced company stores. Mary Owsley, whose husband worked as a dynamiter in the coal mines, recounted life in the towns during the Depression years for an interviewer in the 1960s:

> We lived in a company house.... I bought my food from the company store, and we bought our furniture from the company store, and we paid three prices on it. I've seen my husband have to borry from his next pay check—what they call scrip—to buy just medicine and things like that. And we didn't live extravagant either. We paid over 260 some odd dollars for furniture from the coal company. We paid it all back but $20. And when he went and got another job, he bought a truck down there for the furniture. And they took the whole thing away from us. They wouldn't let us pay the $20.

Although union activity could be harshly punished—an activist worker would lose not only his job, but most likely his house, too—union activity persisted. The United Mine Workers formed in 1890, and Kentucky's miners joined nationwide strikes in 1894, 1919, 1922, and 1924. But companies enjoyed the upper hand during the 1920s as coal prices fell from their high WWI levels and UMW membership dwindled from 19,000 in 1912 to less than 1,000 in 1931.

The Depression, however, kicked the coal counties from hard times to desperate times. Workers decided the risks of sitting idle outweighed the risks of confronting the coal operators. Harlan County soon attracted national attention in the confrontation because of the intransigence of the operators and the violence that followed.

During the early 1930s, one third of the county's mines closed and four thousand miners lost their jobs. Miners tramped around the county seeking work or food for their families. Federal relief programs had not yet begun, and the companies—intent on cutting costs—evicted workers from their houses, leaving them homeless, jobless, hungry, and enraged. "The miners, their wives and children live in crumbling shacks, many of them clapboard, through whose cracks pour the lashing mountain winds, rain and snow," wrote one sympathetic observer. "A few crumbs of cornbread usually—a piece of salt pork occasionally—a few pinto beans for the more fortunate—this is their food. 'Last summer we ate grass—this winter I guess we'll eat snow,' said [one] mother."

In May 1931, the rage boiled over into violence in the town of Evarts. Miners ambushed company cars, and miners

Famous Sons and Daughters:
Loretta Lynn

Musician (born April 14, 1935)

A coal miner's daughter—as she sang in one of her songs—Loretta Webb was born at Butcher Holler, Kentucky. She walked several miles everyday to attend school in the town of Van Lear, where she finished the eighth grade. She married Oliver Lynn, age twenty, when she was just thirteen years old. She had four children by the time she was eighteen and learned to play the guitar while singing them lullabies. Shortly after her marriage, she and her husband moved to the state of Washington. In 1960, she appeared briefly on a radio station in Bellingham, Washington, which helped launch her career at Nashville's Grand Ole Opry.

An admirer of Patsy Cline, Lynn took on Cline's mantle as the preeminent female country music singer after Cline's death. She has recorded over fifty albums and had her life documented in an Academy Award-winning film, *Coal Miner's Daughter*, which was based on her autobiography. She has also won a Grammy and several awards from the Country Music Association.

and company guards exchanged gunfire. Four people died. The Communist-controlled National Miners' Union set up soup kitchens to feed hungry miners and proselytize for the workers' revolution. Few miners embraced the cause, even if they did eat the soup, but the Communist presence agitated company owners. "They'll bring a union in here over my dead body," declared one owner. But the next dead body was that of a NMU organizer. This death was followed by beatings of writers who came to report on the conflict and a refusal by county authorities to allow activist student groups into the county to investigate the conditions there. As beatings and threats against union organizers continued, more murders took place. Worker activists car-bombed the county attorney, killing him.

Soon nationally known labor-friendly writers such as John Dos Passos arrived to tour the county and denounce company tyranny. "Everybody knows that the coal industry is sick and that the men working at our most dangerous

Literary Extracts: John Dos Passos

As part of the Writers' Committee (chaired by Theodore Dreiser) of the Communist-controlled National Committee for the Defense of Political Prisoners, leftist writer and journalist Dos Passos visited various Harlan county communities in November 1931, during the miners' strike against the coal operators. In the following excerpt from an essay called "Harlan County Sunset," Dos Passos describes the feeling in the coal towns during the conflict:

Members of the Writers' Committee assured the workers a little shakily that public opinion the whole country over was being aroused in favor of the striking miners of eastern Kentucky. A collection was taken up. But all the time a curious lonesomeness was coming over the hall.

There had been warnings that the gunthugs were coming from Black Mountain to break up the meeting, that Sheriff Blair and his deputies were coming over to arrest everybody present. People were listening to the speeches with one ear cocked for noises outside. Once somebody thought he heard a shot outside and a dozen men ran out to see what the trouble was. The clear fall afternoon light through the gymnasium windows was becoming stained with blue. Slowly and lonesomely the afternoon wore on. At last the speakin' broke up.

On the hillside outside people were melting away into the violet dark. The lights were pumpkincolor in the little stores along the road in the creekbottom. The west flared hot with a huge afterglow of yellow and orange and crimson light against which the high dark hills that hemmed in the Cumberland River cut a sharp razoredge.

Walking down the hill we felt the scary lonesome feeling of the front lines in a lull in the fighting. By the time we got to the road the cars had all gone back to Pineville. We went up to a garage a little piece up the road. Dreiser was standing in the door of the garage looking out into the fading flare of the evening. The garageman said a taxi would be coming back soon. We stood a long time in the door of the garage. I could feel the wonderful breathless hush I'd felt years ago on post [during World War I] in the Avocourt wood. This was war all right.

—from *In All Countries* (1934)

occupation... are badly off," Dos Passos wrote in a 1931 *New Republic* article:

... but few Americans outside of the miners themselves

understand how badly off, or how completely the "American standard of living" attained in some sections during boom years... has collapsed. The coal operators, who have been unable to organize their industry commercially or financially along modern lines, have taken effective common action in only one direction: in an attack against the unions, the wage scales and the living conditions of the men who dig the coal out for them.

A state investigation in 1935 blamed the conflict on the coal operators working in collusion with county officials—together, the report said, they created "a virtual reign of terror." In 1937, a congressional investigation undertaken to stop abuses of the Wagner Act also blamed the hostility of the owners for the violence. Finally, the owners gave in to the law's requirements. The Harlan County Coal Operators' Association signed an agreement recognizing the union, and UMW membership in the county soared to 15,000 by 1940.

The labor movement in other areas of the state did not have the drama or receive the attention that "bloody Harlan" did. Statewide, overall union membership increased in solid if not spectacular fashion. By 1939, Kentucky ranked thirteenth nationally in terms of union membership, with a higher percentage of unionized workers than other southern states. Still, because of its rural character, it was not a hotbed of union activity like the more industrial areas of the Midwest. In fact, lamenting the slow progress of unionization in Louisville, the state's industrial center, one labor leader labeled the city "an open shop town. Labor's been dead, just no nerve at all."

Louisville might have been spared some of the labor troubles that other cities witnessed, because by the late 1930s it was actually doing fairly well compared to other towns of its size, particularly those dependent on a single industry. Louisville's diverse industrial base provided some cushion from the freefall in industrial production, because the Depression affected different industries unevenly. Louisville's tobacco companies, for example, saw few layoffs during the Depression years as Americans lit up increasing numbers of cigarettes to calm their jangled nerves. Louisville produced 85 percent of the nation's supply of ten-cent packs of cigarettes.

The city and the state also got help from the New Dealers' repeal of Prohibition in 1933. Kentuckians enthusiastically supported repeal and the distilleries that had survived the long dry spell restarted production. In 1935, Joseph E. Seagram and Son selected Louisville as the site for their new distillery, the world's largest at the time

By 1937, Louisville seemed to be recovering from the worst effects of the early 1930s. Then it started to rain. In a single month the skies disgorged half of Louisville's average

Madison Street junk yard during the 1937 flood

annual rainfall. The Ohio River began to rise, flooding the city. The Army Corps of Engineers called it a "calamitous inundation of almost Biblical proportions." When the river crested on January 27 at nearly 41 feet—11 feet over the previous record rise of 30 feet in 1884—water covered three quarters of the city. Ninety people died, and the flood

Must-See Sites: Traveling Through Mining's Past

The Barthell Mining Camp

The camp dates back to 1902, when it was the first camp established by the Stearns Coal and Lumber Company. The company got its start when Justus Stearns of Ludington, Michigan, was persuaded to invest in 30,000 acres of southeastern Kentucky timberlands. The company soon discovered coal, opened the Barthell camp, and built the town of Stearns as the hub of a logging and mining empire. At its peak, the Stearns Company controlled over 200 square miles of Kentucky land and employed some 2,200 people in its various mining operations.

Barthell was one of at least 18 mining camps belonging to the company. It closed down for good in 1961, but its closing had been foreshadowed for at least a decade by the decline of neighboring camps. In 1984, the Koger family purchased the land and remaining buildings and opened the site as a living history museum. They have rebuilt, restored, or rehabilitated many of the original buildings, including the miners' houses, the bathhouse, the barbershop, and the doctor's office. Overnight guests today can stay in cottages built on the original sites according to original floor plans, with the significant additions of central heating, air conditioning, and bathrooms. The family also offers guided tours.

Barthell coal camp is located seven miles west of Stearns on State Route 742 in McCreary County. The Big South Fork Scenic Railway also passes through Barthell. The camp is not open to visitors from January through March. For information, call (888) 550-5748 or visit www.barthellcoalcamp.com.

The Blue Heron Mining Camp

Located inside of the Big South Fork National River and Recreation Area, Blue Heron, also known as Mine 18, was another of the camps owned and operated by the Stearns Coal and Lumber Company. The mine operated from 1937 until 1962. Most of the buildings had been dismantled by the time the property came into public hands, so the town was re-created as an interpretive center in the 1980s using "ghost structures," open building shells constructed on the approximate sites of the original buildings.

Each "ghost structure" has an audiotape station with recordings from some of the people who lived and worked Mine 18. With no written records about life at the camp, the National Park Service has reconstructed what life was like from miners' memories and oral histories. The audiotape stations include the train depot, the bath house, the mine entrance, the tipple and bridge, the schoolhouse, the church, the company store, and the superintendent's house. In addition, the recordings provide information on courtship, entertainment, women's lives, and overall impressions of life in a coal camp.

The Blue Heron Mining Camp is located nine miles west of Stearns on State Route 742. It is the stopover point for the Big South Fork Scenic Railway. For more information on Blue Heron, call (606) 376-3787 or visit www.nps.gov/biso/pphtml/facilities.html or visit www.nps.gov/biso/bheron.htm.

The Big South Fork Scenic Railway

The railway takes visitors along the old Kentucky and Tennessee railroad line through the scenic Big South Fork river valley. The Stearns Coal and Lumber Company built the original line to bring timber and coal out of its camps and to take people and supplies into the camps. As the coal began to play out, so did the railroad's purpose. In 1976, the Stearns Company sold out to the Blue Diamond Coal Company, and the last rail car of coal left the Blue Diamond mines in 1987. Soon after that, the Big South Fork Scenic Railway opened as a tourist attraction.

Currently the three-hour round-trip train ride takes visitors to the old coal camps of Barthell and Blue Heron. The train boards at the old Stearns Company headquarters building in the town of Stearns itself. Purchase of a train ticket includes admission to the neighboring McCreary County Museum, which houses historic documents and photographs of coal-mining life.

The Big South Fork Scenic Railway is located on State Route 92 off US Highway 27 in Stearns. The train operates seasonally, with no excursions from November to May. Call (606) 376-5330 or (800) 462-5664 or visit www.bsfsry.com.

The Kentucky Coal Mining Museum

Aiming to collect and preserve the history of the coal camps in Kentucky, the four floors of exhibit space at the museum try to capture both mining history, with displays on the development of the coalfield and the technology of coal mining, and social history, with displays on the workplace, the home, the community, and the company store. The exhibits include a simulated coal mine (the "Mock Mine"), the floor plan of a typical underground mine, showing all the aspects of a mining operation, and several pieces of the heavy machinery used in the mines. The third floor is devoted to the "coal miner's daughter," country singer Loretta Lynn, with photographs and memorabilia from Lynn's life.

The Coal Mining Museum operates in partnership with the Lamphouse Museum and Portal #31 Underground Mine Tour in the neighboring town of Lynch. During the Portal #31 Tour, visitors don the same protective gear worn by underground coal miners and venture by rail car into an actual underground coal mine.

The Coal Mining Museum is housed in the commissary building built by the International Harvester company in the 1920s. (International Harvester sold much of the machinery used in mining operations.) The Museum is located at 231 Main Street in Benham. Information is available at (606) 848-1530 or on the web at www.kingdomcome.org/museum.

caused nearly $50 million in property damage. The rising water had floated houses near the river off their foundations and deposited them willy-nilly over the landscape. "The danger of typhus has been great," stated Louisville author Alice Hegan Rice, "as dead rats, cats, and dogs float in the streets, and a dead horse has been lying in an alley back of us for days."

Such a disaster could have been catastrophic during the early years of the Depression. But Louisville was now economically resilient. Boosted by $1.2 million in disaster loans from the federal government and WPA-funded cleanup workers, the city rebounded. When Louisville hosted the 63rd Derby in May 1937, visitors "found few reminders of the greatest flood known in the Ohio Valley," wrote one Louisville historian.

WORLD WAR II

Despite the good economic news in Louisville and New Deal-inspired optimism in other parts of the state, the Depression lingered. The American economy performed far below capacity through the late 1930s. FDR had stopped the decline, but it was not clear whether the New Deal could trigger total recovery and new growth.

Japanese and German militarism kept the nation from finding out the answer. The wartime mobilization that followed the decision to give aid to the Allies fighting Hitler and then, after Pearl Harbor, to join in the struggle dwarfed anything the nation had seen before. The role of the federal government in boosting the economy during the Depression looked like small potatoes compared to the mushrooming federal role during World War II. Good jobs, good wages, and economic security followed in quick succession.

Louisville benefited the most. The government announced plans in July 1940 to build a smokeless powder plant for artillery shells across the river in Charlestown, Indiana, to be operated by Dupont. Employment for thousands of Louisvillians resulted. Later in 1940 the government announced it would open a Naval gun factory in Louisville itself, adjacent to the train yards—a $26 million project that eventually employed 4,000 people. In early 1941, a series of announcements came that won Louisville the title of largest producer of synthetic rubber in

Must-See Sites: WWII Military Museums

The Patton Museum of Cavalry and Armor

The Patton Museum honors the famed World War II tank commander General George Patton, and demonstrates part of the impact the wartime mobilization had on Kentucky. With the urgent need to develop its armored vehicle capability to confront the Nazi threat, the US Army turned Fort Knox into the training ground for its mechanized cavalry and artillery troops. The museum was established in 1949 to preserve materials related to the development of the army's mechanized divisions.

The exhibits interpret the whole history of American mechanized warfare. There are displays on the tank corps in World War I, and the subsequent scaling-back of armored capability during the so-called lean years, when the United States turned away from international entanglements. The displays then show the rebuilding of that capability during World War II and its subsequent deployment not only in that war but in the Korean and Vietnam Wars and more recently in the conflicts in Iraq. The museum also houses personal items and memorabilia from General Patton himself, and several pieces of artillery. It is one of the largest museums in the US Army museum system.

The Patton Museum is located in Keyes Park near the main entrance of Fort Knox. Keyes Park is located off the Chaffee Avenue exit from US Highway 31W. For more information, call (502) 624-3812 or visit www.knox.army.mil/museum.

The Don F. Pratt Museum

The Don F. Pratt is the official museum for Fort Campbell, located in southwestern Kentucky. The museum highlights the history of the 101st Airborne (Air Assault) Division—the "Screaming Eagle"—which is based at the fort. The division was established in 1942, having a significant effect on the regional society and economy. The museum was established in 1956 as the divisional museum for the 101st. Its mission was broadened in 1965 to cover the history of Fort Campbell and its surrounding communities.

Exhibits include a number of military artifacts, such as a restored World War II cargo glider that carried soldiers and equipment into combat. There are also several items from the D-Day invasion of Normandy, including some captured Nazi items. Other displays tell the story of the development of airborne warfare. Outside the museum are numerous restored aircraft, including vehicles used by the 101st and items captured from enemy fighters.

The museum is named in honor of Assistant Divisional Commander Brigadier General Don F. Pratt, who was killed during the invasion of Normandy, and holds some of Pratt's personal memorabilia. The museum is located on US Highway 41A on the Fort Campbell Military Reservation. For more information, call (270) 798-3215 or (270) 798-4986, or visit www.campbell.army.mil/pratt.

Louisville skyline

the nation. Dupont chose Louisville in March for its synthetic rubber plant and by the end of the year two more companies had announced plans to build rubber plants in the city's southwestern region. Louisville christened the new industrial region Rubbertown.

Other wartime developments quickened the economic pace around Louisville. The Army Air Corps moved into Bowman Field, the municipal airport, in 1940, prompting construction of a second airport, Standford Field. During 1941 and 1942, the new airport saw construction of a plant operated by Curtis-Wright Corporation to manufacture wooden cargo planes. When the wooden planes did not work out (the first test flight ended in a fatal crash), the plant switched to conventional aluminum-bodied cargo planes. Louisville "was no longer the quasi-romantic, slightly seedy place that a writer in the thirties had called 'an American museum piece,'" *Fortune* magazine opined in 1944. "The defense boom… brought in new industries and new workers."

It was not just new plants that boosted Louisville's economic fortunes. Established companies switched to a wartime footing too. Ford Motor Company, which had been manufacturing cars in Louisville since 1916, turned out 100,000 jeeps during the war. Hillerich & Bradsby, manufacturers of the Louisville Slugger baseball bat, began manufacturing gunstocks. By 1944, workers in defense-related industries numbered 80,000 in Louisville.

The war drew workers to the city from struggling rural communities all over Kentucky, and when the demand for labor still could not be met, it drew women of both races into jobs traditionally occupied by men. "You are now the husband of a career woman," a Louisville wife wrote to her soldier husband. "Just call me your little ship yard Babe!" The boom also increased opportunities for older black men (most young black men were off to war) to move into higher-paying jobs.

As the US Army watched German Panzer divisions slash through French defenses in 1940, it resolved to create a new American armored force on the German model. In 1940, the Army announced that Fort Knox (Camp Knox until 1932) would be home to one division of the new force and would add 20,000 acres to its size. In November 1940 the initial group of draftees arrived. Newly formed Fort Campbell, which straddled the Kentucky–Tennessee border in the western portion of the state, also grew rapidly. Other communities saw other new wartime facilities—an ordnance factory in Henderson, an army hospital in Boyle County, and the Blue Grass Ordnance Depot in Lexington.

For all the new facilities, new jobs, and dramatic changes, Kentucky could not hold its own compared to other regions of the country. Although workers from all over Kentucky flocked to the new defense jobs in the state, thousands more flocked to those same jobs outside the state. Some thirteen percent of the population left the state between 1940 and 1950, leaving for high-paying jobs in the North and in the East. Few came back once the war ended. One Kentuckian remembered his rural Floyd county community as being fairly quiet and unchanging "until the war came along and then... it sorta broke all that up. Everyone started the outward migration."

Famous Sons and Daughters: Alben Barkley

Politician
(November 24, 1877–April 30, 1956)

Alben Barkley was the most prominent Kentucky politician of the New Deal era. Born on a farm near the small town of Lowes, in Graves County, Kentucky, Barkley attended public schools and went to Marvin College in Clinton, Kentucky. He graduated from there in 1897. After attending law school out of state, he returned to Kentucky, was admitted to the bar in 1901, and began practicing law in Paducah. He turned to politics soon afterwards.

A lifelong Democrat, he first served as prosecuting attorney for McCracken County, then moved on to become judge of the County Court in 1909. He ran for Congress in 1913, winning a seat in the House of Representatives, which he held for the next 14 years. He resigned his House seat to run for the Senate in 1926. He went on to win re-election to the Senate in the next three elections. During the time of national Democratic preeminence under the leadership of Franklin Delano Roosevelt, Barkley served as Senate majority leader from 1937 to 1947 and as minority leader in 1947 and 1948.

During the 1948 presidential election, he ran as the vice presidential candidate on the ticket with Harry Truman. He was inaugurated as vice president in January 1949. When the Republicans took back the White House in 1952, Barkley campaigned again for his old Senate seat and won a fifth time. He served from 1955 until his death just over a year later and is buried in a cemetery just outside Paducah.

Wartime mobilization during WWII, as in WWI, broke down barriers of isolation and provincialism. People left rural areas for cities; people from all over the state pulled together in a broad national effort to buy bonds and conserve gas, steel, food, and other items; and Kentucky soldiers fought and died together with soldiers from all over the nation. The isolation and localism of traditional rural Kentucky had been irrevocably breached.

Just over 300,000 Kentucky citizens fought during WWII, compared to just 84,000 in WWI. Kentuckians battled in every theater of the war. A military chaplain from Murray, Kentucky, spoke the famous line, "Praise the Lord and pass the ammunition" at Pearl Harbor. And one of the marines who raised the flag over Iwo Jima in the iconic scene hailed from Fleming County, Kentucky. Nearly 8,000 soldiers from the state died during the war.

Harlan county man Jim Hamlin was almost one of them. He had joined the Navy to "get something to eat," but found himself on the USS *California* in Pearl Harbor on December 7, 1941. When his ship took two torpedoes and a bomb, Hamlin stayed to fight the fires but eventually had to abandon the sinking ship. Initially reported as dead—his family even held a memorial service—he went on to serve through the war in the Pacific theater. At sea near Pago Pago, he remembered crying when he heard "My Old Kentucky Home" playing on the radio.

When the war ended in August 1945, people were not sure what to expect. The recent past fed current anxieties— the wartime generation had faced an agricultural depression, a general economic depression, a severe drought, an unprecedented flood, and a global war. Policy officials laid postwar plans, but many feared that economic depression would reappear once military demobilization took place. "What is to happen when the war is over?" the *Courier-Journal* asked in 1942. "Can the powder plant and the naval gun plant and the other war materials plants be readily converted? If so will there be industrial tenants willing to convert them?" In 1943, Louisville formed the Louisville Area Development Association in part to "safeguard the enormous industrial expansion" of the war years.

Enormous social challenges existed as well. Having fought a war to overthrow the repugnant racist ideology of Nazism, how could the repugnant system of racial segregation at home be justified? Many returning African-American veterans—and the African-American community in general, which had seen new doors open during the wartime emergency—swore that the old ways would not stand. Women, too, had sampled new opportunities during the war years and many were not ready to give way to the returning men. Depression and war had indeed changed the face of Kentucky, but the implications of those changes for the postwar world had yet to be fully realized.

Postwar Kentucky

The Depression did not return. Pent-up demand due to wartime restrictions on consumer products combined with the good wages paid to war workers meant a consumer-driven postwar economic boom. This time more Kentuckians participated than in the economic surge that followed World War I. Automobiles, better roads, rural electrification, and mass communication brought the postwar largesse to many previously isolated parts of Kentucky. The same technologies that brought postwar amenities to rural people, however, also sucked people out of rural areas. Mechanization reduced employment in coal mines and on farms, and television and the national media offered portraits of the good life far away from the state's rural communities.

Since the economic struggle against Depression appeared won, issues of equality and opportunity moved to the fore. A broad-based movement to gain for blacks the same rights as whites slowly overturned the state's segregation laws. And the parts of Kentucky that did seem left behind, especially Appalachia, became targets of federal reform efforts designed to share with them the wonders of an affluent society.

Not all Kentuckians greeted these developments with enthusiasm. The civil rights movement faced significant—and sporadically violent—resistance. The spread of automobiles, the growth of suburbs, and the decline of main streets triggered worries about fraying community ties. And as in the 1920s, a group of writers emerged who gave voice to these anxieties, who expressed concern for what was being lost in the hurried pursuit of postwar gain.

A CHANGING ECONOMY

Kentucky has a few signature economic activities—

Literary Extracts: Michael Harrington

Michael Harrington was America's most prominent socialist intellectual from the 1960s until his death in 1989. His 1962 book *The Other America*, from which the following excerpt comes, questioned the smugness of the many postwar politicians who believed American affluence had solved the problem of poverty in the United States. Harrington said that tens of millions of Americans remained mired in poverty, and one of the places he singled out for attention was Appalachia:

> Beauty can be a mask for ugliness. That is what happens in the Appalachians.
>
> Driving through this area, particularly in the spring or the fall, one perceives the loveliness, the openness, the high hills, streams, and lush growth. Indeed, the people themselves are captivated by their mountain life. They cling to their patches of land and their way of living. Many of them refuse to act "reasonably;" they stay even though misery is their lot....
>
> But, the traveler may say, granted that there is a low level of income, isn't it still true that these folk have escaped the anxiety and the rigors of industrialism? Perhaps this myth once held a real truth. Now it is becoming more false every day. Increasingly, these are a beaten people, sunk in their poverty and deprived of hope. In this, they are like the slum dwellers of the city.

distilling whiskey, growing tobacco, raising thoroughbreds, and mining coal. While these traditional mainstays remained significant after World War II, important changes also came to the state's economy. Over the course of the twentieth century, agriculture's economic contribution declined and the state economy began to look more like the overall national economy. By 1990, the percentage of workers in each major category of economic activity was more or less the same as the percentage nationwide.

Kentucky is still a leading national producer of tobacco, ranking second behind North Carolina, and tobacco is still the number-one crop in Kentucky. However, the number of people directly involved in farming has fallen dramatically, as has farming's importance in the overall state economy. In 1990, less than four percent of the state's workers labored on farms, compared to about one third in

1940. Tractors and other farm machinery have replaced human labor in the fields.

But the continued dominance of tobacco has helped preserve the state's rural character, even as agriculture's relative economic weight has declined. Tobacco requires nearly continual care during the growing season and provides good returns per acre (especially with Federal price supports), so it allowed farmers with smaller landholdings to survive. The average farm size in Kentucky in 1990 was two-thirds smaller than the typical American farm, and Kentucky ranked fourth in the nation in terms of the number of farms.

In 1985, when much of the rest of the nation's farm economy was squeezed mercilessly by scarce and expensive credit, the state legislature issued a report stating that:

> ... the Kentucky farm economy has experienced less of the farm credit crisis than have many of our fellow agricultural states. That this has been the case is explainable primarily, if not solely, by the presence of the tobacco industry. Even in its present dire condition tobacco can be counted on to provide a cash flow for thousands of Kentucky farmers who would otherwise be unable to meet their financial obligations.

That same 1985 report pronounced that "tobacco is at the heart of Kentucky agriculture." But the state is now undergoing a heart transplant. The recent demise of the old system of production quotas, price supports, and guaranteed purchasers has left tobacco with a very uncertain future. Given tobacco's ill effects on public health and the success of anti-smoking campaigns, the future of Kentucky agriculture may lie with agribusiness giants and factory farms—including Tyson Foods' immense poultry farms in Henderson County—that already dominate so much of the nation's agriculture. Or it may lie with the part-time farmers that already make up half of the agricultural labor force. Over half of the state's farms in 1990 had sales of less than $10,000, providing only supplementary income to the owners who tended them.

The other segment of the agricultural economy permanently associated with Kentucky is the thoroughbred horse farm. Horse country centers in the Bluegrass and "the whole social and economic fabric" of the region is "colored by the industry," writes Thomas Clark. Lexington's Kentucky Horse Park, a celebration of the equine industry and the animals themselves, draws thousands of tourists each year. The state does not dominate the production of racing champions as it did in the early years of the twentieth century, but it still has produced a good share of winners in recent decades. Troubles in the racing industry, however, have adversely affected horse country. Declining revenues at the racetracks—triggered by scandals, the expansion of other forms of gambling, and other causes—have caused declines in horse-breeding revenues. In 1989, in fact, the unthinkable occurred: Money made from horse sales and stud fees fell behind the money generated by cattle sales. For at least one year, the thoroughbred was the second most important animal (economically speaking) in the state.

Many of the same trends that affected agriculture affected the state's other rural industry—coal mining. Boom-and-bust pricing cycles contributed to financial instability, and mechanization dramatically decreased the number of people working in the mines. Demand increased during the 1940s, then fell during the 1950s, then jumped again following the oil embargo in the 1970s. Miners lost jobs every time the coal economy tanked, but they lost vastly more jobs through mechanization. "The thousands of jobless men faced their situation with astonishment," wrote Harry Caudill, a mountain-born lawyer turned state legislator turned social reformer, in 1962. "Never before in the experience of the oldest miner had there been mass unemployment in the midst of booming coal production."

From well over 60,000 workers in 1950, the industry employed less than one third that number just 15 years later. Harlan County, in the heart of the eastern coalfield, saw coal employment fall from over 13,000 in 1950 to just over 2,400 in 1965. At the same time, production increased; Kentucky produced 88 million tons of coal in 1947 and almost twice that amount in 1990, over 17 percent of the nation's coal.

The coal industry—like the tobacco industry—had other problems. When in the 1960s and 1970s it turned wholesale to strip mining, which spared workers the dangers of cave-ins and black-lung disease, it got lambasted

Must-See Sites: The Kentucky Horse Park

Paying homage to one of Kentucky's signature industries, the breeding and racing of horses, the park is unique in the world in that it is dedicated to the long relationship between humans and horses. A working horse farm on 1,200 acres in the heart of the Bluegrass region of the state, it houses two museums, two theaters, and nearly 50 different breeds of horses, and it attracts nearly one million visitors per year.

The park's two museums are the International Museum of the Horse and the American Saddlebred Museum. The first highlights the 55-million-year history of the horse, with exhibits on "The Horse in Sport," showcasing contemporary competitive uses of horses; on Calumet Farm, one of Kentucky's most famous producers of racing champions; and on thoroughbred owner and breeder W. Paul Little. It also has changing exhibitions of equine art and a collection of nineteenth-century horse-drawn vehicles. The American Saddlebred Museum highlights Kentucky's only native breed of horse. Exhibits focus on the sights and sounds of the world of saddlebred breeding and racing, both historically and in the present day.

Other attractions at the park include the 23-minute video on horses, "Thou Shall Fly Without Wings," the Man o' War Memorial, honoring one of the world's greatest racehorses, and the Breeds Barn, which houses many of the park's different horse breeds. The "Parade of Breeds," in which handlers show the horses and highlight differences among the breeds, takes place twice each day between March 15 and October 31. The park has a Hall of Champions, where some of today's racing elites are housed after their track careers are over, and a Draft Horse Barn, which houses the big workhorses that pull the park's horse-drawn trolleys.

The Kentucky Horse Park is located at 4089 Iron Works Parkway, off Exit 20 from Interstate 75. Call (859) 233-4303 or (800) 678-8813, or visit www. imh.org.

for scarring the mountain landscape. By the 1990s, most Kentucky coal again came from underground mines. In more recent years, some coal operators have adopted the aptly—unhappily so—named technique of "mountaintop removal." meaning literally what it says. Mountains are bulldozed to expose coal seams, the fill being dumped into the valleys, leaving a blighted landscape behind.

Must-See Sites:
Automobile Manufacturers

Large national and international corporations sited manufacturing facilities in Kentucky after World War II, helping transform the state's economy. Three automobile manufacturers have factories in the state—Ford, General Motors, and Toyota. The latter two offer regular public tours of their facilities.

Toyota Motor Manufacturing Kentucky

Toyota began operations in 1986, producing the Toyota Camry and currently employing over 7,000 people. Over 300,000 people have toured the plant since tours began in 1990. In 1994, the company opened a 11,500-square-foot visitor center to help accommodate the tourist traffic. The visitor center includes several exhibits on the production and design process and some interactive computer activities.

Toyota Motor Manufacturing Kentucky is located at 1001 Cherry Blossom Way off US Highway 62 (exit 126 off Interstate 75) in Georgetown, Kentucky. More information on factory tours is available at (502) 868-3027 or (800) 866-4485, or at www.toyotageorgetown.com.

General Motors' Corvette Assembly Plant

Opened in Bowling Green in 1981, the General Motors plant offers a one-mile walking tour that allows visitors to see the Corvette assembly process, including the industrial robots that weld together the car's underlying steel structure and the assembly line where workers add parts to the trim and the chassis. The tour then shows the "marriage" of the body and the chassis to create the final product. The Cadillac XLR is also manufactured at the plant.

The Corvette Assembly Plant is located at 600 Corvette Drive (exit 28 off Interstate 65) in Bowling Green. Call (270) 745-8419, or visit www.bowlinggreenassemblyplant.com. The plant encourages visitors to pre-book tour reservations online because there is not always space to accommodate walk-up visitors.

National Corvette Museum

For those who cannot get enough of the Corvette, this museum is located right across the street from the assembly plant. The Corvette has been around since 1953, and the museum houses more than 50 Corvette models, as well as thousands of items of Corvette memorabilia in its 68,000 square-foot exhibit space. It is the largest nonprofit museum in the world devoted to a single automobile,

The National Corvette Museum is located at 350 Corvette Drive. For more information, call (270) 781-7973 or (800) 538-3883, or visit www.corvettemuseum.com.

The industry also lost most of its markets as fewer homes heated with coal and railroads turned to diesel. That left coal-fired utilities, which soon came under fire for polluting the air. "Coal is unlikely ever again to be a prime industry," Caudill predicted in the 1960s. "Its path is downward, and the men and communities who are dependent upon it are tied to a descending star." In just the first three years of the 1990s, over one thousand mines closed, leaving some 750 open. Despite substantial untapped reserves, coal's future in the state's economy can only be guessed.

Liquor production bounced back from Prohibition and is probably the most stable of the state's traditional economic mainstays. Kentucky produces around 70 percent of all the distilled spirits in the country and 90 percent of the bourbon. Unfortunately for the industry, bourbon consumption began to decline in the 1960s as more and more consumers turned away from the "hard stuff." A voluntary ban on television advertising also caused a decline in market share compared to wine and beer, ads for which saturated the airwaves. Increasing international sales and boutique bourbons (premium small-batch bourbons) have staved off some of the decline in the domestic market, but wave after wave of consolidation in the distilling industry has dramatically reduced the number of small local distilleries.

Smoking, drinking, horse-racing, and (in the case of coal) polluting are not exactly the soundest foundations for a healthy lifestyle, much less a healthy economy. One of the main storylines of Kentucky in the postwar period has been the turning away from these traditional mainstays and toward other sectors of the economy. It did not come easily and made the business leaders of the state seem blander than in the past, but the state's economy began to look more like the nation's after 1945.

Louisville had a leg up on this process owing to wartime industrial development. The corporate operators of government plants in Rubbertown bought the facilities after the war and maintained production, leaving Louisville's status as synthetic-rubber champion unchanged. Plastics and chemical producers also came to Rubbertown. International Harvester bought the airplane factory and converted it to peacetime tractor production. In 1951 came the biggest news of all. General Electric announced that it was moving its entire home-appliance manufacturing operation to Louisville. The 1,000-acre Appliance Park soon rose up just south of the city. Ford Motors had been the only national corporation with a significant manufacturing presence in Louisville before the war; by the early 1950s there were several.

While Louisville stood at the center of the postwar transformation, other areas saw similar corporate invasions. IBM came to Lexington; Fruit of the Loom opened plants in Campbellsville, Bowling Green, and Frankfort; General Motors opened a Corvette plant in Bowling Green in 1981; Toyota opened a manufacturing plant in Georgetown in 1988. Both Toyota and General Motors offer plant tours for visitors; in addition, the National Corvette Museum across the street from the factory gives sports-car enthusiasts ample opportunity to celebrate the 'Vette.

Corporate giants also bought up local firms. Pillsbury bought local Louisville flour miller Ballard & Ballard; Gannett Communications bought the Louisville *Courier-Journal*; Pepsi bought Kentucky Fried Chicken (although it later spun it off—along with Taco Bell and Pizza Hut—into Tricon Global, now renamed Yum! Brands, headquartered in Louisville).

As early as 1959, the *Louisville Times* reported that

> … the attrition of local ownership of industry here—and elsewhere—has been no economic accident. Inexorable forces have been at work to cause some 50 locally owned firms to pass to absentee ownership since World War II and make of Louisville a "branch plant" city. The major force for merger has been the necessity to compete in a larger and increasingly national market. This means a national distribution system, national advertising, more plants, and sometimes the production of a firm's own raw material.

Over the succeeding decades, Kentucky became a "branch-plant state," and the "national market" of 1959 became the global market of the 21st century.

A few homegrown corporate giants did emerge in Kentucky during the postwar period, notably Ashland Oil,

Humana (health care), and Brown-Forman (liquor and wine). The dominant trend, however, remained the same as it had been since the end of the Civil War—a trend toward outside capital and outside management. These corporations created jobs, and many of them acted as good corporate citizens, but they represented the supplanting of the local by the national and, by the 1980s, the global.

National and global corporations, of course, have a national and global perspective on their corporate interests. So even as Kentucky shifted to manufacturing from agriculture, several large corporations closed up their factories in the state and shifted production overseas in the 1980s and 1990s to reduce costs. Fruit of the Loom closed its plants during the 1990s, for example, and GE moved several appliance production lines to Mexico and elsewhere.

In the late 1980s, the state legislature's research division looked back at the previous twenty years of economic change and noted that "the most significant changes in the Kentucky economy... include the growth of the service sector as a source of earnings and jobs, the growth of the trade sector as a source of jobs... and the decline of the manufacturing sector as a source of earnings and jobs." The state increasingly finds itself trying to lure high-tech and high-wage service jobs to Kentucky.

All these economic changes wrought important changes in people's lives. With the rise of the manufacturing economy came the rise of the managerial class, many of them non-locals. Well educated and well paid, they fed the demand for automobiles and suburban housing, which transformed the landscape around Kentucky's cities. A speedy commute required expressways, which soon encircled Louisville, Lexington, and Cincinnati's suburbs in northern Kentucky. In 1957, *Holiday* magazine wrote about one of the old plantations in eastern Jefferson county: "Oxmoor, near the junction of Route 60 and the Watterson Expressway, is the home of William Marshall Bullitt, who was Solicitor General under Taft.... Until recently Bullitt's fief was surrounded by open country. Now the horizon is dark with prim new developments occupied by suburbanites."

By 1970, the growth of suburban shopping malls had eroded downtown Louisville's position as the center of

Famous Sons and Daughters: Thomas Merton

Monk and author
(January 31, 1915–December 10, 1968)

The French-born son of artist parents—his father a New Zealand-born watercolorist, his mother an American designer—Merton grew up in a bohemian milieu and in the late 1930s was a forerunner of the Beat movement. In 1938, however, he converted to Roman Catholicism, and in 1941 he joined the Order of Cistercians of Strict Observance (the Trappists) and entered the Abbey of Our Lady of Gethsemani near Bardstown.

The order follows a severe discipline of silent work and prayer, but Merton continued to write as he had before entering the monastery. The publication of his autobiography, *The Seven Storey Mountain*, in 1951 gained him international recognition. Through the 1950s and 1960s, Merton emerged as an important social critic and prolific religious writer. He met with students from all religious traditions and delved deeply into eastern religions.

In 1965, the Order allowed Merton to pull out of the regular life of the community to live in solitude in a small cabin on the abbey's property. On a pilgrimage to Asia—where he met with the Dalai Lama and attended a conference on monasticism in the Buddhist and Christian traditions—he accidentally electrocuted himself by touching a fan with bad wiring while still wet from the shower. He was transported home and is buried at the Abbey of Gethsemani.

---

retail trade. Thirty-four acres of Oxmoor itself became the site of a shopping mall in 1971. In 1972, the population of Jefferson County outside Louisville outstripped the city's population for the first time since the earliest days of settlement, and the city has continued to lose ground ever since.

Like many older cities around the nation, Louisville has embraced the usual laundry list of projects designed to bring people back downtown—neighborhood revitalization, economic incentive zones, and government-subsidized cultural attractions. And, as in other cities, these projects had some success in keeping downtown vibrant.

Louisville's Fund for the Arts, established in 1949, was the nation's first unified arts fund, distributing money from a central pool of funds to a variety of arts organizations. The fund has helped keep the arts scene more lively in Louisville than it is in comparably sized cities. The Actors' Theatre of Louisville, for example, has helped revitalize playwriting nationally through its annual Festival of New American Plays and is widely regarded as one of the preeminent regional theaters in the nation.

Such developments downtown, however, have done little to halt or reverse the sprawl of suburbia to the east and south of the city. "The bulldozer," wrote Thomas Clark in 1968, is "the fiercest varmint ever to exist in Kentucky.... A frog pond today becomes a subdivision or a shopping center tomorrow."

As the urban and then the suburban population climbed, the rural population of Kentucky shrank. Machines replaced people in the tobacco fields and the coalfields, and a great rural-to-urban migration resulted. Rural people filled many of the new manufacturing jobs in Kentucky's cities and in cities elsewhere. In the 1940s, so many Kentuckians poured into Chicago's Uptown neighborhood and Dayton, Ohio's East End that they earned their own nickname—"O-Tucks." During that decade, nearly a quarter of a million people left Kentucky's Appalachian counties. In the 1950s, another 340,000 people left, almost a third of the area's population. The coal-mining counties of Harlan and Letcher lost nearly half their population in the years between 1940 and 1970. Mostly the young and the better educated, the rural emigrants left behind a region that had been largely bypassed by postwar affluence.

"Since the end of the war," wrote Harry Caudill, "there had been a steady trickling away of highland families. Miners and farmers 'took off' for Ohio, Michigan, Indiana, Illinois, California and Florida. Most important of the émigrés, however, were the annual classes of high school graduates. Fully three quarters of each county's spring crop of brighter boys and girls left immediately in quest of jobs in other states."

After a decade of rosy economic reports about the booming economy and the steady climb in the US standard of living, the nation "rediscovered" poverty in the 1960s.

One of the places it was "rediscovered" was Appalachia. Michael Harrington's book *The Other America* and Harry Caudill's *Night Comes to the Cumberlands*, both published in 1962, called attention to the persistence of poverty in rural mountain communities.

Caudill quoted "a 56-year-old jobless miner" who came into his law office on a rainy day and began discussing the "hopelessness" of his prospects:

> I hain't got no education much and jist barely can write my name. After I lost my job in 1950 I went all over the country a-lookin' fer work. I finally found a job in a factory in Ohio a-puttin' televisions inside wooden crates. Well, I worked for three years and managed to make enough money to keep my young-'uns in school. Then they put in a machine that could crate them televisions a whole lot better than us men could and in a lot less time.... I got laid off again and I jist ain't never been able to find nothing else to do.... I come back home here to the mountains and raised me a big garden ever' year and worked at anything I could find to do. I sold my car fer seventy-five dollars and I sold all the land my daddy left me and spent the money on my children. They didn't have much to eat or wear, but at least they didn't miss no school.

The mountaineer's hopes for his children were dashed, however, when his oldest boy, a newly minted high school graduate, went to California and could not find factory employment because of his low educational level. "I reckon they jist ain't no future fer people like us. Me and my wife ain't got nothin' and don't know nothin' hardly. We've spent everything we've got to try to learn our young-'uns something so they would have a better chance in the world, and now they don't know nothin' either!"

Caudill's book blistered the outside corporations and coal operators that exploited the land and left the people poor and the environment polluted. He wrote:

> From the beginning, the coal and timber companies insisted on keeping all, or nearly all, the wealth they produced. They were unwilling to plow more than a tiny part of the money they earned back into schools, libraries, health facilities and other institutions essential

Winchester

to a balanced, pleasant, productive and civilized society. The knowledge and guile of their managers enabled them to corrupt and cozen all too many of the region's elected public officials and to thwart the legitimate aspirations of the people. The greed and cunning of the coal magnates left behind an agglomeration of misery.

Federal anti-poverty programs undertaken in the Kennedy administration bloomed into Lyndon Johnson's War on Poverty during the late 1960s. Somewhat like the New Deal, the War on Poverty tried a lot of different approaches with mixed results. Some programs tried to empower local residents to overthrow elites in the thrall of the coal operators; other programs tried to funnel money through local governments to build needed infrastructure like roads and schools. Local elites welcomed the infusion of federal money but resented the intrusions of outside do-gooders who meddled in local politics.

Janice Holt Giles, a Kentucky writer who married a man of Appalachian stock and eventually moved with him in the late 1940s to a mountain farmstead, reflected on the prospects of the new federal programs in her 1967 book *Forty Acres and No Mule*:

> The Appalachian is courteous and hospitable, and, in these days of intensive research into Appalachia following John F. Kennedy's discovery of the area in 1960, he allows himself to be interviewed, surveyed, measured, charted, polled and tabulated. But behind his courtesy and hospitality he remains inscrutable and his very courtesy and hospitality are themselves his barrier and protecting wall. He uses an affable manner and agreement in all that is said as a shield for his own integrity, and as a mask for his contempt for the questioning outsider.

In the end, the War on Poverty helped slow the out-migration and raised the region's per-capita income, but the region still ranks high on the list of the poorest places in America.

Other parts of Kentucky besides Appalachia also saw infusions of federal money and new federal projects after World War II. Unlike the government retrenchment seen after WWI, the newly expanded national government did not wither away in the post-WWII period. It channeled

Famous Sons and Daughters: Harland Sanders and his Café & Museum

The famed Colonel Sanders behind the Kentucky Fried Chicken franchise was born on September 9, 1890, in Henryville, Indiana, and quit school after the sixth grade. He first learned to cook when his mother had to find a job following the death of Harland's father, leaving the six-year-old Harland in charge of his younger brother and sister. After working a variety of jobs, he landed in Corbin, Kentucky, in 1930 and opened a service station with a small lunch counter out back. His food was so popular that he then opened a restaurant and motel across the street from the service station. By 1937 the restaurant business had grown rapidly, due mostly to Sanders' fried chicken, with its now-famous "secret recipe" of 11 herbs and spices. Sanders also innovated by using a pressure cooker, thus speeding the cooking process.

Sanders' business thrived until Interstate 75 bypassed Corbin. Realizing the loss of much nearby traffic would dry up his roadside trade, Sanders sold his buildings and began to sell franchises based on his fried-chicken recipe. Franchising was a relatively new idea that took a while to catch on, but by 1959, Sanders had 200 such franchisees. He also was an early devotee of takeout food, an idea he credited to his oldest daughter.

Although he was first given the honorary "Kentucky Colonel" title in 1934, after about 1950 Sanders began to dress in the stereotypical fashion of the Kentucky colonel—with a white suit, goatee, and string tie—as part of the promotion of his brand's image. In 1964, he sold out to two Louisville businessmen for $2 million, though he remained as part owner and spokesperson for the restaurants. Since then, Kentucky Fried Chicken has passed through several corporate owners. The Colonel died on December 16, 1980, and is buried in Louisville's Cave Hill Cemetery.

The Colonel Harland Sanders Café and Museum

Recounting the life and career of Harland Sanders, the café and museum sit at the site where the founder of Kentucky Fried Chicken perfected his recipe for fried chicken, and emphasizes Sanders' humble roots. The old restaurant building has now been restored to its 1940s appearance and outfitted with a modern kitchen to serve up the Colonel's fried chicken. The café and museum house a variety of Kentucky Fried Chicken memorabilia.

The café and museum is located on US Highway 25 West (exit 29 off Interstate 75) in Corbin. Call (606) 528-2163 or visit www.chicken festival.com/sanders.htm.

money to Louisville for the construction of an Ohio River floodwall, for new public housing, and for slum clearance. The interstate highway network, justified as a Cold War national-defense expenditure, brought more federal money into Kentucky.

Indeed, it was the construction of Interstate 75 that indirectly gave the world one of Kentucky's most recognizable icons—Colonel Sanders of Kentucky Fried Chicken. Having run a restaurant in Corbin for 26 years, at age 66, Sanders hit the road peddling his "secret recipe" for fried chicken and recruiting franchisees. In 1964, Sanders sold out to businessman John Y. Brown for $2 million. KFC eventually passed through the hands of several corporations, achieving a global presence in the process, but the chain's humble beginnings can still be viewed at the Harland Sanders Café and Museum in Corbin (see page 262).

Federal money also flowed into western Kentucky with the construction of Barkley Dam on the Cumberland River, which was built between 1957 and 1966 by the Army Corps of Engineers. With its companion dam on the neighboring Kentucky River, Barkley Dam created an inland peninsula—the Land Between the Lakes—that the Tennessee Valley Authority proposed turning into a national recreation area. TVA argued that government oversight of the area "will stimulate tourist and recreation travel to a far greater extent than would any number of private developments within the area." President Kennedy named the Land Between the Lakes a federal "demonstration site" to show "how an area with limited timber, agricultural, and industrial resources could be converted to a recreational asset."

Crucial to TVA's plan was buying out all the privately held land inside the boundaries of the proposed recreation area. "On private lands within parks you will find lumberyards, pig farms, gravel pits, logging operations, and sheep and cattle ranches," argued one government official. Not all of the 950 families in the area were hospitable to the idea, however. "Many of our ancestors settled here in the 1700s. We need our homes, businesses, churches and schools much more than we need our land bought up for a haven for opossums, coons, rattlesnakes, and mangy buffalo," one group of residents stated in a letter to Congress. A court fight resulted in a victory for the government. Of the 95,000 acres that had to be purchased from private owners, just over ten percent were taken through court-ordered condemnation because of refusals to sell.

Money and power from outside the state—both federal and corporate—thus engineered a true transformation of Kentucky's economy and society in the postwar years. Many local customs fell away under the onslaught as government programs, improved transportation, and mass communication linked Kentucky inextricably to the larger national society. The bleakest of these local customs—racial segregation—likewise came under renewed attack.

The Crusade for Civil Rights

Kentuckians learned in segregated schools, swam in segregated pools, played in segregated parks, ate in segregated restaurants, watched movies in segregated theaters, and lived in essentially segregated neighborhoods. "When I came to Louisville," recalled Lyman Johnson, a black teacher and civil rights activist who later played a large role in the desegregation of the University of Kentucky, "Negroes couldn't use the main public library at Fourth and York. If you were a black janitor, you could go in to clean up, of course, but you couldn't go in to read a book."

That all changed in the 25 years following the end of World War II. The civil rights movement overturned the state's segregation laws and got new laws passed outlawing racial discrimination. The successes seemed stunning since the prewar struggles of blacks against segregation had borne so little fruit.

Two factors loomed especially large in the movement's postwar success: numbers and attitude. The wartime economy had resulted in a great number of African Americans living in the state's major communities, especially Lexington and Louisville. Louisville's African-American population grew during the 1940s from 47,200 to 57,800. Kentucky had never taken away black voting rights, as other states in the South did, so numbers, especially concentrated numbers, meant more political clout. Anne Braden, a white journalist and movement activist who moved to Louisville in 1947 from Alabama and Mississippi, remembered her shock upon learning that she "was now

Literary Extracts: Wendell Berry

A native Kentuckian and author of more than 50 books of fiction, essays, and poetry, Wendell Berry is one of America's most eloquent defenders of the simple life rooted in a local environment. His essays, one of which is excerpted below, often combine a close observation of the landscape with a tragic sense of how it has been misused and misunderstood by humans:

> The Kentucky is a river of steep high banks, nearly everywhere thickly grown with willows and water maples and elms and sycamores. Boating on it in the summer, one is enclosed in a river-world, moving as though deep inside the country....
>
> Once, before the man-made floods of modern times, and before the automobile, all the river country turned toward the river. In those days our trip would probably have had more witnesses than it did. We might have been waved to from house windows, and from barn doors. But now the country has turned toward the roads, and we had what has come to be the back view of it. We went by mostly in secret. Only one of the fine old river houses is left on this side of the river in the six miles of our trip, and it is abandoned and weathering out; the floods have been in it too many times in the last thirty-five years, and it is too hard to get back to from the road. We went by its blank windows as the last settlers going west passed the hollow eyes of the skulls of their predecessors' oxen.
>
> —from *Long-Legged House* (1969)

living in a place where Negroes voted!" She asked a fellow reporter whether it was true. "It's pretty much an accepted thing," he told her. "In fact, the Negro vote in Louisville is often the balance of power."

Attitudes also changed. Few African Americans had accepted segregation as just, but for many before the war it seemed futile (and possibly dangerous) to fight actively against that injustice. That changed after the war. African-American veterans returning from an overseas fight against a blatantly racist ideology were unwilling to accept Kentucky's own racism. African-American war workers, having gained access to good jobs and good wages and having worked alongside whites, would not accept a return to the more menial, lower-paid positions many had occupied during the prewar era. White attitudes had also changed. The war had demonstrated the bankruptcy of racist ideology and had demonstrated that blacks could work and fight as well as whites.

"I always thought colored people were something to look down on," one white factory worker told Anne Braden. "But when I went to work at Harvester I saw something different. The Negroes were some of the best leaders the union had…. You can't help but respect them, and pretty soon you get to like them, and the first thing you know you almost forget they're colored and you think of them as just people like yourself."

Still, the downfall of segregation did not just happen. It had to be dismantled piece by piece by legal action and by direct protest. The Day Law—the 1904 statute forbidding interracial education at Kentucky colleges—fell first. In 1948, Lyman Johnson applied to graduate school at the University of Kentucky. Predictably denied admission, he filed suit in federal court and won. "The state of Kentucky had maintained that Negroes were being adequately provided for at Kentucky State [a black college] in Frankfort," Johnson remembered. At the trial, Thurgood Marshall, the attorney for Johnson and the other plaintiffs, asked the president of the University of Kentucky, who was the main witness for the state, whether he honestly thought the two institutions were equal educational facilities. "Dr. Donovan shook his head," Johnson wrote. "The judge said: 'Why drag this out? The state has won the case for you.'"

University trustees hotly debated whether to appeal the decision and after a rancorous meeting decided against it. In the summer of 1949 Johnson and a dozen other African Americans began taking classes at the state's flagship university. By 1954 almost 600 African Americans had enrolled at formerly white colleges all over the state. The state supreme court finally ruled the Day Law unconstitutional the following year.

Integration at the elementary and secondary schools came next. In 1954, the US Supreme Court declared segregation unconstitutional in the *Brown vs. Board of Education* decision. Kentucky's schools began desegregating in the summer of 1955, when a young black woman enrolled at Lexington's Lafayette High School. But most attention focused on Louisville, the largest city in the state, which planned to integrate its schools in the fall of 1956. The city's school board redrew school district lines without regard to race and assigned students to the school nearest them. It also allowed voluntary transfers by both races as a safety valve.

The national media came to watch the first day of school on September 10, 1956. Expecting trouble, they got only a normal school day—no riots, no National Guard troops, no politicians standing in the schoolhouse door. The ordinariness of it all made headlines. "Segregation died quietly," the *New York Times* reported. Amid the violent protests that rocked other southern cities, Louisville emerged as a national model of peaceful school integration.

Integration did not always go smoothly. In 1956 there had been disturbances in two rural communities in Union County to which the governor had dispatched the National Guard, but these proved to be exceptions rather than the rule. Kentucky's leaders had made a choice. They could have joined much of the rest of the South in pledging massive resistance to desegregation of the schools. Instead, perhaps motivated by the fact that they had black voters to whom they had to answer, they chose accommodation. Anne Braden wrote that Louisville's "school officials had said from the beginning they would comply with the Supreme Court decision." The city's elites backed them up. "They let the police know in no uncertain terms that they wanted trouble nipped in the bud."

Racial integration in other areas of Kentucky life came about more slowly and only after a good deal more struggle by the state's African-American community. Civil-rights advocates knew that schools could not be truly integrated if the larger society remained effectively segregated. So campaigns for open housing and for an end to discrimination in public accommodations ranked high on the movement's list of priorities. These were largely urban movements, since most of Kentucky's African Americans lived in the cities.

The movement gained some early successes in Louisville. The main branch of the city's public library desegregated in 1948, and all the other branches followed suit in 1952. Hospitals in Louisville ended segregation in

Must-See Sites: Land Between the Lakes National Recreation Area

An economic development initiative of the Kennedy administration, the Land Between the Lakes (LBL) provides an example of the ongoing federal involvement in the state's economy following World War II. LBL was envisioned as a "demonstration site," where recreational development could foster economic growth in a resource-poor area. It thus offers a wide variety of outdoor recreation activities, from hiking and camping to hunting to boating, spread out on a 170,000-acre peninsula between Lake Barkley and Lake Kentucky. It is the centerpiece of a $600 million tourism industry in western Kentucky, and it remains the only "demonstration site" of its kind in the nation.

Its architects also built an environmental education initiative into the plans for LBL in an effort to restore an increasingly urbanized people's connection to the land. The Elk and Bison Prairie, for example, is an ongoing effort to restore new-growth forest to its original prairie landscape. In 1975, LBL biologists discovered a small patch of native prairie grasses growing in a region that had been overgrown by forest due to the impact of settlement. Through a series of controlled burns, biologists have sparked the germination of long-dormant prairie grasses, hoping to bring back what was once the eastern edge of the Great Plains ecosystem. The restoration of native prairie animals such as the bison and elk is part of the plan, and the 750-acre prairie project demonstrates the complex task of habitat renewal.

LBL also administers Homeplace, just over the Tennessee line in Stewart County. Homeplace is a working 1850s-style farmstead, and is meant to show the rural lifestyle of the early settlers in the region. The Woodlands Nature Station is another LBL attraction, providing educational exhibits on the flora and fauna in the area. Outside, in the Backyard, there are several live-animal exhibits of species found within LBL. Another LBL highlight, found at the Golden Pond visitor center, is the planetarium and observatory. Far from the light pollution of large cities, visitors can see and learn about the night sky.

LBL is located between Barkley and Kentucky Lakes, off State Highway 453 (exit 31 off Interstate 24). Call (270) 924-2000 or (800) 525-7077, or visit www.lbl.org.

1948, golf courses in 1952, and municipal parks in 1955. In 1955, civil-rights activists scored a major statewide victory when the state court of appeals outlawed segregation in all public recreational facilities.

The struggle for equal treatment in stores, restaurants, and other public accommodations took longer. As early as 1949, demonstrators in Louisville had protested against the segregated seating in the city's movie theaters. As Lyman Johnson recalled of his involvement in those early struggles, "I was a civil rights activist before I ever heard the term." Sit-ins at segregated lunch counters and restaurants began in the early 1960s, particularly in Louisville and Lexington. Frustration with downtown merchants resulted in the Nothing-New-for-Easter boycott in 1961 in Louisville. In Lexington, advocates campaigned against the city's department stores for not hiring black workers. Slowly, grudgingly, white resistance gave way. Two years after the Easter boycott, for example, Louisville passed a public-accommodations ordinance.

At the state level, a 1964 public-accommodations bill failed to make it out of committee, despite a rally drawing Martin Luther King, Jr., Ralph Abernathy, Jackie Robinson, and thousands of others to the state capitol. Two years later, however, a much stronger bill, the Kentucky Civil Rights Act, passed easily. The law forbade discrimination in public accommodations and in employment. It was the first such act passed by a southern state.

The fight for open housing also involved a long and difficult struggle. Again the movement centered in Louisville. One of the opening acts in the drama occurred in 1954 when a WWII vet named Andrew Wade wanted to buy a house in the suburbs south of Louisville. When nobody would sell him one because he was black, Wade asked Anne Braden and her husband Carl to buy the house for him. The Bradens did so, in an all-white neighborhood near Shively, and transferred the title to Wade. He moved in with his family in May. Anne Braden remembered the transaction very simply: "One man wanted a house. We were helping him get it. It seemed a small thing."

Over the next few weeks, the Wades endured constant harassment, including gunfire and a cross-burning across the street. On June 27, a bomb exploded underneath the house.

State capitol at Frankfort

The Wades, unhurt but shaken, never returned to the house. "Charlotte [Andrew Wade's wife]… insisted that she would never move back into that house with her children," Anne Braden wrote. "She said she would never be able to sleep there peacefully for a night—not knowing what minute a bomb might explode again." Braden recorded it as the "failure of a community," as the failure of Louisville, when "Andrew finally put a 'For Sale' sign in the yard of his house."

The Bradens, attacked editorially for "forcing the issue" of residential segregation, soon became targets of a sedition prosecution. The state attorney general alleged that the bombing was actually a Communist plot designed to increase racial strife in Kentucky. He indicted the Bradens, well known for their socialist sympathies, under a never-used Kentucky sedition statute. "We felt we were living in a fantasy," Anne recalled. "We knew the whole theory of the prosecution was ridiculous…. We were caught up in an hysteria we could not dissipate." Found guilty, Carl Braden served seven months of a fifteen-year sentence before the case was thrown out on appeal.

Over the next decade and a half, Louisville saw repeated demonstrations on behalf of open housing. Local organizers planned a Stop-the-Derby protest in 1967 with Martin Luther King's backing, pledging to send a phalanx of demonstrators to sit in on the track on Derby Day, but canceled the protest at the last minute. Louisville eventually bowed to the pressure and passed an open-housing ordinance in 1967. Bardstown, Covington, and Lexington also passed fair housing ordinances in 1966 and 1967. In 1968, the movement achieved statewide victory when Kentucky adopted a wide-ranging Fair Housing Act. It was, again, the first southern state to do so.

By the late 1960s, Kentucky was patting itself on the back for having avoided most of the beatings, bombings, and unrest that accompanied the civil rights movement in other southern states. Despite the grudging acquiescence of its white community to the demands for civil rights, the state looked pretty good compared to the rest of the South.

That comforting optimism allowed many to misperceive the deep frustration in the African-American community, particularly in the younger generation. Many lamented the lack of real change that had occurred with the

Famous Sons and Daughters: Anne Braden

Civil-rights activist
(July 28, 1924–March 6, 2006)

Anne McCarty was born in Louisville and traced her ancestry on both sides to some of Kentucky's oldest and most prominent families. Her family left Louisville for Alabama when she was a girl, and she grew up in a strictly segregated Alabama community. After graduating from college in 1945, she worked on several newspapers until she returned to Louisville in 1947 to join the staff of the *Louisville Times*.

She married Carl Braden in 1948, a fellow reporter and a crusader for social and racial justice. Never comfortable with segregation, Anne soon left journalism to work in various civil-rights and labor organizations alongside her husband. In 1954, the Bradens touched a nerve when they bought a house in an all-white neighborhood on behalf of a black acquaintance. The house was subsequently bombed and the family driven out, and the Bradens found themselves indicted for "criminal syndicalism and sedition." The prosecutor's theory was that the bomb was the Bradens' Communist plot to inflame racial tensions within Louisville.

Her husband was the only "conspirator" of the seven indicted to stand trial. Convicted and sentenced to fifteen years, he was released on bail after seven months, and in June 1956 the appellate court threw out the case.

The Bradens next joined the southern Conference Educational Fund, trying to bring whites into the civil rights movement and forge a biracial coalition. When the fund began agitating in Pike County against strip mining, the Bradens again were indicted for sedition. Their appeal in that case resulted in the court declaring the sedition law unconstitutional. Throughout the 1960s and 1970s, the Bradens were active in all aspects of the movement for civil rights, free speech, and social change.

Carl died in 1975, and Anne continued to live in Louisville and work in local and national civil-rights organizations. In 1990, the American Civil Liberties Union made her the first recipient of the Roger Baldwin Medal of Liberty for her contributions to civil liberties.

downfall of legal segregation. And while whites talked about the speed of the changes, from the perspective of many civil-rights activists the pace of change appeared glacial. These frustrations led many younger activists to turn away from the nonviolent integrationist philosophy of King and other early generation civil-rights leaders and toward a more aggressive black-nationalist philosophy.

These frustrations finally boiled over into violence in May 1968, popping the bubble of those who believed Kentucky had solved its racial problems. Racial tensions already ran high in the spring of 1968 owing to the Vietnam War and the assassination of Martin Luther King, Jr. in Memphis in April. Then, early in May, a white police officer in Louisville slapped an African-American business-man and was suspended from the force. On May 27, as the officer awaited a decision on whether he would be allowed to return to the force, a crowd of about 400 people gathered in the city's Parkland neighborhood to protest the possible reinstatement.

Later that evening, black student leaders announced that no decision had yet been reached, and the crowd began to disperse. Suddenly, a rumor spread that white authorities had forbidden the plane of nationally known black activist Stokely Carmichael—an expected speaker at the protest—from landing in Louisville. Just as suddenly, several bottles rained down on the crowd from the roof of a nearby building. Spontaneously, the crowd erupted into violence, looting stores, igniting fires, and vandalizing the streets.

When the police arrived, they were completely overwhelmed by the size of the crowd. The riot spread. The mayor imposed a nighttime curfew and called in 700 National Guardsmen. Things calmed down by morning, but violence flared again the following afternoon. More Guardsmen came in and the mayor tightened the curfew. By the third day with the mayor in negotiation with black community leaders, the curfew was lifted and the troops departed. The city's worst racial violence of the century had ended with two deaths (both young African-American boys), 472 arrests, and some $400,000 of property damage. Louisville had not burned like Detroit, Newark, and Washington, DC, burned in 1968, but the riot reminded everyone that the city's—and the state's—pursuit of racial equality could not end with the end of legal segregation.

Other episodes of unrest tarred the state's reputation for racial moderation as the 1960s wore on into the 1970s. During the summer of 1968, bombs exploded in African-Americans businesses and churches in various communities across the state. And near Berea in September, a group of blacks traded gunshots with a white supremacy group, leaving two whites dead.

In the mid-1970s, Louisville again attracted unwanted national attention when activists challenged the de facto resegregation of its schools in federal court. The court case brought to light the dirty little secret behind Louisville's earlier apparent success. The school board had desegregated by creating neighborhood schools that students of either race could attend. That worked fine aslong as the neighborhoods themselves were integrated. But increasingly they were not. Before passage of fair housing laws, restrictive covenants in property deeds that forbade white property owners to sell to blacks maintained pre-existing racial patterns. Even with open-housing laws, however, the white exodus to the suburbs outside the city limits increased residential segregation. By 1968, 35 schools in the city had essentially resegregated, with either blacks or whites making up at least 95 percent of the student body.

As a remedy for this situation, the court ordered the merger of the city and county school districts and mandated busing to desegregate the student body. At the start of the 1975 school year, angry whites violently protested the busing decision, looting stores, attacking buses, and damaging school property, particularly in southwestern Jefferson County. Again the National Guard came in to help restore order. Protests continued for the next two years, some drawing thousands of people, with Ku Klux Klansmen putting in an appearance at some rallies.

In a speech made during the height of the antibusing agitation, Lyman Johnson said that

> ... in Louisville we have grown accustomed to their [whites'] clamor and their violence. It is the price the black community still has to pay to live a decent life. We know that not all white people are mean and malicious.... But we wish that you people of goodwill would not hide your good wishes under a bushel. The

black people of Louisville depend on the rulings of the federal courts to guarantee us equality of opportunity. We carried this county before the court, and it was found guilty of inequality. Now we are merely asking for the benefits the court said we are entitled to.

While the anti-busing protesters grabbed headlines, desegregation did take place. Across the state in 1974, some 29 percent of African-American students went to schools where the student body was over 90 percent African American; by 1980 none did. A national study in 1991 labeled Kentucky's schools the most integrated in the country. In the late 1990s, in fact, a federal judge vacated the desegregation order in Louisville largely at the instigation of African American parents unable to enroll their children in nearby Central High (the first African-American high school in Louisville). The school had to turn away numerous black students to meet the school district's rules on maintaining racial balance, which the judge ultimately declared unfair.

"Polite racism" is the most frequently used term to describe Kentucky's race relations. Subtle, informal, undeniably present for the majority of African Americans and easy to deny for many whites, the style of polite racism discourages outspoken challenges to prevailing race relations by vocal opponents, whether black or white. When Lyman Johnson challenged the segregation of the University of Kentucky, for example, someone pointed out that he was light-skinned enough to pass as a Latin American or other foreign exchange student. "You didn't have to raise all this hell to get on campus," the person said. Johnson, of course, refused. "I've been a Negro all my days," he retorted, "and I'm not thinking about changing my race now."

Similarly Muhammad Ali—born Cassius Clay in Louisville in 1942—was hated by many white Kentuckians when he was the brash loudmouth boxer who joined the Nation of Islam, criticized the country as racist, and refused induction into the Army. They lauded the decision by boxing authorities to strip Ali of his world title and deny him a boxing license. They criticized Ali when he spoke out against the war in Vietnam. "[You] are fighting those people in their own land, fighting Asian brothers," Ali said in 1971. "You got to shoot them, they never lynched you, never called you nigger, never put dogs on you, never shot your leaders." As Jackie Robinson had noted a few years earlier, Ali "just might be one of the greatest heavyweight champions this country has ever produced. One thing is certain. He is the most hated. He is hated because he is a Muslim. He is also hated because he speaks his mind.... [W]hat they seem to dislike most is that [he] is a Black Muslim and outspoken black man." But he was just as well loved after his retirement from boxing, when he became a global spokesman for harmony and goodwill among all peoples and a benign symbol of a Louisville boy made good.

Another Kentucky sports legend—longtime University of Kentucky basketball coach Adolph Rupp—also became a vehicle for discussing race relations in the state. Rupp began coaching at UK in 1930 and stayed 42 years, winning 875 games and four national championships. His success transformed the state's budding love affair with the sport of basketball into an intense passion. For a remarkable decade between 1945 and 1955, Rupp's teams never lost a game at home. But even as the university itself desegregated, the basketball team did not. Despite the abundance of black high-school basketball talent in the state, Rupp did not recruit black players until the mid-1960s and even then he did it halfheartedly. Rupp was not an outspoken racist; his view was just that the UK teams got along fine without black players—polite racism at work.

STILL ON THE BORDER?

In the six decades since the end of WWII, Kentucky's residents have probably gone through more changes than at any other time in their collective history. Long a rural state, Kentucky became predominantly an urban/suburban state. At first a slave state and then a segregated state, Kentucky finally legislated equality between the races. And a state long focused on local and state government issues found itself with a massive federal presence in its midst.

Many state residents welcomed these changes. African Americans relished the breaking of segregation's shackles. Many rural residents doubtless never looked back as they fled the poverty of the farms of their childhoods. Those who remained enjoyed being plugged in and turned on to

Famous Sons and Daughters:
Muhammad Ali and The Ali Center

Proclaimed by himself and then others as "The Greatest," Ali was born on January 17, 1942 as Cassius Clay in the black section of the Parkland neighborhood in Louisville. When Ali was 12 years old, his bicycle was stolen, and this injustice prompted him to take up boxing. His first coach, an Irish-American policeman, paid Ali four dollars each time one of his fights appeared on "Tomorrow's Champions," a local television show. His studies at Louisville's Central High School suffered, but his boxing flourished, as he won six Kentucky Golden Gloves tournaments in various weight classes, two national Golden Gloves tournaments, and two national AAU titles.

His AAU championship earned him a spot on the 1960 US Olympic team, and he won a gold medal in the light heavyweight division. (Stung by the persistent racism and segregation in his hometown, Ali later told the story that he threw his gold medal into the Ohio River.) Turning professional in 1960, Ali defeated nineteen straight opponents, earning him a shot at Sonny Liston, the world heavyweight champion. Loudmouthed and cocky, Ali boasted that he would knock Liston out, which he did in the seventh round. Right after the fight, he announced his membership in the Nation of Islam and officially changed his name from Cassius Clay to Muhammad Ali.

Controversial as a boxer, Ali became more controversial for his actions outside the ring. He refused induction into the army, and the army denied him conscientious-objector status. Although he never served prison time for draft evasion, the World Boxing Association banned him from boxing, took away his heavyweight title, and awarded it to Joe Frazier on April 28, 1967. In 1970, the Supreme Court ruled in Ali's favor and he regained his boxing license. On March 8, 1971, he fought Frazier in New York City for the title and a $1 million purse. Frazier won in a 15-round decision, giving Ali the first loss of his professional career.

Ali did recapture the title in 1974, besting then-champ George Foreman with an eighth-round knockout. Ali fought Frazier again in 1975 in one of the greatest boxing matches of all time—the "Thrilla in Manila." It ended at the opening of the fifteenth round when Frazier did not come out of his corner. Ali lost the title three years later to Leon Spinks, then won it back a few months later—the only man to win the heavyweight title three times. He fought for the last time in December 1981, losing to Trevor Berbick—only the fifth loss in his 61-bout career.

As a vocal and proud young black man in the 1960s and 1970s, Ali transcended the boxing ring to become a symbol and role model for thousands of young men. His stand against the military and his up-front talk about racism in America also earned him plaudits from civil-rights and antiwar activists. After his retirement from boxing, slowed by Parkinson's disease, he became a global ambassador of goodwill and one of the most recognized people on the planet.

The Ali Center

One of Louisville's newest attractions, the $41 million Ali Center honors both the boxing career and the spiritual values embraced by Muhammad Ali and combines exhibits that show off Ali's greatest fights with ones that show his controversial actions outside the ring and the values that motivated them. Determination, perseverance, and self-discipline helped Ali rise to the pinnacle of heavyweight boxing, but his concerns for social justice, for international peace, and for brotherhood among men also led him to take stands on issues such as racism and the Vietnam War. The center continually gives visitors opportunities to reflect on these values and how they might apply them in their own lives.

The center features a good deal of video footage of Ali's boxing matches, as well as highlights from his numerous press conferences and celebrity appearances. It also chronicles his life in segregated Louisville, his disaffection with his home country after winning the gold medal in the 1960 Olympic Games and still finding himself a second-class citizen, and his turn to Islam. Stressing his self-disciplined training regimen, it also shows much of the work that goes into being a heavyweight boxer.

The Ali Center is located at Seventh Street and River Road on the waterfront in downtown Louisville. Call (502) 584-9254, or visit www.alicenter.org.

the conveniences of modern life. Other residents (if not their political representatives) welcomed the loosening grip of local political machines as federal money, federal rules, and federal administrators occupied a permanent place in different regions of the state.

But, as in the 1920s, when modern America also intruded into Kentucky's rural byways, there was discomfort with the changes. As the busing protests in Louisville and the harassment and violence endured by civil-rights activists showed, not all welcomed disruptions in the established way of doing things. "Who gave you the right to compel our children to sin Against God, by compelling them to intermix with Negro's?" wrote one distraught Kentuckian to a UK dean once the university began allowing black students to enroll. A woman in Hopkinsville wrote to the state governor that if the elementary schools integrated, "we might as well open the doors of Hell." To these minds, racial division made up a natural part of the social order.

And just as in the 1920s, questioning was not confined to rednecks and racists. Many watched with dismay as rural towns dwindled away to almost nothing, as suburban developments devoured farmland, and as once-proud community high schools folded into large consolidated school districts. In 1952 tiny Cuba, Kentucky—with a team that emulated the Harlem Globetrotters during pre-game warm-ups—stormed miraculously to the state high school basketball championship. The little school represented for many the revenge of rural Kentucky on the highfalutin urban and suburban high schools. Interviewed years later, however, Cuba's players lamented that such a miracle could never happen again. The widespread shuttering of community high schools—made possible by improved roads and bus transportation—precluded such an unlikely run and symbolized for many the unraveling of community.

What bothered many Kentuckians about the postwar world was the apparent loss of control over their lives and their destinies as big government and big corporations exercised more political and economic power. By the last quarter of the twentieth century, the idea that Kentucky was a "colonial economy" beholden to outsiders who took more from the state than they returned gained wide credence as an explanation for the state's second-rank economic status and as justification for stronger government oversight of companies.

In the 1920s, similar feelings had motivated the Agrarian literary movement, which extolled the virtues of rural life in opposition to the rising tide of industrialism and consumerism. In the 1960s and 1970s, another group of Kentucky writers rose to national prominence raising questions about the triumph of modern urban/suburban culture over rural traditionalism. In the late 1950s, many members of this group had coalesced around the University of Kentucky in the same way the earlier Agrarians had coalesced around Vanderbilt. The later group was more diverse than the Agrarians, however, and never formed a self-conscious literary movement.

No one raised the concerns about the direction of

postwar America—and postwar Kentucky—as explicitly and as forthrightly as Wendell Berry. More as an essayist than a novelist, Berry decried the supplanting of the local by the global and the resulting loss—for many people—of a sense of place. He criticized the postwar worship of technology and the constant quest for the most efficient method of producing something. "My work has been motivated by a desire to make myself responsibly at home in this world and in my native land and chosen place," he has written. A living embodiment of the injunctions contained in his writing, Berry resides on a farm in rural Henry County, writing, teaching, and staying close to the land.

Bobbie Ann Mason, born in western Kentucky in 1940, also attended the University of Kentucky during the late 1950s. Her work has covered themes of love, loss, and alienation in different ways, but she has repeatedly returned to her rural roots for material. *Shiloh and Other Stories*, the collection that first brought her widespread notice, painted a portrait of the people of western Kentucky confronting the oddities and marvels of modern American life, from rock music to video games. In *Feather Crowns*, the 1993 winner of the southern Book Award, a rural couple in turn-of-the-century Kentucky gives birth to quintuplets. Repeated invasions and exploitations by the national culture follow: a media frenzy over the "miracle babies," a hucksterish and macabre lecture tour after their deaths, and a final surrender of the tiny corpses to a scientific institute.

Of course, Berry, Mason, and other Kentucky literati write for national—even global—audiences; their concerns and the anxieties to which they give voice are not uniquely Kentuckian. But it is significant that these writers return repeatedly to Kentucky settings and Kentucky people, especially rural settings and rural people, to explore these concerns and anxieties. These writers give a Kentuckian voice to a widely held ambivalence about modern American society.

This ambivalence fits well a state that still straddles a cultural border. Kentucky's history could be told as a northern story—slow but steady progress, increasing economic complexity, rising levels of political and cultural sophistication. Boosters of the state, from politicians to real-estate agents, like to peddle this version to out-of-state northerners looking to relocate.

Must-See Sites: The University of Kentucky Basketball Museum

University of Kentucky basketball constitutes an important bond among many of the state's citizens. Basketball games broadcast over radio and television—particularly as Kentucky rose to prominence under Coach Adolph Rupp—provided a shared core of experience for citizens all across the state. The important role played by Kentucky basketball in the social glue that binds many Kentuckians together is honored at the University of Kentucky Basketball Museum.

The museum attempts to be more than just a storehouse for Wildcat memorabilia, providing an interactive look at the world of UK basketball from the perspectives of coaches, players, and fans. An introductory video provides an overview on what UK basketball means to those closest to it. Exhibits at the museum honor the great teams and players in UK's past, show a typical day in the life of a college basketball player today, and provide fans an opportunity to play a game of virtual one-on-one. There are also exhibits on Kentucky's coaches, on sports nutrition, and on the science of basketball. Other exhibits cover the obsessive relationship fans maintain with the Wildcats and chronicle the media coverage of the basketball team. Reservations can also be made through the museum to tour Rupp Arena, where the Wildcats play their home games.

The Basketball Museum is located in downtown Lexington on Vine Street just off Broadway (US Highway 27) in the Civic Center shops. For more information, call (859) 225-5670 or (800) 269-1953, or visit www.ukbballmuseum.org.

The state's history would just as easily fit a southern frame—hobbled by slavery, exploited by outsiders, nostalgically longing for a return to the civility of an agrarian past. Older Kentuckians, leaders in traditional industries (tobacco, bourbon, etc.), and tourist industries favor this version.

But Kentucky seems to fit most comfortably between these two. The progress and the sophistication have been real developments, as have the hesitancy, the reluctant embrace of modernity, and the nostalgia. Kentucky has long been a state of ambivalence and contradiction. Just as it served as the border between Shawnee and Cherokee, between Union and Confederate, it still serves as the border where Midwest gives way to Southeast—not all at once, but bit-by-bit, so there is always present a mix of disparate regional cultures. Kentucky is still on the border, after all these years.

Chronology of Major Events

BCE

12,000	Initial Paleoindian migration into present-day Kentucky
8,000	End of the Ice Age. Beginning of the Archaic Period
1,000	Beginning of the Woodland Period. Native Americans learn how to make pottery
500	First burial mounds constructed

CE

700	Use of bows and arrows for hunting
900	Beginning of maize cultivation
1000	Beginning of the Late Prehistoric Period. Mississippian culture flourishes in western Kentucky; Fort Ancient culture develops in eastern part of the state
1575	Appearance of first European trade goods
1673	Jesuit missionary Jacques Marquette stops at the mouth of the Ohio River
1680s	First documented epidemic of European disease, probably smallpox
1739	French Canadian Charles Lemoyne de Longueil collects fossils at Big Bone Lick
1749	French force under Pierre-Joseph de Bienville ascends the Ohio
1750	The Loyal Company sends Dr. Thomas Walker to explore Kentucky
1750s	Re-establishment of permanent Shawnee settlements in Kentucky
1763	End of the French and Indian War; Proclamation Line of 1763 established
1768	Treaty of Fort Stanwix signed with the Iroquois
1769	Daniel Boone's first trip to Kentucky
1773	Virginia sends two surveying expeditions to Kentucky
1774	March: First European settlement, Harrodsburg, is laid out; October: Lord Dunmore's War
1775	March: Treaty of Sycamore Shoals signed with the Cherokees April: Boone blazes the Wilderness Trail. Establishes Fort Boonesborough
1776	July 4: The American colonies declare their independence from England
1777	Shawnee chief Blackfish leads warriors across the Ohio; November: Murder of Shawnee peace chief Cornstalk by settlers
1778	February: Boone is captured and adopted by Shawnee

	chief Blackfish
	May: George Rogers Clark establishes camp at Corn Island
	July: Clark's force takes Kaskaskia in the Illinois Country
	September: Siege of Boonesborough
1779	February: British surrender Fort Vincennes to George Rogers Clark
1780	Combined British/Native American invasion of Kentucky
1782	The "Year of Blood"; Intertribal confederation invades Kentucky
	August: Battle of Blue Licks
1783	Treaty of Paris ends the war for American independence; Virginia creates the judicial district of Kentucky
1784	Mississippi River closed to American trade by Spanish authorities; John Filson publishes *The Discovery, Settlement, and Present State of Kentucke.*
1787	James Wilkinson attempts to engineer Kentucky's secession from the United States
1789	Bourbon-making process developed
1792	June: Kentucky admitted to the Union as the fifteenth state
1793	First Kentucky novel, *The Emigrants*, published by Gilbert Imlay
1794	July: Battle of Fallen Timbers in Ohio ends Native American threat to Kentucky
1796	Pinckney Treaty signed with Spain, opening Mississippi river to US goods
1797	Henry Clay arrives in Kentucky; organization of the Kentucky Jockey Club in Lexington
1798	A landless Daniel Boone leaves Kentucky for Missouri; November: Kentucky Resolutions passed, denouncing the Alien and Sedition Acts
1799	Constitutional convention revises state constitution
1800	Thomas Jefferson elected president of the United States
1801	"Old Captain" establishes first black church in Kentucky; August: Huge religious revival meeting at Cane Ridge
1803	United States negotiates Louisiana Purchase with France
1806	Aaron Burr may (or may not) have plotted to take Kentucky out of the Union; shaker colony at Pleasant Hill established
1807	Shaker colony at South Union established; John James Audubon sets up a store in Louisville
1808	June: Birth of Jefferson Davis in Fairview

1809	February: Birth of Abraham Lincoln in Hodgenville
1811	First steamboat, the *New Orleans*, arrives in Louisville; Henry Clay first elected to Congress
1812	June: War of 1812 begins
1813	October: Battle of the Thames in Upper Canada.
1814	War of 1812 ends.
1818	Jackson Purchase negotiated with Chickasaw
1820	Henry Clay engineers the Missouri Compromise
1824	The first of Henry Clay's three unsuccessful campaigns for president
1830	The four-mile Maysville-to-Washington macadam-surfaced road opens; the Louisville and Portland Canal opens
1832	Henry Clay runs for president and loses (again)
1833	Nonimportation Act passes, prohibiting the import of slaves in order to resell them
1839	*American Slavery As It Is* published by Theodore Dwight Weld
1844	Delia Webster and Calvin Fairbank arrested for assisting slaves to escape; Henry Clay's final unsuccessful campaign for the presidency
1845	Cassius Marcellus Clay publishes the antislavery newspaper, the *True American*
1846	The Mexican War begins
1848	Mexican War hero and Kentuckian Zachary Taylor elected president
1849	Nonimportation Act repealed
1850	Kentucky adopts its third constitution; Henry Clay engineers the Compromise of 1850; tougher Fugitive Slave Law passed by Congress
1851	Law passed requiring slaves who are freed by their owners to leave the state; Jenny Lind, the "Swedish Nightingale," performs in Louisville
1852	Henry Clay dies; *Uncle Tom's Cabin* published by Harriet Beecher Stowe
1853	The song "My Old Kentucky Home, Goodnight" penned by Stephen Foster
1855	August: "Bloody Monday" riots in Louisville
1859	Louisville and Nashville railroad completed
1860	Abraham Lincoln elected president; Kentucky Senator John Crittenden's compromise fails to stop secession of South
1861	Civil War begins. Kentucky initially declares itself neutral; western Kentucky town of Columbus occupied by Confederate troops; Bowling Green occupied by Confederate troops

September: End of neutrality. Legislature orders withdrawal of Confederate troops
October: Battle of Wildcat Mountain in Laurel county
November: Provisional Confederate state government formed at Bowling Green

1862   January: Battle of Mill Springs; Confederate General Felix Zollicoffer killed
February: Union troops take Forts Henry and Donelson; Confederates evacuate Bowling Green.
July: First raids into the state by John Hunt Morgan
August: Battle of Richmond ends in Confederate victory
September: Lexington and Frankfort occupied by Confederate forces
October: Battle of Perryville turns back Confederate invasion
December: John Hunt Morgan's "Christmas raid"

1863   January: President Lincoln issues the Emancipation Proclamation
March: Nathan Bedford Forrest leads cavalry raid against Paducah
July: John Hunt Morgan's "Great Raid" crosses into Indiana and Ohio

1864   March: Lincoln allows recruitment of black soldiers within Kentucky
June: John Hunt Morgan's last raid
September: Morgan killed in Tennessee; "Sue Mundy" begins guerrilla raids inside Kentucky against Unionists

1865   April: End of the Civil War; Kentucky legislature rejects Thirteenth Amendment, which would abolish slavery

1866   Freedmen's Bureau begins operations in Kentucky

1867   Kentucky legislature rejects the Fourteenth Amendment, which would establish civil rights

1869   Kentucky legislature rejects the Fifteenth Amendment, which would establish voting rights; Freedmen's Bureau closes down operations in Kentucky

1870   Federal court forbids racial discrimination on Louisville streetcars

1872   State legislature gives African Americans equal legal standing in state courts

1875   First Kentucky Derby (Aristides wins)

1877   Great Railroad strike affects Louisville; John Marshall Harlan appointed to the US Supreme Court

1881   Formation of the Kentucky Woman Suffrage Association

1882   Beginning of the famous feud between the Hatfields and McCoys

1883   Southern Exposition held in Louisville

1888   Kentucky Equal Rights Association organized by
        Laura Clay
1891   Adoption of Kentucky's fourth constitution; founding
        of the Populist Party in Kentucky
1892   State law requires racial segregation of railroad cars
1893   Panic of 1893 touches off nationwide depression
1895   Kentucky's first Republican governor, William O.
        Bradley, elected; "Tollgate War" begins in Washington,
        Anderson, and Mercer counties
1899   Gubernatorial race between William Taylor and
        William Goebel
1900   Goebel assassinated. Legislature declares him governor
        before he dies.
1902   Hindman Settlement School founded; Matt Winn
        takes over Churchill Downs
1903   John Fox, Jr., publishes *The Little Shepherd of Kingdom
        Come*, the first novel in the United States to sell a
        million copies
1904   Day Law passed, banning racially integrated
        institutions of higher education
1905   Black Patch War begins. Violence persists for four years
1908   Legislature passes child-labor law
1911   Cora Wilson Stewart starts first Moonlight School, in
        Rowan county
1913   Louisville passes a housing-segregation ordinance;
        Ford Motor Company opens a Model T plant in Louisville
1915   D.W. Griffith, from Oldham county, releases the film
        Birth of a Nation
1917   The United States enters World War I; Louisville's
        housing segregation ordinance overturned by US
        Supreme Court
1919   Statewide Prohibition passed
1920   Nineteenth Amendment ratified, granting women the
        right to vote
1921   First female state legislator in Kentucky elected, Mary
        Elliott Flanery
1922   The South Union Shaker colony—the last in
        Kentucky—closes; WHAS radio station begins
        broadcasting from Louisville
1925   Floyd Collins cave-rescue saga and accompanying
        media circus
1927   Musical pioneer Bill Monroe first performs on radio, in
        North Carolina
1928   "My Old Kentucky Home" named state song
1929   Stock market crash, beginning Great Depression
1930   Harland Sanders opens a service station in Corbin and

starts serving fried chicken

1931   Labor troubles between coal miners and mine
        operators in Harlan county
1932   Election of Franklin Roosevelt to the presidency
1933   End of national Prohibition
1934   Tobacco Control Act sets crop quotas and minimum
        prices; *Man with a Bull-Tongue Plow*, Jesse Stuart's first
        book, published
1935   First African American elected to state legislature,
        Charles Anderson of Louisville; state Prohibition
        repealed
1937   Ohio River floods, damaging Louisville and other
        Ohio River towns; Cumberland National Forest (later
        renamed Daniel Boone) established; *Renfro Valley Barn
        Dance* radio show begins broadcasting
1939   Bill Monroe's "Bluegrass Boys" perform on The Grand
        Ole Opry radio show; Robert Penn Warren publishes
        Night Rider, a novel about the Black Patch War
1941   Beginning of Rubbertown industrial area in Louisville;
        US enters World War II after attack on Pearl Harbor;
        Mammoth Cave National Park established
1942   Fort Campbell military base established
1944   Tennessee Valley Authority builds Kentucky Dam on
        the Tennessee River
1945   End of World War II
1947   Robert Penn Warren wins the Pulitzer Prize for *All the
        King's Men*
1948   Kentucky Senator Alben W. Barkley elected as Harry
        Truman's vice president; University of Kentucky wins
        its first national championship in basketball;
        Louisville's WAVE becomes Kentucky's first television
        station
1949   University of Kentucky admits Lyman Johnson, an
        African American
1951   General Electric's Appliance Park established in Louisville
1954   After *Brown v. Board of Education*, the state orders
        public school desegregation
1955   All-white Lafayette High School in Lexington admits
        its first black student; State Supreme Court overturns
        the Day Law; Harriette Simpson Arnow wins the
        National Book Award for *The Dollmaker*
1956   Desegregation of Louisville's public schools
1959   Dedication of Cumberland Gap National Historical Park
1960   Cassius Clay wins an Olympic gold medal in boxing;
        Loretta Lynn performs at the Grand Ole Opry in
        Nashville

1961	First black woman elected to state legislature, Amelia Tucker
1962	Harry Caudill's *Night Comes to the Cumberlands* and Michael Harrington's *The Other America* draw national attention to Appalachian poverty
1963	Louisville forbids racial discrimination in public accommodations; President Kennedy establishes Land Between the Lakes National Recreation Area
1965	Congress creates the Appalachian Regional Commission
1966	Kentucky legislature passes a statewide Civil Rights Act
1968	May: Race riot erupts in Louisville
1975	Anti-busing riots occur in Louisville
1976	The Humana Festival of New American Plays debuts in Louisville
1981	Corvette Assembly Plant opens in Bowling Green
1983	Kentucky elects its first woman governor, Martha Layne Collins
1986	Toyota manufacturing plant opens in Georgetown
1990	Kentucky Education Reform Act passed
1992	Louisville replaces busing with a modified school-choice plan to achieve racial balance in public schools
2000	Court dissolves 1974 desegregation order for Louisville's public schools
2003	Republican Ernie Fletcher elected governor, symbolizing growing power of Republican party in state politics
2004	Tobacco buyout enacted, ending federal price supports and production quotas
2005	Investigation of politically motivated hiring by Fletcher administration
2006	Number of Kentucky soldiers killed since war in Iraq began in March 2003 reaches 34

Cultural Highlights

Kentucky Movies

With a few exceptions, movies set in Kentucky generally reflect commonly held images of the state. The courage of the early frontier settlers, the conflict between traditional rural life and modernity, feuds, horse racing, and coal mining have been the dominant subject matter. The following is a chronological list of some of the most notable films about the state.

The Romance of Happy Valley (1919) D.W. Griffith, dir. Starring Lillian Gish and Robert Harron. This early silent feature tells the story of John Logan, who leaves his sweetheart and the rural hamlet of Happy Valley to make his fortune in the city. He returns a wealthy man, but his embittered father, not recognizing him, vows to kill the "stranger" for his money.

Our Hospitality (1923) John Blystone and Buster Keaton, dirs. Starring Buster Keaton and Natalie Talmadge. A silent-era comedy about a feud between rival clans, the Canfields and the McKays. As a young Canfield man returns to his mountain home, he falls in love with a McKay girl, not realizing that her family has pledged to kill the members of his family.

Uncle Tom's Cabin (1927) Harry Pollard, dir. Starring James B. Lowe, Virginia Grey, and George Siegmann. Billed as "the $2 million motion picture," this silent film retells the story of Harriet Beecher Stowe's famous novel, supposedly based on Kentucky events.

Mountain Justice (1930) Harry Joe Brown, dir. Starring Ken Maynard and Otis Harlan. A man returns to the small town of Kettle Creek in the Kentucky mountains to find his father's killer.

The Great Meadow (1931) Charles Brabin, dir. Starring Johnny Mack Brown and Eleanor Boardman. When Daniel Boone talks up Kentucky in a small Virginia town in 1777, a young couple makes the dangerous trek to the new land. Based on the novel by Elizabeth Madox Roberts.

In Old Kentucky (1935) George Marshall, dir. Starring Will Rogers and Dorothy Wilson. A horse trainer is caught between feuding clans, who agree to settle their differences with a horse race.

The Little Colonel (1935) David Butler, dir. Starring Shirley Temple and Lionel Barrymore. Based on the immensely popular novel of Annie Fellows Johnston, a charming little girl melts the heart of her crusty old grandfather—a former Confederate colonel—and helps reconcile him to his daughter's marriage to a "Yankee."

The Trail of the Lonesome Pine (1936) Henry Hathaway, dir. Starring Henry Fonda, Fred MacMurray, and Sylvia Sidney. Based on the novel by John Fox, Jr., the movie shows mountain people grappling with modern culture through the love story of a young mountain woman and a man from "outside."

Kentucky Moonshine (1938) David Butler, dir. Starring the Ritz Brothers and Jerry Wade. Radio producer Tony Martin goes to the Kentucky mountains to recruit new talent for his radio show, but he finds the Ritz Brothers who, although actually from New York, are posing as hillbillies to gain an appearance on the show.

The Fighting Kentuckian (1949) George Waggner, dir. Starring John Wayne and Vera Ralston. John Breen is a Kentucky militiaman in Alabama in 1818 who falls in love with a French exile, but discovers a plot to steal the land upon which the small group of exiles had intended to settle.

The Story of Seabiscuit (1949) David Butler, dir. Starring Shirley Temple and Barry Fitzgerald. A horse trainer and his daughter come to Kentucky to begin a new life, and the trainer must persuade Seabiscuit's owner to take a chance on the undersized horse.

The Kentuckian (1955) Burt Lancaster, dir. Starring Burt Lancaster and Dianne Foster. A frontiersman in 1820s Kentucky, finding the state becoming too "civilized," plans to leave for the Texas frontier with his son.

The Little Shepherd of Kingdom Come (1961) Andrew McLaglen, dir. Starring Jimmie Rodgers and Luana Patten. One of several film versions of John Fox, Jr.'s, novel about a young mountain orphan adopted by a Bluegrass family that is sharply divided by the Civil War.

Goldfinger (1964) Guy Hamilton, dir. Starring Sean Connery. A film in which Kentucky is treated merely as setting, not as metaphor, as secret agent James Bond foils an attempt to raid the US Gold Depository at Fort Knox.

Harlan County USA. (1976) Barbara Kopple, dir. An Oscar-winning documentary about a bitter and violent coal miners' strike in Harlan county in 1973, placing that strike in the context of the long history of the county's labor troubles.

Coal Miner's Daughter (1980) Michael Apted, dir. Starring Sissy Spacek and Tommy Lee Jones. The story of country singer Loretta Lynn's rise from poverty in the Kentucky mountains to become the premiere female country vocalist of her day.

Beloved (1998) Jonathan Demme, dir. Starring Oprah Winfrey and Danny Glover. Based on the novel by Toni Morrison, a former slave woman is visited by the spirit of her deceased daughter, whom she killed rather than having her returned into bondage. Based on the true story of Margaret Garner, a Kentucky slave.

Simpatico (1999) Matthew Warchus, dir. Starring Nick Nolte, Jeff Bridges, and Sharon Stone. A horse-racing drama set in Kentucky, adapted from a play by Sam Shepard.

Nice Guys Sleep Alone (1999) Stu Pollard, dir. Starring Michael Greene and Sean O'Bryan. A sex and dating comedy set in contemporary Louisville.

Ali (2001) Michael Mann, dir. Starring Will Smith, Jamie Foxx, and Jon Voight. The life of Muhammad Ali from 1964, when he defeated Sonny Liston for boxing's world heavyweight championship, to 1974, when he won it back from George Foreman.

Seabiscuit (2003) Gary Ross, dir. Starring Toby Maguire, Jeff Bridges, Chris Cooper. Another version of the story of the misfit race horse—with accompanying misfit trainer, jockey, and owner—who rise to prominence in Depression-era America. Set partially in Kentucky and many of the race scenes were filmed in the state.

Elizabethtown (2005) Cameron Crowe, dir. Starring Orlando Bloom and Kirsten Dunst. A light romance set in the context of a young man returning to his Kentucky hometown from the West Coast to attend his father's funeral and settle his affairs.

Glory Road (2006) James Gartner, dir. Starring Josh Lucas. A feel-good, underdog-wins sports movie that tells the story of the all-black Texas Western University's basketball team's defeat of Adolph Rupp's all-white Kentucky Wildcats team for the national championship.

Kentucky Music

Kentucky's rich musical heritage has been fattened by the contributions of various social and ethnic groups, at times coexisting in separate spheres, at times coming together in bursts of syncretic creativity. Categorizing and organizing these different musical strands can be difficult. The Kentucky Music Museum and Hall of Fame in Renfro Valley and the International Bluegrass Museum in Owensboro are two good places to start diving into the state's musical history.

During the nineteenth century, many upper-class homes had a piano, and it was considered desirable for upper-class young ladies to take music lessons. Lexington was an early musical center, and there are notices advertising private voice lessons and music schools dating from as early as 1800. A Lexington tavern hosted a concert in 1817 that opened with a piece from Beethoven's First Symphony, and the Speed family in Louisville played host to composer Anton Philip Heinrich. Early formal musical tastes thus tended to be classical and conservative.

Sheet music, however, was also popular. And many popular songs from composers such as Stephen Foster and Samuel Woodworth would be played and sung as entertainment in upper- and middle-class homes. Many of these early popular songs have become part of the American pop-music canon. Foster's "My Old Kentucky Home" is played every year before the start of the Kentucky Derby. Perhaps the most familiar Kentucky song of all is "Happy Birthday," originally written by two Louisville sisters in 1893 as "Good Morning to You" and still under copyright.

In terms of folk music, European immigrants, rural dwellers, and African Americans have all made important contributions to Kentucky's legacy. All-male German singing societies were a strong community-building force in Louisville, Covington, and elsewhere. Annual Saengerfests—national conventions of these singing societies—frequently met in Louisville, with the 1914 event drawing some 3,000 singers and musicians.

African-American music has a long history in Kentucky. Slave spirituals influenced the development of the blues and jazz in the early twentieth century, out of which grew the modern gospel music movement. The blues began as work songs by black field workers, and early music folklorists have documented stage performances of the blues going back to the end of the nineteenth century. As the center of African-American life in Kentucky, the city of Louisville produced many of Kentucky's bluesmen and ladies. Vocalists Sarah Martin, Edith Wilson, and Edmonia Henderson came out of Louisville, and Martin helped get Sylvester Weaver's "Guitar Rag" recorded in the 1920s, the first blues guitar instrumental.

Jazz, influenced by the blues but morphing into something totally new, probably came via the rivers and railroads to Kentucky from places like New Orleans, Memphis, and Chicago. A subversive music associated with brothels and bars in the early days, jazz moved into mainstream clubs in the 1920s. By the 1950s, Kentucky had a native-born jazz tradition, again largely centered in Louisville. Trumpeter Jonah Jones, born and raised in Louisville, played locally before moving on to some of the best jazz bands in the nation during the 1940s. Vocalist Helen Humes, another Louisvillian, sang with the Count Basie Orchestra and recorded several hit records.

Church music has, of course, always been important in the African-American community. By the 1960s, several black Baptist churches in Kentucky had multiple choirs. With the introduction of electronic instruments and percussion to the traditional piano and organ, the modern gospel music movement arose. Leading choirs in the gospel scene included the choirs from Louisville's Cable Baptist Church and Canaan Missionary Baptist Church.

The largely white rural dwellers of Kentucky's small towns and mountains also had a long musical tradition stretching back to the English, Scotch, and Irish folk tunes that their ancestors brought over from the old country. For many years, this had been "front porch" music, one of the few forms of free entertainment in small, isolated hamlets. Beginning in the early twentieth century, musical folklorists—seeing the penetration of modern industrial life into these communities—began collecting and preserving their musical legacy. In 1911, the book *A Syllabus of Kentucky Folksongs* was published, followed in 1920 by *Kentucky Folk Songs*. Louisvillian John Jacob Niles traveled all across Appalachia gathering songs in the 1910s and again in the early 1930s, then wrote them down and performed them on the dulcimer for audiences all across the nation. Jean Ritchie, another musical folklorist, was born in the mountains, left them to go to college, then returned to record hundreds of traditional ballads in their original form during the 1950s.

Such "hillbilly music" went out to a national audience through radio shows like the Grand Ole Opry in Nashville, the National Barn Dance in Chicago, and in 1939 Kentucky's own Renfro Valley Barn Dance. Kentuckians Red Foley and Grandpa Jones became regular performers and national stars on these programs. Foley's "Chattanoogie Shoe Shine Boy" was the first country recording to reach the top of the popular music charts.

Over time, "hillbilly music" produced two different modern genres—country music and bluegrass music. Country music, generally considered more commercial and more open to modern influences like electronic instruments, has produced Kentucky stars including Loretta Lynn, Crystal Gayle, Tom T. Hall, Dwight Yoakam, and Naomi and Wynonna Judd. Bluegrass music, generally considered to be more traditional "roots" music and more reliant on acoustic stringed instruments, got its start with Bill Monroe, whose Bluegrass Boys became regulars on the Grand Ole Opry. Bluegrass music has produced Kentucky-born stars such as the Osborne Brothers, Merle Travis, and Ricky Skaggs.

Of course, as with all musical genres, there is substantial crossover and cross-fertilization among these musical styles, as well as between them and other traditions, such as African-American music. Several more recent Kentucky musicians have gained fame as crossover artists, such as Rosemary Clooney (jazz and pop), the Everly Brothers (rockabilly), the Kentucky Headhunters (rock and country), and Nappy Roots (rock and hip-hop). Kentucky's legacy to American music is a large one, and the current musical scene continues to be creative and vital.

KENTUCKY BOOKS AND WRITERS

Most noteworthy among the early Kentucky travel guides and promotional literature is John Filson's *The Discovery, Settlement, and Present State of Kentucke* (1784), largely because it contains Daniel Boone's "autobiography." Although written by Filson himself from material told to him by Boone, it still makes for interesting reading.

By the turn of the nineteenth century, colorful nonfiction accounts of particular localities or regions were very much in favor with the reading public. Two books of such sketches, James Lane Allen's *The Blue-Grass Region of Kentucky and Other Articles* (1900) and John Fox, Jr.'s, *Blue-Grass and Rhododendron: Out-Doors in Old Kentucky* (1901) are notable for their focus on rural Kentucky life—in the Bluegrass for Allen, in Appalachia for Fox—on the cusp of modern intrusions.

In 1874, Richard H. Collins produced a two volume *History of Kentucky* that built on a similar antebellum work by his father. Collins was a great compiler of lists, and the book is filled with facts that became the foundation for much later historical writing on Kentucky. But the real dean of Kentucky historians was Mississippi-born Thomas D. Clark, who attended graduate school in Kentucky, and eventually returned to teach at the University of Kentucky from 1931 until 1968. Clark was professionally trained, but he also knew how to write and how to tell a good story. His *History of Kentucky*, first published in 1937 and revised in 1950 and again in 1960, was the standard account for 60 years. Clark also produced numerous specialized and non-specialized works on Kentucky history, southern history, and frontier history. *Kentucky: Land of Contrast* (1968) sums up much of his thoughts about the state.

Novelist Harriette Simpson Arnow produced two fine social histories in the 1960s of the region of Kentucky where she grew up, *Seedtime on the Cumberland* (1960) and *Flowering of the Cumberland* (1963). Another nonfiction essayist associated with Kentucky, but whose work addressed universal spiritual themes, was the Trappist monk Thomas Merton, who lived at the Abbey of Gethsemani near Bardstown. A prolific writer, Merton's best known work is the story of his life, *The Seven-Storey Mountain* (1948).

Wendell Berry and Harry Caudill bear mentioning as two standout historical and cultural essayists of more recent vintage. Not professional historians, but excellent writers and passionate advocates, Berry and Caudill have borne witness to the ravages of the modern age on the Kentucky landscape. In a series of books, most notably *Night Comes to the Cumberlands* (1962), Caudill has drawn attention to the exploitation of eastern Kentucky's environment and people by outside economic interests and their local collaborators. Wendell Berry has been an eloquent critic of modern society's divorce from a sense of place and its lack of rootedness in the land in such books as *The Unsettling of America* (1977) and *What Are People For?* (1990).

In terms of fictional literary output, Kentucky has had at least three historical moments when a corps of state writers have made waves on the national literary scene. Many of these writers eventually left the state to reside elsewhere, but they often returned to Kentucky and Kentucky themes in their writing. The list below is not intended to be comprehensive; it focuses on Kentucky writers who have presented Kentucky to the broader literary world. Many writers from Kentucky are not described below; even though they lived in the state, Kentucky did not appear to have much of an influence on their literary output. Two good recent anthologies of Kentucky writing are *The Kentucky Anthology: Two Hundred Years of Writing in the Bluegrass State* (2005), edited by Wade Hall, and *Home and Beyond: An Anthology of Kentucky Short Stories* (2001), edited by Morris Grubbs.

The first of Kentucky's literary-historical moments came around the turn of the nineteenth century, with writers such as Fox and Allen in Lexington and a group of women authors, including Annie Fellows Johnston and Alice Hegan Rice, in Louisville. James Lane Allen had published several works of fiction before *The Choir Invisible* (1897) gained him national renown. Dealing with a man's love for a married woman, it explored the conflict between traditional standards of morality and modern manners. John Fox, Jr., set his fiction, like many of his essays, among the mountain people of Kentucky. *The Little*

Shepherd of Kingdom Come (1903) was his most popular novel, but *Trail of the Lonesome Pine* (1908) surpassed it in literary quality. The story of a mountain girl's love for an "outsider," the book dealt with Appalachia's own confrontation with the modern industrial age.

In Louisville at about the same time, a group of women writers produced a collection of popular novels. *The Little Colonel* (1895) by Annie Fellows Johnston was not great literature but told a sweet story about a little girl whose charm healed the festering wounds of the Civil War within her own family. Such stories of sectional reconciliation were popular at the time. Alice Hegan Rice was another writer of this group. Active in settlement house work among Louisville's poor, she wrote a fictionalized portrait of a cheery, optimistic slum dweller for whom everything worked out in the end. *Mrs. Wiggs of the Cabbage Patch* (1901) was wildly successful, as were Rice's treacly follow-up novels.

The second "moment" came in the 1920s and 1930s when Kentucky writers Elizabeth Madox Roberts, Robert Penn Warren, and Jesse Stuart began their sustained literary production. Roberts published her first novel, *The Time of Man*, in 1926, about the inner strength and simple grace of country people, though she wrote it in sophisticated prose. Her book *The Great Meadow* (1930) is an historical novel about the settling of the Kentucky frontier. Robert Penn Warren wrote his first novel, *Night Rider* (1939), about the Black Patch War. In *World Enough and Time* (1950), *Brother to Dragons* (1953), *Band of Angels* (1955), and *The Cave* (1959), he returned to Kentucky for his settings and subject matter. Jesse Stuart splashed on to the literary scene with *Head o' W-Hollow*, a collection of short stories, in 1936. His first novel, *Trees of Heaven*, appeared in 1940. *Taps for Private Tussie* (1943) was an often comic portrait of a mountain family that sold over a million copies. Stuart was a prolific writer, producing stories, novels, essays, and poetry with immense energy. James Still was another writer of this period, although his output was fairly limited. His best-known work is the novel *River of Earth* (1940).

A third moment came in the 1950s and 1960s when such writers as Harriette Simpson Arnow, Wendell Berry, Janice Holt Giles, and Walter Tevis confronted postwar America. (Penn Warren and Stuart were still going strong in this period, as well). Arnow's classic work, *The Dollmaker* (1954), is a tragic tale of the sapping of one woman's will by modern industrialism. Janice Holt Giles was born in Arkansas but moved to Kentucky with her husband in 1939. *The Enduring Hills* (1950) was a tale of urban/rural conflict, while historical novels *The Kentuckians* (1953) and *Hannah Fowler* (1956) explored Kentucky's frontier experience. Wendell Berry, noted above as an essayist, also produced several fine novels about Kentucky. Of particular note is *The Memory of Old Jack* (1974). Tevis explored a grittier side of life in his work, building on his experience among small-town pool sharks in smoky billiard halls to write *The Hustler* (1959).

Besides the ever-productive Berry, Bobbie Ann Mason is probably the most prominent of the more recent crop of Kentucky writers. She came of age with Berry and Tevis, but got a late start on her writing career, publishing her first collection of short stories, *Shiloh and Other Stories* (1982), when she was forty-two years old. She followed that with, among other works, *In-Country* (1985) and *Feather Crowns* (1993), which won the southern Book Award. Mason moved back to rural Kentucky in 1990 to devote herself to writing.

Another prominent writer from Kentucky, Barbara Kingsolver, seems to be weaving her way back to Kentucky in her writing. The heroine of her first novel, *The Bean Trees* (1988), is a Kentucky native fleeing the provincialism of her home state for the desert Southwest. While her later books *Animal Dreams* (1990) and *The Poisonwood Bible* (1998) took, respectively, the Southwest and the Belgian Congo as their milieu, *The Prodigal Summer* (2000) told the story of three intertwined lives in southern Appalachia.

Up-and-coming Kentucky writers include Fenton Johnson, Silas House, and Sena Jeter Naslund. Johnson's *Crossing the River* (1989) and *Scissors, Paper, Rock* (1994) have both dealt with Kentucky characters coming to grips with the wider world. *Clay's Quilt* (2002), by Silas House, a rural mail carrier in eastern Kentucky, tells of a young man's struggle to feel settled on his home ground, a small town in Kentucky's coal country. Naslund is probably the least "Kentuckian" of these three; her most recent work, *Four Spirits* (2003), tells the civil-rights-era story of the 1963 Birmingham, Alabama, church bombing that killed four little girls.

Many of Kentucky's best-known poets come from the ranks of its fiction writers. Robert Penn Warren produced several fine volumes of poetry, winning a Pulitzer Prize for *Promises: Poems, 1954–1956* (1957). Jesse Stuart's first published work was the large collection of poems entitled *Man with a Bull-Tongue Plow* (1934). Wendell Berry, too, has produced much good poetry, as evidenced in *The Collected Poems of Wendell Berry, 1957–1982* (1987). A modern Kentucky poet of note is Frank X. Walker, whose collection *Affrilachia* (2000) reflects on his experience as an African American living in Appalachia.

Special Events

Signature sporting events, community festivals (celebrating a region's distinctive food, product, or culture), ethnic festivals, arts and crafts shows, music and theater festivals, and Civil War reenactments occur throughout the year. The following list is by no means comprehensive. For additional events, consult www.kyfestivals.com or the state and county tourism websites.

January–February
Sporting Events:
College Basketball. University of Kentucky Southeastern Conference Games. Rupp Arena. Lexington. (800) 928-2287.
College Basketball. University of Louisville Big East Conference Games. Freedom Hall. Louisville. (800) 633-7105.

March
Arts and Crafts:
My Old Kentucky Home Festival of Quilts. Bardstown. Phone: (800) 638-4877.

Music/Theater:
Humana Festival of New American Plays. Actors Theater of Louisville. Phone: (502) 584-1205. World premieres of original plays by both new and established writers.

April
Sporting Events:
Thoroughbred horse racing. Keeneland Race Course spring meet. Lexington. (800) 456-3412.
Rolex Three-Day Event. Kentucky Horse Park. Lexington. (859) 254-8123. A major equestrian competition.
Thoroughbred horse racing. Churchill Downs spring meet. Louisville. (502) 636-4400.

Community Festivals:
Hillbilly Days Festival. Pikeville. (800) 844-7453.
Kentucky Derby Festival. Louisville. (800) 928-3378.
Springfest. Mammoth Cave National Park. (270) 758-2254.

Arts and Crafts:
American Quilter's Society National Quilt Show. Paducah. (270) 575-9958.

MAY
Sporting Events:
Kentucky Derby. Churchill Downs. Louisville. (502) 636-4400.

Community Festivals:
International Bar-B-Q Festival. Owensboro. (800) 489-1311.
Poke Sallet Festival. Harlan. (606) 573-4717. "Poke" is a
naturally growing weed, the leaves of which can be used in
"sallet" (salad).

Ethnic Festivals:
Kentucky Scottish Weekend. General Butler State Resort Park.
Carrollton. (800) 325-4290 or (502) 732-4384

Arts and Crafts:
Kentucky Guild of Artists and Craftsmen Spring Fair. Berea.
(800) 598-5263.

Music/Theater:
Bill Monroe Memorial Day Weekend Bluegrass Festival.
Rosine. (270) 298-3551.

JUNE
Community Festivals:
Appalachian Celebration. Morehead State University.
Morehead. (606) 784-6221.
W.C. Handy Blues and Barbecue Festival. Henderson. (800)
648-3128.

Music/Theater:
Festival of the Bluegrass. Kentucky Horse Park. Lexington.
(859) 846-4995.
Great American Brass Band Festival. Danville. (859) 236-7794.

JULY
Arts and Crafts:
Berea Craft Festival. Berea. (800) 598-5263.

Music/Theater:
Official Kentucky Championship Old-Time Fiddler's Contest.
Rough River State Park. Falls of Rough. (800) 325-1713.

AUGUST

Community Festivals:
Western Kentucky State Fair. Hopkinsville. (270) 885-5237.
Kentucky State Fair. Louisville. (502) 367-5000

Ethnic Festivals:
Strassenfest. Louisville. (502) 561-3440. Celebrating Louisville's
German heritage.

Arts and Crafts:
Annual Kentucky Western Waterland Arts and Crafts Festival.
Golden Pond. Land Between the Lakes National Recreation
Area. (800) 448-1069.

Civil War Re-enactment:
Battle of Richmond. Richmond. (800) 866-3705.

SEPTEMBER

Community Festivals:
Gaslight Festival. Jeffersontown. (502) 267-2070.
Kentucky Bourbon Festival. Bardstown. (800) 638-4877.
Simon Kenton Frontier Festival. Old Washington Village.
Maysville. (606) 759-7409.
World Chicken Festival. London. (606) 878-6900.

Ethnic Festivals:
Oktoberfest. MainStrasse Village. Covington. (859) 491-0458.
Kentucky Highland Folk Festival. Prestonsburg. (800) 844-7404.
Celebrating the Scots-Irish heritage of the mountains.
Kentucky Folklife Festival. Frankfort. (502) 564-1792.
Honoring all the ethnic communities in the state.

Music/Theater:
Poppy Mountain Bluegrass Festival. Morehead. (606) 784-2277.

OCTOBER

Sporting Events:
Thoroughbred horse racing. Keeneland Race Course
fall meet. Lexington. (800) 456-3412.

Community Festivals:
Kentucky Wool Festival. Falmouth. (859) 654-3378.
Logan County Tobacco Festival. Russellville. (270) 726-2206.
Trigg County Ham Festival. Cadiz. (270) 522-3892.
Lincoln Days Annual Festival. Hodgenville. (270) 358-3411.

Ethnic Festivals:
Trail of Tears Indian Pow-Wow. Hopkinsville. (270) 886-8033.

Arts and Crafts:
St. James Court Art Show. Louisville. (800) 792-5595.
Kentucky Guild of Artists and Craftsmen Fall Fair. Berea.
(859) 986-2540.

Civil War Re-enactment:
Battle of Perryville. Perryville Battlefield State Historic Site.
(859) 332-8631.

NOVEMBER

Sporting Events:
Thoroughbred horse racing. Churchill Downs fall meet.
Louisville. (502) 636-4400.

Arts and Crafts:
Festival of the Mountain Masters. Harlan. (606) 573-2900.
Demonstrations of traditional mountain crafts by master artisans.
Christmas in Berea. Berea. (859) 986-2540.

DECEMBER

Sporting Events:
College Basketball. University of Kentucky vs. University of
Louisville. At Lexington or Louisville. UK: (800) 928-2287. U of
L: (800) 633-7105. The premier in-state rivalry.

Community Festivals:
Frontier Christmas. Washington. (606) 759-7411.

Contact Information

State Tourism Agencies
Kentucky Travel: (800) 225-8747 or
www.kentuckytourism.com

Kentucky State Parks: (800) 255-7275 or
www.kystateparks.com

City and County Tourism Bureaus
Ashland Area: (800) 377-6249 or www.visitashlandky.com

Bardstown: (800) 638-4877 or www.bardstowntourism.com

Bell County: (800) 988-1075

Berea: (800) 598-5263

Bowling Green–Warren County: (800) 326-7465 or
www.bowlinggreen.ky.net/tourism

Cadiz-Trigg County: (888) 446-6402 or www.gocadiz.com

Carrollton–Carroll County: (800) 325-4290 or
www.carrollcountyky.com

Cave City: (800) 346-8908 or www.cavecity.com

Corbin: (606) 528-6390

Cumberland: (606) 589-5812

Danville–Perryville–Boyle County: (800) 755-0076 or
www.danville-ky.com/BoyleCounty/tourism.htm

Elizabethtown: (800) 437-0092 or www.touretown.com

Frankfort–Franklin County: (800) 960-7200 or
www.visitfrankfort.com

Franklin–Simpson County: (270) 586-3040 or
www.franklinky.com

Georgetown–Scott County: (888) 863-8600 or
www.georgetownky.com

Glasgow–Barren County: (800) 264-3161 or
www.glasgowbarrenchamber.com

Grand Rivers–Livingston County: (800) 977-0325 or
www.grandrivers.com

Grant County: (800) 382-7117

Grayson County: (270) 259-2735

Greater Louisville: (888) 568-4784 or www.gotolouisville.com

Harlan: (606) 573-4156 or
www.lawrencecomputer.com/harlan

Harrodsburg: (800) 355-9192 or www.harrodsburgky.com

Henderson County: (800) 648-3128 or www.go-
henderson.com

Hopkinsville–Christian County: (800) 842-9959 or
www.commercecenter.org

Lexington: (800) 848-1224 or www.visitlex.com

Logan County: (270) 726-2206 or www.visitlogancounty.com

London–Laurel County: (800) 348-0095 or
www.laurelkytourism.com

Louisville: (888) 568-4784 or www.gotolouisville.com

Lyon County: (800) 355-3885 or www.lakebarkley.org

Marshall County: (800) 467-7145 or www.kentuckylake.org

Maysville–Mason County: (606) 564-9411 or
www.cityofmaysville.com

McCreary County: (888) 284-3718 or
www.mccrearycounty.com

Morehead: (800) 654-1944 or www.moreheadchamber.com

Mount Sterling: (859) 498-8732 or www.mountsterling-
ky.com/tourism

Mount Vernon–Rockcastle County: (800) 252-6685 or
www.rockcastlecokytourism.com

Murray: (800) 651-1603 or www.murraylink.com

Northern Kentucky: (800) 447-8489 or www.nkycvb.com

Owensboro–Daviess County: (800) 489-1131 or
www.visitowensboro.com

Paducah–McCracken County: (800) 723-8224 or
www.paducah-tourism.com

Pendleton County: (859) 654-4834

Pikeville–Pike County: (800) 844-7453 or
www.tourpikecounty.com

Powell County: (606) 663-1161 or
www.powellcountytourism.com

Prestonsburg: (800) 844-4704

Radcliff–Fort Knox: (800) 334-7540 or
www.ltadd.org/radcliff

Richmond: (800) 866-3705 or www.richmond-ky.com

Russell County: (888) 833-4220 or
www.lakecumberlandvacation.com

Shelbyville: (800) 680-6388 or www.shelbyvilleky.com

Shepherdsville–Bullitt County: (800) 526-2068 or www.ltadd.org/bullitt

Somerset–Pulaski County: (800) 642-6287 or www.lakecumberlandtourism.com

Taylor County: (800) 738-4719 or www.campbellsvilleky.com

Williamsburg: (800) 552-0530

Winchester–Clark County: (800) 298-9105 or www.winchesterky.com/tourism

SOURCES AND FURTHER READING

NON-FICTION

Memoirs, Diaries, Journals, Letters, etc.

Barkley, Alben. *That Reminds Me*. Garden City, NY: Doubleday, 1954.

Bibb, Henry. *The Life and Adventures of Henry Bibb: An American Slave*. Madison: University of Wisconsin Press, 2001. (Originally published 1849).

Braden, Anne. *The Wall Between*. New York: Monthly Review Press, 1958.

Caudill, Harry. *The Mountain, the Miner, and the Lord, and Other Tales from a Country Law Office*. Lexington: University Press of Kentucky, 1980.

Collins, William. *Ways, Means, and Customs of Our Forefathers*. New York: Vantage Press, 1976.

Eslinger, Ellen, ed.. *Running Mad for Kentucky: Frontier Travel Accounts*. Lexington: University Press of Kentucky, 2004.

Filson, John. *The Discovery, Settlement, and Present State of Kentucke*. Bowie, MD.: Heritage Books, 1996. (Originally published 1784).

Giles, Janice Holt. *40 Acres and No Mule*. Boston: Houghton Mifflin, 1967.

Guerrant, Edward O. *Bluegrass Confederate: The Headquarters Diary of Edward O. Guerrant*. Baton Rouge: Louisiana State University Press, 1999.

Hall, Wade. *The Rest of the Dream: The Black Odyssey of Lyman Johnson*. Lexington: The University Press of Kentucky, 1988.

Merton, Thomas. *The Seven-Storey Mountain*. New York: Harcourt, Brace (1948).

Peter, Frances. *A Union Woman in Civil War Kentucky: The Diary of Frances Peter*. Lexington: University Press of Kentucky, 1999.

Polk, Jefferson J. *Autobiography of Jefferson J. Polk*. Louisville: J.P. Morton and Co., 1867.

Purviance, Levi. *The Biography of Elder David Purviance*. Dayton, OH: B.F. and G.W. Ells, 1840.

Stedman, Ebenezer. *Bluegrass Craftsman: Being the Reminiscences of Ebenezer Hiram Stedman, Papermaker, 1808–1885*. Lexington: University Press of Kentucky, 1959.

Stewart, Cora Wilson. *Moonlight Schools for the Emancipation of Adult Illiterates*. New York: E.P. Dutton and Co., 1922.

Stoddart, Jess, ed.. *The Quare Women's Journals: May Stone and Katherine Pettit's Summers in the Kentucky Mountains and the Founding of the Hindman Settlement School*. Ashland, KY:

Jesse Stuart Foundation, 1997.

Stuart, Jesse. *Thread that Runs So True*. New York: C. Scribner's Sons, 1949.

_____. *God's Oddling: The Story of Mick Stuart, My Father*. New York: McGraw Hill, 1960.

Warren, Robert Penn. *Portrait of A Father*. Lexington: University Press of Kentucky, 1988.

Watterson, Henry. *The Editorials of Henry Watterson*. Compiled by Arthur Krock. Louisville: Louisville Courier-Journal Co., 1923.

Encyclopedias, Histories, etc.

Allen, James Lane. *The Blue-Grass Region of Kentucky and Other Kentucky Articles*. New York: Macmillan, 1900.

Arnow, Harriette Simpson. *Seedtime on the Cumberland*. New York: Macmillan, 1960.

_____. *Flowering of the Cumberland*. New York: Macmillan, 1963.

Aron, Stephen. *How the West Was Lost: The Transformation of Kentucky from Daniel Boone to Henry Clay*. Baltimore: Johns Hopkins University Press, 1996.

Bailey, Bill. *Kentucky State Parks: A Guide to Kentucky State Parks*. Saginaw, Michigan: Glovebox Guidebooks, 1995.

Berry, Wendell. *The Unsettling of America: Culture and Agriculture*. San Francisco: Sierra Club Books, 1977.

_____. *Long-Legged House*. New York: Harcourt, Brace and World, 1969.

_____. *What Are People For?* San Francisco: North Point Press, 1990.

_____. *Home Economics: 14 Essays*. San Francisco: North Point Press, 1987.

Caudill, Harry. *Night Comes to the Cumberlands: A Biography of a Depressed Area*. Boston: Atlantic Monthly Press, 1962.

Clark, Thomas D. *History of Kentucky*. New York: Prentice Hall, 1937. (Revised 1954, 1960, 1992).

_____. *Kentucky: Land of Contrast*. New York: Harper and Row, 1968.

_____. *Agrarian Kentucky*. Lexington: University Press of Kentucky, 1977.

Dos Passos. John. *In All Countries*. New York: Harcourt, Brace and Co., 1934.

Faragher, John Mack. *Daniel Boone: The Life and Legend of an American Pioneer*. New York: Holt, 1992.

Fox, John, Jr. *Blue-Grass and Rhododendron: Outdoors in Old Kentucky*. New York: C. Scribner's Sons, 1901.

Fuller, Paul. *Laura Clay and the Woman's Rights Movement*.

Lexington: University Press of Kentucky, 1975.

Harrison, Lowell. *George Rogers Clark and the War in the West*.
Lexington: University Press of Kentucky, 1976.

Harrison, Lowell, ed. *Kentucky's Governors*. Lexington:
University Press of Kentucky, 2004.

Harrison, Lowell, and Dawon, Nelson L. *Kentucky Sampler:
Essays from the Filson Club History Quarterly, 1926–1976*.
Lexington: University Press of Kentucky, 1977.

Harrison, Lowell and James Klotter. *A New History of
Kentucky*. Lexington: University Press of Kentucky, 1997.

Henderson, A. Gwynn. *Kentuckians Before Boone*. Lexington:
University Press of Kentucky, 1992.

Irvin, Helen. *Women in Kentucky*. Lexington: University Press
of Kentucky, 1979.

Kleber, John, ed. *The Kentucky Encyclopedia*. Lexington:
University Press of Kentucky, 1992.

Kleber, John, ed. *The Encyclopedia of Louisville*. Lexington:
University Press of Kentucky, 2001.

Lewis, R. Barry, ed., *Kentucky Archaeology*. Lexington:
University Press of Kentucky, 1996.

Klotter, James. *Kentucky: Portrait in Paradox, 1900–1950*.
Frankfort: Kentucky Historical Society, 1996.

Lucas, Marion. *A History of Blacks in Kentucky, Volume I: From
Slavery to Segregation, 1760–1891*. Frankfort: Kentucky
Historical Society, 1992.

McDonough, James. *War in Kentucky: From Shiloh to Perryville*.
Knoxville: University of Tennessee Press, 1994.

Remini, Robert. *Henry Clay: Statesman for the Union*. New York:
W.W. Norton, 1991.

Smith, Frank. *Land Between the Lakes: Experiment in Recreation*.
Lexington: University Press of Kentucky, 1971.

Stoddart, Jess. *Challenge and Change in Appalachia: The Story of
Hindman Settlement School*. Lexington: University Press of
Kentucky, 2002.

Tapp, Hambleton, and Klotter, James. *Kentucky: Decades of
Discord, 1865–1900*. Frankfort: Kentucky Historical Society,
1977.

Woodson, Urey. *The First New Dealer: William Goebel*.
Louisville: The Standard Press, 1939.

Wright, George. *A History of Blacks in Kentucky, Volume II: In
Pursuit of Equality, 1890–1980*. Frankfort: Kentucky
Historical Society, 1992.

_____. *Life Behind a Veil: Blacks in Louisville, Kentucky,
1865–1930*. Baton Rouge: Louisiana State University Press,
1985.

_____. *Racial Violence in Kentucky, 1865–1940:*

Lynchings, Mob Rule, and "Legal Lynchings." Baton Rouge: Louisiana State University Press, 1990.

Wright, John, Jr. *Lexington, Heart of the Bluegrass*. Lexington: Lexington-Fayette County Historic Commission, 1982.

Yater, George. *Two Hundred Years at the Falls of the Ohio: A History of Louisville and Jefferson County*. Louisville: The Filson Club, 1987.

Fiction, Poetry, etc.

Allen, James Lane. *A Kentucky Cardinal*. New York: Harper Brothers, 1894.

_____. *The Choir Invisible*. New York: Grosset and Dunlap, 1897.

_____. *The Reign of Law: A Tale of the Kentucky Hemp Fields*. New York: Macmillan, 1900.

Arnow, Harriette Simpson. *Hunter's Horn*. New York: Macmillan, 1944.

_____. *The Dollmaker*. New York: Macmillan, 1954.

Berry, Wendell. *The Memory of Old Jack*. New York: Harcourt, Brace, Jovanovich, 1974.

_____. *Jayber Crow*. Washington, DC: Counterpoint, 2000.

_____. *Hannah Coulter: A Novel*. Washington, DC: Shoemaker and Hoard, 2004.

_____. *The Collected Poems, 1957–1982*. San Francisco: North Point Press, 1985.

Cobb, Irvin S. *Back Home: Being the Narrative of Judge Priest and His People*. New York: George H. Doran Co., 1911.

_____. *Old Judge Priest*. New York: George H. Doran Co., 1916.

Fox, John, Jr. *The Little Shepherd of Kingdom Come*. New York: C. Scribner's Sons, 1903.

_____. *The Trail of the Lonesome Pine*. New York: Grosset and Dunlap, 1908.

Giles, Janice Holt. *The Enduring Hills*. Lexington: University Press of Kentucky, 1988. (Originally published 1950).

_____. *The Kentuckians*. Lexington: University Press of Kentucky, 1987. (Originally published 1953).

_____. *Hannah Fowler*. Boston: Houghton Mifflin, 1956.

_____. *The Land Beyond the Mountains*. Atlanta, GA.: Cherokee, 1990. (Originally published 1958).

Grubbs, Morris, ed. *Home and Beyond: An Anthology of Kentucky Short Stories*. Lexington: University Press of Kentucky, 2001.

Hall, Wade, ed. *The Kentucky Anthology: Two Hundred Years of Writing in the Bluegrass State*. Lexington: University Press of Kentucky, 2005.

Johnson, Fenton. *Scissors, Paper, Rock*. New York: Pocket Books, 1993.

_____. *Crossing the River*. Secaucus, NJ: Carol
  Publishing Group, 1989.
Johnston, Annie Fellows. *The Little Colonel*. Bedford, MA:
  Applewood Books, 1998. (Originally published 1895).
Kingsolver, Barbara. *The Bean Trees*. New York: Perennial
  Library, 1988.
_____. *Prodigal Summer.* New York: HarperCollins, 2000.
Mason, Bobbie Ann. *In Country*. New York: Harper and Row, 1985.
_____. *Feather Crowns*. New York: HarperCollins, 1993.
_____. *Shiloh and Other Stories*. New York: Harper and
  Row, 1982.
Rice, Alice Hegan. *Mrs. Wiggs of the Cabbage Patch*. New York:
  Century, 1901.
Roberts, Elizabeth Madox. *The Time of Man*. New York:
  Grosset and Dunlap, 1926.
_____. *The Great Meadow*. New York: The Viking
  Press, 1930.
Still, James. *River of Earth*. New York: The Viking Press, 1940.
_____. *On Troublesome Creek*. New York: The Viking
  Press, 1941.
Stuart, Jesse. *Man with a Bull-Tongue Plow*. New York: E.P.
  Dutton and Co., 1934.
_____. *Head o' W-Hollow*. New York: E.P. Dutton
  and Co., 1936.
_____. *Taps for Private Tussie*. New York: E.P. Dutton
  and Co., 1943.
_____. *Thirty-two Votes Before Breakfast: Politics at the
  Grass Roots, as seen in Short Stories*. New York: McGraw
  Hill, 1974.
Tevis, Walter. *The Hustler*. Cutchogue, NY: Buccaneer Books, 1959.
Walker, Frank X. *Affrilachia*. Lexington: Old Cove Press, 2000.
Warren, Robert Penn. *Night Rider*. Boston: Houghton Mifflin,
  1939.
_____. *All the King's Men*. New York: Grosset and
  Dunlap, 1946.
_____. *World Enough and Time*. New York: Random
  House, 1950.
_____. *Brother to Dragons: A Tale in Verse and Voices*.
  New York: Random House, 1953.
_____. *The Cave*. New York: Random House, 1959.
_____. *Promises: Poems, 1954–1956*. New York:
  Random House, 1957.
_____. *Now and Then: Poems 1976–1978*. New York:
  Random House, 1979.
_____. *New and Selected Poems, 1923–1985*. New York:
  Random House, 1985.

Index of Place Names

Must-see sites are highlighted in bold